Choice and Competition in American Education

Choice and Competition in American Education

Edited by
Paul E. Peterson

ROWMAN & LITTLEFIELD PUBLISHERS, INC.
Lanham • Boulder • New York • Toronto • Oxford

The articles in this volume previously appeared in *Education Next: A Journal of Opinion and Research*, published by the Hoover Institution, Stanford University. Copyright is held by the Trustees of Leland Stanford Jr. University. Permission to reprint this material is gratefully acknowledged.

ROWMAN & LITTLEFIELD PUBLISHERS, INC.

Published in the United States of America
by Rowman & Littlefield Publishers, Inc.
A wholly owned subsidiary of The Rowman & Littlefield Publishing Group, Inc.
4501 Forbes Boulevard, Suite 200, Lanham, Maryland 20706
www.rowmanlittlefield.com

PO Box 317
Oxford
OX2 9RU, UK

British Library Cataloguing in Publication Information Available

Library of Congress Cataloging-in-Publication Data

Choice and competition in American education / edited by Paul E. Peterson.
    p. cm.
    ISBN 0-7425-4580-6 (cloth : alk. paper)—ISBN 0-7425-4581-4 (pbk. : alk. paper)
    1. School choice—United States. 2. Educational change—United States. I. Peterson, Paul E.
    LB1027.9.C47 2005
    379.1'11'0973—dc22

                                                                2005017447

Printed in the United States of America

♾ ™ The paper used in this publication meets the minimum requirements of American National Standard for Information Sciences—Permanence of Paper for Printed Library Materials, ANSI/NISO Z39.48–1992.

Contents

Section I: The Profit Motive: Will It Benefit Kids?

Introduction: The Use of Market Incentives in Education   3
    Paul E. Peterson
1 The Private Can Be Public   13
    John E. Chubb
2 The Costs of Privatization   23
    Henry M. Levin

Section II: The Education Profession

Part A: Should We Deregulate Entry into the Profession?

3 Regulations Do More Harm than Good   33
    Frederick M. Hess
4 In Defense of Regulation   43
    Mary E. Diez
5 We Need New Types of Administrators   55
    Frederick M. Hess
6 New Leaders: Will Public Schools Hire Them?   69
    Alexander Russo

Part B: Making Teacher Pay More Competitive

7 Fringe Benefits: AFT and NEA Teacher Salary Surveys   79
    Michael Podgursky

8 Low Pay, Low Quality   93
    Peter Temin
9 The Case for Merit Pay   102
    Lewis C. Solmon
10 Wage Compression and the Decline in Teacher Quality   111
    Caroline M. Hoxby and Andrew Leigh

Part C: Do Teacher Unions Stifle Reform?

11 A Union by Any Other Name   123
    Terry M. Moe
12 Reform Unionism Is Here   136
    Charles Taylor Kerchner

Section III: School Choice

Part A: Charter Schools

13 Charter Schools: Mom and Pops or Corporate Design   149
    Bryan C. Hassel
14 Charter School Politics   161
    Bruno V. Manno
15 A School Built for Horace: Tales from a Start-up Charter School   172
    Nancy Faust Sizer and Theodore R. Sizer

Part B: School Vouchers

16 The Impact of Vouchers on Student Performance   183
    William G. Howell, Patrick J. Wolf, Paul E. Peterson,
    and David E. Campbell
17 Do Vouchers and Charters Push Public Schools to Improve?   194
    Caroline M. Hoxby
18 School Choice and Social Cohesion   206
    David E. Campbell
19 How Vouchers Came to D.C.   219
    Spencer S. Hsu

Part C: Other Ways of Increasing School Choice

20 Contracting Out: The Story behind Philadelphia's
    Edison Contract   233
    Jay Mathews

21 Home Schooling: The Nation's Fastest-growing Education Sector   243
       Christopher W. Hammons
22 School Choice in No Child Left Behind   255
       William G. Howell
23 Selling Supplemental Services   265
       Siobhan Gorman

SECTION I

The Profit Motive: Will It Benefit Kids?

The Use of Market Incentives in Education

Paul E. Peterson

School reform has long been on the nation's agenda. Earlier strategies tried out new curricular ideas, new management techniques, or the commitment of additional financial resources. But, recently, two more sweeping reforms—one holding schools accountable for specific educational outcomes, the other introducing choice and competition—have been placed on the table. The first involves setting state standards and measuring student performance by means of standardized tests. Given nationwide prominence by No Child Left Behind, the 2002 federal law, this reform strategy asks schools to reach defined achievement goals or suffer the consequences. Many hope that by setting clear goals, and asking schools to meet them, sweeping educational progress will be achieved. But others are skeptical, doubtful that education can be precisely measured or that politically determined rules and regulations can, by themselves, enhance student learning.

The other option, choice and competition, is less well known, though some believe it to be the more promising reform strategy. It takes American business and industry as the appropriate model for schools to follow. In the private economy, consumers make choices, businesses make profits when they satisfy consumers more than their competitors do, and new inventions constantly drive the economy to ever-higher levels of productivity. Choice and competition: it's the American way—most of the time.

But does it work in education? Would students learn more, if instead of attending the neighborhood public school, they went to the school their parents chose? Would teachers and principals be more effective if they, and their

3

employers, were subject to fewer and more flexible rules affecting their train-ing, recruitment, compensation, and retention? Or would the introduction of market-like mechanisms into education aggravate existing inequalities and weaken the effectiveness of one of the nation's greatest public institutions?

These are some of the questions this collection of essays seeks to address. Originally published in *Education Next: A Journal of Opinion and Research*, these focused, succinct essays describe many of the most recent efforts to introduce more choice and competition into American education. They examine both the promise and the potential pitfalls of an idea which appears to be gradually spreading across the educational landscape.

Education, the Largest, Most Costly Government Service

Should choice and competition become widespread practice, it would consti-tute a fundamental change in the organization of public education. With few exceptions, public schools today are operated directly by government agen-cies, which provide needed services by hiring superintendents, principals, teachers, psychologists, teacher aides, crossing guards, bus drivers, and a wide variety of other employees. Indeed, elementary and secondary public educa-tion is the largest service delivery system in the United States directly oper-ated by local governments. In 2002, over 47 million students were being taught by over 3,100,000 teachers hired by nearly 16,000 different school boards, operating within the framework of state and federal law.

To provide millions of students with a broad range of services costs the government (at the federal, state, and local levels) over $430 billion dollars, an amount that exceeds the budget of the U.S. Department of Defense. The Social Security program is more costly, but that program does not operate a substantive service in the same way schools do. It simply distributes monies to the bank accounts of senior citizens. Health care programs, such as Medicare and Medicaid, are very large programs that do offer services, but, for the most part, these services are not delivered by employees of the government but by private contractors, whether they are private doctors and nurses, or for-profit or nonprofit hospitals. After the service has been performed, the contractors are reimbursed by the government. Other domestic services, such as air traf-fic control, garbage collection, and police and fire protection are typically provided directly by the government. But they are much smaller undertak-ings. In 2002, the cost of operating the U.S. Postal Service, next to education the largest domestic service provided directly by the government, was but

$3.8 billion, less than 1 percent of the amount devoted to financing the nation's school system.

Not only are public schools a large and costly government service, but the price tag has risen rapidly over the past thirty-five years. According to the reckoning of economist Caroline Hoxby, per pupil expenditures on public elementary and secondary education in the United States grew (in real dollars that are adjusted for inflation) from $4,500 in 1970 to nearly $9,500 in 2000, a 111 percent increase that more than doubled the nation's public investments in its schools.

Unfortunately, the large increment in public expenditure for education in recent decades did not translate into high student achievement within the classroom. According to an international survey conducted in 2003 by the Organization of Economic Cooperation and Development, the United States ranked twenty-fourth in math and fifteenth in reading (out of twenty-nine participating nations), a sad performance for a country long known as the world leader in education. Even worse, the U.S. high school graduation rate in the United States, once the highest rate in the world, now trails the average of all industrialized countries.

Nor do graduation rates look any better when one ignores what is happening in other countries and just considers trends within the United States. During the 1950s and 1960s, they had climbed steadily, but they reached their peak in 1970 and have declined since, most notably since 1990.

Trends in academic achievement of high school students have also been disappointing. Student achievement has been tracked since 1970 by the federally sponsored National Assessment of Educational Progress (NAEP), a periodic survey of student performance of 9, 13, and 17 year olds in reading, math, and other subjects. The best available yardstick, NAEP is widely considered to be the "nation's report card." During this period of time the scores of whites at the age of 17 remained stagnant, despite the fact that the country was otherwise making remarkable economic and social progress. Younger white students have in recent years been performing at a somewhat higher level than their peers of earlier generations, but when those students reach high school the early gains have disappeared.

But even though white students have only barely held their own, they still outperformed their black peers by a wide margin in 2003. Indeed, the average white fourth grader was doing almost as well as the average black eighth grader. Black students had begun to close this gap during the 1980s, but among high school students, it opened up again during the 1990s.

Unfortunately, one cannot track the scores of Latino or other minority students systematically over this stretch of time, because new waves of immigrants make it difficult to compare early cohorts of students with later ones. But the alarmingly low graduation rates among Hispanic youth make it doubtful that the public education is effectively serving this large and growing segment of the nation's student population.

Nor can one discard this information on the grounds that tests of achievement are a poor measure of genuine learning. How well one does on educational achievement tests is as good a predictor of one's future life chances as the socioeconomic background of the family in which one is born. So important are achievement levels that, when black high school students score as well as their white peers, their earnings later in life are roughly the same. In the words of scholars Christopher Jencks and Meredith Phillips, "If racial equality is America's goal, reducing the black-white test score gap would probably do more to promote this goal than any other strategy that commands broad political support."

Choice and Competition as a Reform Strategy: Strengths and Limitations

Given these signs of persistent inequality and stagnation in American education, many reformers have recommended that school systems borrow ideas and approaches from the much more dynamic private sector. That sector may best be understood as the world of hard knocks, where decisions are driven by the constant search for more profits. Outstanding firms make large profits by inventing or applying new technologies that either cut costs or generate better products. The ones that cannot keep up are taken over by the more prosperous firms—or eventually go out of business. A similar tough approach is taken with employees, especially those in administrative and professional positions. Employers look for effective administrators and highly skilled technical employees who can help them compete effectively. Employees who perform well receive bonuses and promotional opportunities. Weak ones are dismissed. And when a company goes bankrupt, the jobs of all employees, competent or not, are placed at risk.

Of course, this is an over-simplified portrait of the way in which the private economy works. Business competition is contained and channeled by state and federal laws that regulate the impact of commerce and industry on the environment as well as on worker health, safety, and working conditions. Other laws restrict accounting practices, the flow of information to stockholders (to limit stock-price manipulation) and the advertisement of products to consumers (so that false and misleading claims are not made). Nor is competition uniform in all sectors of the private economy. Some industries are controlled by only one or a few firms, and others are influenced by political connections between government and industry. But if the private marketplace is not perfectly competitive, for the most part the most innovative and efficient tend to squeeze out the out-dated and less productive—at least in the long run.

Public schools march to quite another drumbeat. It is true that schools are built by private contractors, most textbooks are prepared by large corporate entities, and school cafeterias are often run by privately owned dining services. But the core operations of most public schools are operated directly by the government. As a result, choices are limited, competition constrained, and regulation pervasive. Except in a few places (as discussed later), most students have little choice in the public school they are to attend. Either they attend the school serving the neighborhood in which they live or another school assigned to them by the school district. Since school boards assign students to schools, individual schools do not need to worry about their enrollments or finances. Payments come not from parents but from local and state taxpayers as well as some additional funding from the federal government.

For public schools, there is no such thing as profits. Schools seldom receive additional money for doing an excellent job, and money is hardly ever withdrawn for failure. So schools have little monetary incentive to strive for a higher level of performance.

Working conditions are highly regulated by state law and collective bargaining agreements, protecting teachers from the harshest forces of the marketplace. In general, school districts are not free to hire any college graduate they wish but must select from among those who pursue a well-defined educational program that conforms to state regulations. Those granted temporary exceptions must take designated courses within a year or two after beginning their teaching career. Nor are teachers paid according to how effectively they perform in the classroom. Instead, they are paid a standard salary based on their educational credentials and years of experience. Further, most bargaining contracts between school districts and teacher unions prevent the dismissal of ineffective teachers, except after a long grievance process has transpired.

School districts generally have more choice in the recruitment and the retention of the principals of their schools, but even these decisions are often subject to regulatory controls. In most parts of the country, principals must first have taught school themselves and then pursued a set of principal preparation courses required by state law. This makes it difficult to bring into education expertise and skills acquired in other industries.

Would education benefit from the introduction of techniques and strategies drawn from the harder world of business? Many shrink at the prospect, in part because schools have long been public institutions that symbolize equality of opportunity and shelter children from the world's harsher realities. Choice and competition in education raise other disturbing questions as well. Do we really want private firms to make a profit on a child's education? Can parents evaluate school quality in the same way customers can readily tell whether a shoe fits? Even if desirable, is school choice realistic? How can enough schools be provided in any one area so that parents have a wide range of alternatives? And what would happen to those schools that no one chose? Or to those students left behind in poor schools abandoned by the most astute shoppers? It is one thing for a restaurant or a clothing store to close its doors; it is quite another for children to be denied access to their school. These are just some of the issues addressed in the essays that follow.

Organization of the Essays in the Collection

The collection is organized into three major sections. The first section examines some of the large issues associated with school choice and competitiveness in education, with John Chubb, the chief education officer of Edison Schools, a for-profit corporation, making the case that for-profits can operate more efficiently and effectively. Henry Levin, a Columbia University education professor, wonders whether a shift toward a more competitive system would in fact yield the benefits that are often claimed.

Section II examines the way in which market incentives might be used to enhance teaching and educational administration. In the first part of this section, the focus is on entry into teaching and educational administration. Frederick Hess, a senior fellow at the American Enterprise Institute, argues that school districts should be able to hire any qualified college graduate, regardless of whether they have followed a particular curriculum prescribed by state law. In a separate essay, he makes the same point about principals, superintendents, and other school leaders. In her reply, Mary Diez; a professor of education at Alverno College in Milwaukee, Wisconsin, argues, in response, that all teachers need a certain amount of pedagogical training, if they are to be effective. Meanwhile, reporter Alexander Russo looks at an experiment that is providing an alternative route into educational administration. Although those trying this alternative route appear exceptionally talented, he says, they appear to be having a surprising amount of trouble finding jobs within school systems wedded to traditional recruitment practices.

The next topic involves teacher pay. Most teachers feel that they are poorly paid, but University of Missouri economist Michael Podgursky, in a provocative analysis, points out that the hourly earnings of teachers compare favorably with those of other professions requiring similar qualifications, when one takes into account the length of the school year and the length of the school day. But Peter Temin, an economist at the Massachusetts Institute of Technology, points out that teacher quality has slipped, because teacher pay has not kept up with rising compensation in other professions. Other essays in this part take a look at how teacher pay could be modified in a way that would enhance teacher quality. Lewis Solmon discusses the virtue of merit pay, while economists Caroline Hoxby and Andrew Leigh report that able women are increasingly avoiding the teaching profession, because higher-quality teachers are paid no more than lower-quality teachers. In their view, the rise of teacher unions is the major explanation for this trend.

That suggestion provides an apt introduction for the third part of this section, which takes up the controversial question of the role of the union in American education today. On the one side, Terry Moe, a Stanford political scientist, argues vigorously that unions are the major obstacle to school reform, simply because unions, as organizations, must almost always defend all teachers, even when they are ineffective in the classroom. Charles Kerchner, professor of education at the University of California, Riverside, on the other side, finds encouraging signs that the old, bread-and-butter unionism is being superceded by a reform unionism more sensitive to educational issues.

The final section of the collection turns to the way in which school choice is being used to enhance competition in American education. In the first part of this section, attention is given to charter schools, widely regarded as one of the most important organizational changes in education in the past fifteen years. In 1990, there were no charter schools in the United States, but by 2005, there were nearly 3,000 charter schools serving over a million students, a large number but still a small percentage of the public school population. The charter school movement is now reaching a critical stage. Either it has reached a plateau that leaves it as a curiosity on the fringes of American public education, or it will continue to grow steadily, thereby decisively changing the shape of American education. The essays in this section throw light on the likely direction that the charter school movement will take. Bryan C. Hassel, a consultant to the charter school industry, explains the relative advantages of two quite different kinds of charter schools—those run by edu-cation management organizations and smaller scale operations run by indi-vidual entrepreneurs. Though each type has its following, Hassel shows that each has its disadvantages as well. Bruno Manno, a foundation officer at the education-minded Casey Foundation, identifies the many problems—fiscal, practical, and political—that charter schools are likely to face in the years ahead. Nancy and Theodore Sizer, well-known scholars and innovators in American education, provide an honest, on-the-ground feel for what it is like to put your ideas into practice and actually create a new school from the very beginning.

If charter schools hold considerable potential, they are not as far-reach-ing—or as controversial—as school vouchers, the topic of the penultimate part of this collection. School vouchers have the potential for introducing the broadest amount of choice and competition into American education, because, unlike charters, which remain public schools, vouchers also give parents the option of placing their children into private school. Many of those who believe that market incentives work to enhance quality and satis-faction think that only through school vouchers can fundamental change in American education be achieved. But critics believe that school vouchers would undermine much that makes public education in this country the prized heritage that it is.

Empirical information that can help resolve such debates is still limited, but included in this part of the collection are a variety of studies that shed important new light on the topic. One set of studies, conducted by Harvard political scientist William Howell and his coauthors, has been able to use high-quality, experimental data to ascertain whether students given vouchers to attend private schools learn more than those remaining in public schools. Their evaluation of small, privately funded school voucher programs in New York City, Washington, D.C., and Dayton, Ohio finds that school vouchers have substantial, positive effects on the achievement of African American students but no discernable effect on those from other ethnic backgrounds. In the next essay, Caroline Hoxby, a Harvard economist, also finds significant positive effects, this time on the performance of students remaining in public schools in places where sizable voucher and charter school programs increase the competitive effects on public schools. Still, questions arise as to whether wider use of private schooling would adversely affect social cohesion and important public values. After reviewing the evidence, David Campbell, a political scientist at Notre Dame University, concludes that the potential for harm is small.

Despite these generally positive results, one cannot expect school vouchers to spread rapidly. As Spencer Hsu, a *Washington Post* reporter, points out in his essay, the obstacles to setting up even a small voucher program in Washington, D.C. were multiple. Only a broad national coalition, backed by strong support within the city, was able to overcome intense opposition. One can hardly expect school vouchers to revolutionize American education in the immediate future.

The collection ends with analyses of less well-known but no less important innovations that are expanding the range of choice in American education. Jay Mathews, another reporter for the *Washington Post*, tells about the conflicts that can occur when a school board writes a contract with a private firm to run a school. In Philadelphia, the school board contracted some of its schools to the Edison Schools. The conflict that ensued was memorable; we do not know whether the ending to this story will be happy or not, because the final chapter has yet to be told. If successful, other school boards may decide that contracting out in education makes just as much sense when it comes to running schools as it does when building them.

But despite the attention that has been given to charters, vouchers, and contracting out, it is home schooling that is the fastest-growing sector in American education, with well over a million children now being educated at home. Educator Christopher Hammons provides us with a sense of the range of experiences that are taking place within a home setting. His findings stand as a warning against any who would draw any simplistic conclusions, either positive or negative.

Finally, the book concludes with an examination of the choice and competition provisions contained in No Child Left Behind. According to the law, parents of students attending schools that failed two years running were to be given a choice of another public school within the district. William Howell explains why that choice, at least in the early years of the program, was exercised by no more than 1 percent of the eligible students. A higher percentage of students are taking advantage of the supplemental service provision of the law, however. According to this provision, students in schools that have failed three years in a row are to have the opportunity to obtain private tutoring or attend an after-school program—run either by the school district itself or by another qualified provider, which can be a private firm. Siobhan Gorman says that many for-profit firms are becoming involved, and the numbers of participating students is growing quite rapidly. Yet it remains to be seen whether a supplemental service program is central enough to the core of American education to constitute a major educational change.

All in all, these essays suggest that the movement for choice and competition in education is taking many forms—from deregulation of the teaching profession to charter schools, home schooling, school vouchers, and privately run after-school programs. Each can be seen as an exciting innovation, but none, by itself, is free from ambiguities and political obstacles. Taken together, they leave us with the impression that the twenty-first century will see a more competitive educational system than existed in the twentieth, but the pace of change will be more that of the tortoise than the hare. Its supporters will have to hope that slow and steady works this time, too.

Many people have assisted in the preparation of the materials that are included in this volume. We wish to thank Chester E. Finn, Jay P. Greene, Frederick Hess, Marci Kanstoroom, and Martin R. West, who served as editors of *Education Next: A Journal of Opinion and Research* for part or all of the period during which these articles were originally published. We especially thank Peter Meyer and Tyce Palmaffy, who, as the manuscript editors, gave shape and tone to the essays that follow. We were also assisted by Carol Peterson, the journal's managing editor, Debbie Styles, its copyeditor, and Susan Pasternack, its proofreader. Mark Linnen and Antonio Wendland assisted in the preparation of the edited collection. The Hoover Institution of Stanford University is the publisher of *Education Next: A Journal of Opinion and Research*. Copyright to the articles included in this volume is held by the Trustees of Leland Stanford Jr. University. All rights except those granted to Rowman & Littlefield are reserved. We wish to thank John Raisian, director of the Hoover Institution, for granting permission to use this material.

PAUL E. PETERSON is Henry Lee Shattuck Professor of Government and director of the Program on Education Policy and Governance at Harvard University, and editor-in-chief of *Education Next: A Journal of Opinion and Research*.

CHAPTER ONE

The Private Can Be Public

John E. Chubb

During the 1999–2000 school year, public school districts spent some $35 billion on goods and services provided by private, for-profit businesses—about 10 percent of the nation's annual K–12 education budget. In other words, districts large and small recognize that for-profit businesses can produce many educational goods and services more efficiently or effectively than districts can themselves. It makes good sense for districts to partner with the private sector. In fact, private businesses now provide not only the pencils, chalk, and computers but also the core of the instructional program in many districts. Most school districts are too small, for example, to develop and produce their own curricula; they buy complete instructional programs from textbook publishers. Teacher training is often provided by the same vendors that publish the textbooks or by firms specializing in various kinds of professional development. States contract with testing companies to develop and administer customized state exams. Districts choose from commercially available standardized tests to measure students against national norms. In short, private business already plays a major supporting role in the provision of public education.

The question now is: Should we give private businesses an even larger role in public education? Companies such as Advantage Schools, Edison Schools, National Heritage, and a dozen or so smaller firms are seeking to actively manage entire public schools—hiring and firing; supervision, evaluation, and compensation; professional development; curriculum, instruction, and assessment; educational technology; plant management—everything. These firms believe that, using economies of scale as well as other tools that are more readily available to the private sector, they can build organizations that use time and resources more efficiently and effectively than public school districts, leading to higher student achievement at a similar cost.

Raising student achievement, of course, is not the only task we assign to the public schools. We also ask them to provide equal educational opportunity to all students and to socialize diverse young people into our democratic culture. Whether private business can fulfill these many roles and still make a profit is a question on which the jury is still out. The very early track record of school management companies was mixed, but recent experience has been more positive. Perhaps 200 public schools are currently under private management, and all of these are schools of choice. At the very least, private managers are offering schools that parents deem worthy of their choosing. And there is preliminary evidence that parents are choosing wisely. Students in schools run by the largest management company, Edison Schools, have, on average, posted meaningful achievement gains in every year those schools have been open. Not all of the schools managed by private firms are doing well; at least a few have closed after experiencing difficulties. It will be some time before the experience of schools under private management is sufficient to permit definitive empirical analysis.

Regardless, as a nation we seem to agree that our schools are not as good as they should be or need to be. Moreover, many academics, policymakers, and even public educators have concluded that some schools cannot or will not make the necessary changes on their own. They may be too paralyzed by politics, bogged down by bureaucracy, or incapable of innovation to move achievement forward rapidly. In this environment, experimentation is called for, particularly the kind that gives parents a wider range of educational options from which to choose. These choices could be charter schools, which are an independent form of public school, or contract schools, public schools that would be operated by private businesses. More radical advocates say private schools should also be available as a choice, reimbursed at taxpayer expense via vouchers. Charters and contract schools, as potentially powerful sources of market influence on a public education system that clearly needs it, deserve a serious trial.

What can or will for-profit firms do differently from public schools? For one, private businesses can make more effective use of scale than public schools. Most school districts are either too small or too large—too small to afford the kind of administrative supports they need, or too large for a public bureaucracy to remain easily governable and accountable. A for-profit firm is more likely to build an effective organization that can serve hundreds or even thousands of schools, giving them the supports they need while leaving more resources to be spent at the school level. For another, the capital-raising ability of private businesses gives them the capability to make the financial investments in research and development and comprehensive school reform that public schools can only dream of. And finally, private businesses have more freedom than public entities to structure their instructional practices and employee contracts in ways that maximize their performance. Their relative freedom from the constraints of state rules and, sometimes, excessively constraining collectively bargained contracts allows them to stay focused on their mission and to steer all their resources toward accomplishing it.

Scaling Up

Critics of private management ask: What can business do that the public sector cannot? The answer is: Anything that requires scale to accomplish. Private, for-profit firms must build organizations that achieve efficient and effective scale. They must deliver quality products and services at reasonable prices or be driven out of business. Firms that built bureaucracy that failed to deliver for the public schools would have no future. The political process often creates and protects bureaucracy; a competitive market discourages it. The market permits society to gain the benefits of scale without paying the costs of bureaucracy.

Most local school systems are very small operations. The average school district contains only six schools—four elementary schools, a middle school, and a high school—and serves 3,100 students. Thousands of school systems are smaller still. Of the nearly 15,000 school districts in America, roughly 7,000 are truly tiny, with fewer than 1,000 students, and 3,500 are well below the national average, with only 1,000–2,499 students. Relatively few school districts—barely 2,500 nationwide—exceed even the moderate size of 5,000 students.

Small size creates two problems. First, a superintendent and staff are clearly capable of supervising districts much larger than the districts that are typical of American education. Yet, with 15,000 mostly small school districts, the nation expends more resources than it should on redundant district administrative operations. At the same time, however, these administrative expenditures aren't enough to provide sufficient services in small districts. Because most districts are small, they have the resources to deliver only the most basic support. It is not unusual, for example, for a school district to have only two professionals to supervise and support the district's full educational program, from the teaching of pre-reading skills in kindergarten to the teaching of Advanced Placement physics in high school. Such a district lacks the scale to offer anything more than essential services—facilities, accounting, payroll, and compliance. The instructional program is designed almost entirely by the teachers and principals. A for-profit firm, by contrast, could provide to hundreds or even thousands of public schools, and their teachers and principals, the support that they need—and that only a large-scale organization could possibly offer.

The idea that most school districts are actually too small may seem counterintuitive. After all, sheer size appears to have been unhelpful to the public schools. Twenty-five American school districts, including New York, Philadelphia, Chicago, and Detroit, possess the size—more than 100,000 students each—and the resources to build the kinds of organizations that might effectively support the schools, by recruiting and training high-caliber teachers, developing a demanding curriculum, and building an assessment system that accurately tracks student progress. But appearances can be deceiving. These school systems do not have vast resources at their disposal to build whatever kind of support system their schools may need. Resources are consumed administering programs and fulfilling mandates over which the local administration has little say. These urban systems contend with the toughest—and most expensive—educational challenges in the nation. Big as they are, moreover, these systems are not big by the standards of private enterprise. Public education has truly not given scale a try.

By serving as a sort of mega-district for a large number of schools, and thus putting scale to good use, a for-profit firm could free up more education dollars for use at the school and classroom level. Not only students but also their teachers would ultimately benefit. Public school systems that are too small to enjoy any economies of scale or too large to avoid the inefficiencies of public bureaucracy cannot maximize the education dollars devoted to teacher salaries. A typical school system spends only 45 percent of its revenue on teacher salaries. Meanwhile, school systems spend anywhere from 5 to 30 percent of their revenue on support systems and administration—what the private sector calls overhead. A private business aims to keep overhead below 5 percent. The point is not that education should work like a private business. The point is that a business has advantages of scale and political autonomy in supporting schools, advantages that ought to enable it to enhance productivity. For instance, teachers in Edison Schools work a school year that is 10 percent longer than the national norm, and Edison is able generally to pay teachers 10 percent more than they would earn in another public school—all for the same dollars that other public schools receive.

Of all students, disadvantaged children could have the most to gain from the efficiencies of private management. Disadvantaged students are concentrated in the larger school systems where politics is most intense and change is hardest to bring about—because there is so much system potentially to change. Private management allows for a large system to contract for change on a limited basis—for, say, several needy schools—without having to change the entire school system, as ambitious internal reforms would demand. Private firms have already shown a great interest in serving the most disadvantaged of students. Edison's 113 schools include contracts with many of the largest school systems, such as Dallas, San Francisco, Minneapolis, Miami, and Wichita. The students in Edison Schools are disproportionately needy or of minority background; 65 percent are eligible for federal free or reduced-price lunches, while 55 percent are black and 17 percent are Hispanic or Latino. Privatization could thus serve as an important equalizer in public education.

Larger scale could also enhance the way that schools purchase goods and services from the private sector. Currently, school districts depend on those textbooks and instructional programs that have proved strong enough to make it in the marketplace. The problem is that the education market is defined not by the nation's 15,000 districts but by a handful of large "adoption" states—mainly California, Florida, and Texas. Their lists of "approved" textbooks and instructional materials largely determine the books and software that will be available to the rest of the states, because the remaining purchasers are too small and heterogeneous to strongly influence publishers. Moreover, as a fundamentally political process, state adoption decisions often focus more on pleasing various interest groups than on enhancing the schools' instructional programs. Publishers frequently lard their products with every bell and whistle that is hot in the world of education, hoping that all of the state decision makers will find their interests represented. The result is textbooks and instructional materials that offer a little bit of everything to everyone, rather than a well-structured, cohesive, and effective program.

A for-profit management firm, by contrast, could not tolerate the kinds of compromises that yield dubious educational materials. A management company's survival would depend on building effective support systems for its instructional programs. It would thus demand that publishers and software makers provide comprehensive and integrated services that contribute to an enhanced educational experience. The entry of for-profit firms into the educational management field could force the purveyors of educational support materials to provide more effective products to the entire education market.

R&D

Making private businesses accountable for raising student achievement also would substantially raise the nation's investment in educational research and development. It is difficult to estimate how much is spent on educational R&D each year, but the total does not exceed $100 million. This is a pitiful .03 percent of public school spending. For-profit firms often spend 100 times that amount in percentage terms. And what little educational R&D does take place is not done by the people running the schools, who might know what research is needed. Education research and development is done mainly by university-based outsiders, with academic agendas of their own. Most of this research, moreover, is just that: research. There is little follow-through, or development, to put the research into practice.

Research and development is a powerful force in the private sector for innovations in goods, services, and productivity. Firms invest heavily in it to maintain competitive advantage. It is difficult to fathom how public education imagines bringing about great advances in teaching and learning when its current structure does not allow it to invest seriously in understanding or improving its practices. If businesses were responsible for running, say, 10 percent of America's schools, spending on education research and development could be expected to reach $1 billion a year—ten times current levels. In fact, public education already puts more faith in the research and development performed by private businesses—textbook publishers and software vendors, to name a few—than it does in research sponsored by the government or foundations. For-profit management firms would expand their R&D efforts in an attempt to integrate all the elements that contribute to student achievement—curriculum, instruction, assessment, professional development, technology. The spending would address areas of schooling that have never been seriously researched before, such as management systems, compensation plans, and school organization. Estimating the impact of all of this new R&D is impossible, but it undoubtedly represents a dramatic upgrade of the unfortunate status quo.

Moreover, the schools have not maximized the potential of the R&D that has been done. Several promising "whole school reform" models, such as "Modern Red Schoolhouse" and "Atlas Schools," both the products of intense R&D efforts, have been placed on the market, but thus far their record in boosting student achievement has been pretty mixed. The disappointments, however, seem to have much more to do with the implementation of the models than with the models themselves.

Privatization could dramatically advance the implementation of comprehensive school reform. Comprehensive school reform has foundered on two obstacles. One is money. To change everything that a school is doing, from its curriculum to its technology, to its training and ongoing support, to its assessment of student progress, is potentially quite expensive. Relative to the normal funding of schools, the costs are simply huge. A typical school receives money for new curricula in perhaps one major subject area every two years. It receives money to pay for two or three days of teacher training per school year. Money for a comprehensive change does not exist, unless it can be raised from a government or philanthropic grant program or from a bond issue approved by local voters. These are tough ways to spur widespread reform. Private businesses, however, could fund comprehensive reform with investment dollars. Edison Schools, for example, invests about $1.5 million in the start-up of each school and earns the investment back during the course of its contract. This money ensures that Edison's comprehensive reform model is launched as effectively as possible.

Another obstacle to comprehensive reform that businesses can help overcome is what is often called "buy-in." Comprehensive reform requires the enthusiastic assent and long-term cooperation of every teacher and administrator in the school. Without this buy-in, the reform breaks down. Teachers can close their doors and do their own thing; they can write off the reform as just another fad. Public schools struggle with the buy-in problem for many reasons, not the least of which is the fact that teachers and administrators have rights as public employees and need only go so far in cooperating with reform. A business's relative freedom from the constraints of traditional school systems allows it to reconstitute public schools with teachers and administrators who choose to do something different. Businesses have the ability to implement a contractually agreed-upon reform model—to garner buy-in and to work collaboratively toward better academic results.

Breaking the Mold

The same freedom from constraints that gives businesses an advantage in implementing whole-school reform also allows them to experiment and innovate in ways that public schools find difficult. Most public schools are organized and managed in pretty much the same way, according to the putatively impartial rules of civil service, often with the added constraints of collective bargaining agreements. These rules, like all other rules in public education, are products of political battles fought and settled over the course of more than a century. To be sure, every rule has some higher public purpose—for example, protecting schools from political patronage or ensuring that teachers are treated equitably. But it is also true that the rules that organize public education were not necessarily established to maximize the ability of schools to help students succeed.

These rules are not going to change substantially or rapidly. There are too many powerful interests vested in the status quo and too much uncertainty about what kinds of changes would truly promote better teaching and learning. The beauty of privatization is that new forms of organization can be introduced into public education without making wholesale changes to public education itself. Businesses can be contracted to run public schools based on alternative models of school organization. Teachers and administrators who want to work under new work rules can do so voluntarily. Educators who want to stick with the current system are free to stay the course.

What innovations might business use? The list is very long. Teachers are currently paid on the basis of seniority and education. A business-run school might introduce merit pay and school-wide performance bonuses. Public education debates these ideas endlessly but usually steps away from the plate before implementing anything meaningful. A business-run school might pay more for teachers in shortage positions, such as math and science, to ensure that skilled professionals cover these courses. This is another innovation that is generally too hot for public education to handle.

Businesses would most likely change the supervision and evaluation structures in a school as well. Most schools are run as flat organizational structures in which only specific administrators are permitted to supervise and evaluate teachers. The problem with this system is that the administrators are generally too few to support the teachers or to hold them accountable. Businesses could organize schools around teams, with senior teachers accountable for supervision and evaluation. Schools could offer the senior teacher post to teachers who want more responsibility and pay but don't want an exclusively administrative position.

Business-run schools could also work creatively with class size. Public education is forever mandating maximum class sizes for different grade levels. But class sizes should vary with the specific needs of the students and teachers. Some students need one-on-one tutoring. Some need small group instruction. Others would prosper in large classes. Some could work independently with lessons delivered over the Internet. Teachers also differ. A veteran teacher might be able to handle a large class, a new teacher a class only half that size.

The point is not that any of these innovations are clearly going to promote school improvement. The point is that many of the organizational tools that the private sector uses to great effect are rejected by the public sector, often because they are simply too controversial for public education to embrace broadly. All of these ideas deserve a chance. Private management provides one.

Public Education's Best Hope

The prospects of substantial improvement in public education without substantial changes in the education system itself are not good. Which is why policymakers are looking for ways to change the system through an injection of market forces, as well as imposing rigorous standards of accountability. But there is reason to believe that current efforts will fall short of their desired effects, and that political pressures for more radical change will continue to mount. The choices that policymakers are now granting parents are not generating the kind of competition that is likely to shake up most school systems or to significantly increase the supply of good schools. Choice now is essentially among existing public schools and a limited number of charter schools— less than 2,000 nationwide, scattered across 36 states. When choice is this limited, even the least successful of schools face little pressure to change what they are doing.

Critics of vouchers fear what the unleashing of market forces and the loss of democratic control might mean for the values of public education. They fear that schools catering to parents will appeal to sectarian or ideological interests, that schools will segregate children more than public education already does, that schools will no longer socialize children into a common democratic culture. These fears may be overblown, given that there is no evidence that private schools now turn out bad citizens or that the public schools now do an effective job of promoting unity, tolerance, or democratic understanding. Still, there is no denying that vouchers will limit the ability of society to govern what is taught and to whom.

For those who worry about the unpredictable consequences of vouchers, but who recognize the need to bring competition, choice, and change to public schools, private management offers a very attractive compromise. Private firms competing with one another for the business of public education are an important source of market influence on education. Add this influence to that of private firms operating schools of choice, and public education could have a powerful engine for school improvement driven by the market. Yet this engine would be governed more by the democratic process than would a market driven by private vouchers. What's more, because private management could be introduced directly into any of the nation's 80,000 public schools, private management might improve the quality of schools more rapidly than would vouchers for private schools, which must change the public schools indirectly through competition. In this sense, private management may be the best hope for keeping public education public.

JOHN E. CHUBB is chief education officer and senior vice president at Edison Schools, Inc.

CHAPTER TWO

‿‿

The Costs of Privatization

Henry M. Levin

The recent entry of for-profit schools into the K–12 arena is an intriguing trend. Their promise is that their endless quest for new customers will drive them to innovate at a faster pace than not-for-profit and public schools. The discipline of market economics supposedly will force for-profit schools to streamline their bureaucracies, retain and reward highly talented administrators and teachers, and raise student achievement on a variety of measures. They will be more responsive to consumers and more accountable to local authorities. In short, they claim to offer a better product at a similar if not lower price. In turn, their siphoning of students will cause not-for-profit and public schools to rethink their approaches to schooling. They will seek to learn from and replicate the more efficient management structures and more effective instructional methods of the for-profits. If all goes according to the free-market theorist's model, introducing the profit motive into education will spark a perpetual discovery process that benefits students, employees, and, let us not forget, investors.

So much for theory. The fact is that we know little about how for-profit schools will operate and how they will affect students and other schools. At least three major questions have yet to be answered satisfyingly:

- If schools are a potentially profitable endeavor, then why did entrepreneurs wait so long to enter the market? Is there something unique about schooling that makes it difficult to earn a profit?

- Now that we do have for-profit schools, how will they achieve cost savings? Will they bring fundamentally different approaches to education through curricular and technological innovations that will "break the mold"?
- Even if they are more effective or less costly, or both, will they earn profits that are comparable to the returns on other investments?

Why Now?

That for-profit schools have only now become players in the K–12 market is puzzling, given that public schools have been around for two centuries, independent schools for four. Among the 28,000 or so independent schools in the United States, probably no more than a few hundred have gone the for-profit route. Many of these specialize in education for the severely handicapped and charge very high fees, which are usually paid by states and school districts to meet the federal special-education mandates. Only in the past decade have we seen the onset of major efforts to establish for-profit schools for a broad range of students in K–12 education. For the most part, education management organizations (EMOs) such as Advantage Schools and Edison Schools, the two best-known EMOs, have sought to manage charter schools or public schools under contract to school districts. (Note that for-profit firms have always had a significant role in K–12 education by providing various products and services to schools, such as supplies, textbooks, transportation, and food services.) What stopped investors, entrepreneurs, and educators from taking advantage of the profitable opportunities in running schools over the past century? In essence, what took so long? Is it possible that few saw potential profits in schooling in the past? Then the question becomes: What has changed to create the opportunities that are perceived today?

One reason that entrepreneurs have been reluctant to enter the schooling market is that they must compete against heavily subsidized public schools, which limits their ability to charge prices that fully cover their costs. Thus, the market has been left to those nonprofit organizations that can raise adequate subsidies to keep tuition low. But that does not explain the existence of private schools that compete very effectively, schools in virtually every metropolitan area and whose tuition levels far exceed public school spending. In my city, New York, elite private schools such as Dalton, Horace Mann, Spence, Brearley, Riverdale Country School, and at least two dozen more levy tuitions in the range of $20,000 a year—exceeding what even the wealthiest New York suburban school districts spend per student. Yet they always have more applicants than openings, a surplus that is maintained in good and bad economic times. Isn't this the kind of niche market that profit-seekers salivate over? But here they are invisible.

The problem for entrepreneurs is that for-profit schools compete at a disadvantage against not only public schools but many nonprofit schools as well. For a variety of reasons, virtually all private schools set tuition below the level that would allow full cost recovery. For instance, I serve on the board of a religious private school that must raise half of its budget, despite a price tag in the $13,000-a-year range for high school. One could argue that this subsidy is necessary to attract an adequate number of students. But this year, its seventh in operation, the school had more than twice as many applications as openings for its freshman class.

Fund-raising remains important for such schools, which often provide scholarships to some portion of their students who cannot afford full tuition. In some of the less expensive independent schools, the fund-raising subsidies are needed to cover operating costs. Moreover, fund-raising often still isn't enough. Many of the nonprofit independent schools are also subsidized with below-market personnel costs, donated facilities, and other payments in kind, benefits that are rarely if ever showered on for-profits.

Further complicating the for-profits' task is the fact that the nonprofits with the highest tuitions also have the highest endowments and most vigorous fund-raising efforts. In conversations with their headmasters, one gets the impression that they see themselves, proudly, as sponsoring activities that are not economically justified by tuition charges. These include extensive community-service programs for students and a much wider range of co-curricular and extra-curricular activities and athletic teams than their school enrollments would justify. They also provide a range of amenities whose costs exceed the tuition allotted for them, from very small classes and seminars (ten or fewer students) to guided independent study.

In short, even the most expensive private schools with the most elite clientele fail to cover their costs with tuition. This goes far in explaining why entrepreneurs have shied away from the K–12 market. This is not to say that an individual, for-profit, family-owned school can't survive. I know of a few for-profit schools at the K–12 level and more at the preschool level that appear to be marginally profitable. But much of what appears as profit is due to the family members' hard work for little pay. The salaries they draw on the school understate the value of their time, leaving the impression that the enterprise is profitable.

Whether this can be replicated on a large scale by corporate entities is doubtful. Historically, economic studies have not identified substantial economies of scale in education at school sites or in multi-school endeavors. Perhaps this is for the reason suggested by John Chubb and Terry Moe in *Politics, Markets, and America's Schools* (1990): that the best results are obtained when schools are given great autonomy. A corporate competitor in schooling must establish brand and product identity, which necessitates relatively uniform operations and services from site to site. This puts the need for quality control and similarity from site to site in direct competition with the need to be responsive to differences among particular clients and settings. Moreover, as the economist Richard Rothstein has observed, as corporate entities expand to more and more schools, they are likely to have to rely on standard operating procedures and monitoring to maintain quality control and brand identification. Paradoxically, this is the argument given by states and school districts for their "over-regulation" of public schools—namely, that equity among schools and students requires uniformity that must be secured by mandates, rules, guidelines, and regulations.

Under New Management

The mandate to cut costs and turn a profit inevitably will dictate some of the for-profits' personnel and instructional practices. Education is a highly labor-intensive activity, with wages usually accounting for 80 percent or more of the school budget. This means that the main cost-cutting opportunities lie in cutting personnel costs by using either cheaper personnel or fewer of them. Thus the for-profits may use more part-time personnel (forgoing staff benefits), less experienced teachers whose salaries are lower, larger class sizes, or shorter school days. Substituting capital for labor in the form of computers and educational technology may also be possible, although there is little evidence in the education industry that this has been an effective cost-cutting strategy.

For now, though, the differences among the for-profit, nonprofit, and public education sectors seem mainly cosmetic. Their approaches to educating children change little from sector to sector. The for-profits generally have adopted curricula that are available commercially to all schools. Many public schools and nonprofit schools have long used similar curricula. Instructional practices also do not seem to differ very much. Some public, some nonprofit, and some for-profit schools use direct instruction while others use more "progressive" approaches. The three sectors overlap so much in their curricula and instructional practices that it is difficult to distinguish them from one another.

Some of the for-profits rely more heavily on sophisticated use of educational technologies. But so do a large number of public schools. Some also provide tutoring services and extended school days and years. But so do many public schools. Given these similarities, it appears that curriculum and instructional practices vary far more within each sector than they do among the three sectors.

Where the three sectors do seem to diverge is in their personnel practices, professional development, and managerial practices. Given that the growth in for-profit schools has been mainly in contracting with public schools or charter schools to operate individual public schools as EMOs, how much they diverge often depends on state laws and school district contracts. Some states and districts require EMO-managed schools to hire certified teachers or even to retain the existing teacher force. They also may require them to enforce the existing collective bargaining agreements, leaving the tenure policy untouched. In other states, for-profit entities have much more leeway in hiring employees and in designing their contracts.

Where the laws have granted them flexibility, for-profit schools have tended to hire their teachers with less concern than public schools for whether they have met certification requirements. In some states they need not meet conventional certification requirements at all. The for-profit schools prefer to hire for a fixed term, renewing only the contracts of teachers who have been judged effective. They also rely on various versions of merit pay, usually rewarding some teachers for subject specialization and other talents in order to retain valued teachers and to provide incentives for improvement. In some cases, the incentives include more-extensive career ladders for classroom teachers than the public schools offer.

Some for-profits, like Edison Schools, the largest EMO, emphasize strong professional development by providing as much as three weeks of training a year for teaching staff. By contrast, public schools typically provide only three to four days of staff development a year, with little follow-up or assessment of results. In my view, this is an important difference between the two sectors, since strong and cohesive professional-development sessions with subsequent mentoring and assessment is one of the most promising methods for heightening school effectiveness.

For-profit schools also give their principals more decision-making powers and provide more incentives for making effective decisions, particularly with regard to personnel practices. They expect principals to monitor the selection and hiring process as well as teacher assessment and to retain only those teachers whom they consider highly productive. This flexibility does not, however, carry over to the academic realm. Corporate entities run many of the new for-profit schools, and to establish their brand identity they have sought relative uniformity in instructional practices from site to site. For example, Advantage Schools uses direct instruction in all of its schools, an approach that relies heavily on teacher lectures and drill. Because the use of direct instruction is one of Advantage's selling points, its school principals have no leeway to deviate from this approach. Other firms have selected specific curricula for each learning domain, and all of their schools are required to use these curricula in the same way.

Attracting Clients

The issue of brand identity raises questions about how for-profit schools will sell themselves in the education market. If their instructional practices don't vary much from those of their public and private competitors, how will they differentiate themselves?

We have too little experience with for-profit schools to answer this question fully. What is clear is that schools will avoid the notion that they are interchangeable, producing similar products and competing on price alone, as the model of perfect competition assumes. Without a voucher system in which parents may supplement the voucher, for-profit schools will be bound by fixed per-pupil allocations, hindering their ability to compete on price. Thus I would expect that they would seek to differentiate themselves from other schools with claims of superior student achievement (difficult to prove in the absence of sophisticated and costly evaluations by third parties) and by using marketing images to persuade parents and school boards that they offer a superior education. If a firm wishes to expand to many schools, then it must have a brand image and at least some evidence that it is succeeding systematically across school sites. The best way to accomplish this is to set unique goals that will appeal to a client niche and claim effectiveness on those goals rather than to compete on similar dimensions with every other school. This is precisely the strategy followed by the middle and upper strata of the non-profit schools. For example, most private high schools refused even to participate in U.S. News & World Report's attempt to rank the nation's best high schools. Likewise, in New York State, a large portion of private schools have sought waivers from the state's requirement that all schools participate in the Regents examinations—for which the state will publicly report the scores.

But, if states and school districts continue to insist on using state standards and tests to judge school performance, then the for-profits will be pushed to compete for contracts and clientele on the basis of a narrower set of criteria. This would give the for-profits, with their more flexible managerial and personnel policies, some advantage in the marketplace. They will be able to hire and maintain a teaching force with the goal of higher test scores in mind, and they will have more flexibility than public schools do to reward or punish their teachers on the basis of test results. For-profit firms are most effective when they focus on tight objectives rather than the normally diffuse activities that we demand from public schools. These narrow goals will also give for-profit schools a powerful incentive to admit and encourage those students whom they expect to do well on achievement tests or who are likely to show the greatest value-added—that is, the greatest improvement in test scores. (There is some reason to believe that it is the lower-middle portion of the student distribution where test scores are most malleable over the short run, as opposed to those students in the least-advantaged or most-advantaged circumstances.) Such policies will pressure the for-profits as well as other schools to "teach to the test" and to provide considerable test practice. If profits are tied to test scores, then the pressure will only build.

There is one area in which costs will most certainly be higher than for public schools: that of marketing and promotion. For-profit schools, especially those with regional and national ambitions, must establish a brand identity for their schools and must also promote themselves intensively to penetrate their markets. Currently this marketing effort is devoted mainly to school districts and charter school prospects in order to obtain contracts. At the district level, this means considerable lobbying of board members and administrators as well as parents. It also may mean informational retreats at pleasant venues for board members and superintendents and many meetings with stakeholders such as teachers and other unions and parents. Even under a system of vouchers, the emerging competition will require intense marketing to distinguish one EMO's schools from the crowd. All in all, marketing and promotion inevitably will absorb resources that could have gone to instruction.

My observations here are limited by our lack of experience with for-profit education. But there is much to be learned from the case of Chile, where a voucher system has been in place for two decades. In Chile, students are found in four types of schools: elite schools that do not accept vouchers and charge considerably more than the voucher; for-profit voucher schools; nonprofit (usually religious) voucher schools; and municipal schools. Since vouchers were introduced, voucher schools have grown considerably—from only about

15 percent of enrollments in 1981 to about one-third of total enrollments in 1996—and for-profit schools accounted for the majority of the growth. For-profit voucher schools have lowered their costs by hiring part-time teachers (who are often teaching full-time in municipal schools), paying lower salaries, and enlarging class sizes. They devote considerable effort to differentiating themselves in the marketplace, often by choosing English names that lend a patina of prestige. Studies show that after adjusting for student characteristics, the for-profit schools achieve at a slightly lower level in Spanish and mathematics than both the municipal and Catholic schools. Since their costs are lower, however, they are also somewhat more cost-effective. There are no dramatic differences among the three voucher-funded sectors.

Will for-profit education evolve here as it has in Chile? The lack of extensive experience with for-profit schools in the United States means that almost any assertions are speculative. We are going through a period of great experimentation as more and more for-profit firms enter the market to manage schools for the public sector or establish their own schools. Unfortunately, none of the EMOs has been around long enough for us to draw any firm conclusions. And, given their current balance sheets (none has announced profits yet), many may not be around for the long haul.

HENRY M. LEVIN is William Heard Kilpatrick Professor of Economics and Education at Teachers College, Columbia University.

SECTION II

~~

The Education Profession

Should We Deregulate Entry into the Profession?

CHAPTER THREE

~~~

Regulations Do More Harm than Good

Frederick M. Hess

Picture Gerard, a 28-year-old business consultant who majored in economics at Williams College and graduated with a 3.7 GPA. Gerard has been working for a consulting firm in Stamford, Connecticut, but is looking for a new, more fulfilling position. He has demonstrated strong interpersonal skills and work habits. In addition, though he didn't major in math, he aced several calculus courses in college. Yet if Gerard were to apply through normal channels to teach math at a junior high school in the Hartford public school system, his application wouldn't even be considered. Why? Because he isn't a certified teacher.

Why shouldn't a principal or a faculty hiring committee in the Hartford schools even be allowed to look at Gerard's application, to judge his qualifications against those of other candidates? The assumption undergirding the contemporary approach to teacher certification is that public school hiring personnel are either unable or unwilling to gauge the quality of applicants. Our response has been to embrace a bureaucratic solution that handcuffs the capable and incapable alike and supposedly keeps weak teachers out of the classroom. As a result, having discouraged or turned away Gerard and hundreds like him, many large school systems resort to last-minute fill-ins who teach on emergency certificates.

This is not to suggest, even for a moment, that candidates with "real world" experience or high GPAs are necessarily qualified or equipped to become teachers or that professional preparation for teachers is unimportant.

It is only to say that some potential applicants might be more effective teachers than the alternatives that are currently available to public schools.

The central premise underlying teacher certification is that—no matter what their qualifications are—anyone who has not completed the specified training is unsuited to enter a classroom and must be prohibited from applying for a job. Presumably, the danger is that, in a moment of weakness, a school official otherwise will mistakenly hire such an applicant rather than an appropriately trained teacher. It is essential to remember what we often seem to forget, which is that allowing someone to apply for a job is not the same as guaranteeing him employment. Making applicants eligible for a position simply permits an employer to hire them in the event that they are deemed superior to the existing alternatives. The argument against certification is not that unconventional applicants will be good teachers; it is only that they might be. If one believes this, case-by-case judgments are clearly more appropriate than an inflexible bureaucratic rule.

Imagine if colleges and universities refused to hire anyone who lacked a Ph.D. They would lose the talents and insights of "lay practitioners" like poet Maya Angelou, journalist William Raspberry, or former public officials such as Alan Simpson, Julian Bond, and Al Gore. The artists and writers "in residence" at dozens of public universities would fail to meet the criteria implicit in the public school certification model. Do we really believe that these universities are ill-serving their students by hiring people whom the public schools would consider unqualified?

What is needed is a competitive certification process that establishes key criteria for entry into the teaching profession; gives public schools greater freedom to hire and fire teachers; and treats teachers like professionals.

Competitive Certification

The theory behind certifying or licensing public school teachers is that this process elevates the profession by ensuring that aspiring teachers master a well-documented and broadly accepted body of knowledge and skills important to teaching. Supporters of teacher certification often make analogies to professions like law and medicine, where being an effective professional requires the acquisition of vast knowledge and skills. Licensure in these professions ensures at least minimal competency and boosts the public's confidence in members of the profession.

The problem is that no comparable body of knowledge and skills exists in teaching. Debate rages over the merits of various pedagogical strategies, and even teacher educators and certification proponents have a hard time defining a clear set of concrete skills that makes for a good teacher. Yet most aspiring teachers are still forced to run a gauntlet of courses, requirements, and procedures created by accredited training programs that vary dramatically in quality.

This is not to deny that teacher education can provide valuable training. After all, one may think that journalism schools produce better journalists without requiring all journalists to complete a mandatory set of courses before seeking work in the profession. Instead, it is assumed that a candidate's training is factored into the hiring process, along with considerations like aptitude, diligence, and energy.

Clearly some sort of screening process for aspiring teachers is essential; parents and the public rightly expect safeguards for those working with youngsters. What is needed is a competitive certification process that establishes key criteria for entry into the teaching profession; gives public schools greater freedom to hire and fire teachers; and treats teachers like professionals and their schools like professional institutions by allowing them to tailor professional development to meet the needs of teachers. Under such a model, aspiring teachers ought to be able to apply for a teaching job if they:

- Possess a B.A. or B.S. degree from a recognized college or university.
- Pass a test that demonstrates competency in knowledge or skills essential to what they seek to teach. The definition of "essential" knowledge or skills is obviously a loose one that can be interpreted in myriad ways and rightly should be different for those wishing to teach younger children or older students. The key point is to demand that teachers at least have an appropriate academic knowledge of the material they will be teaching.
- Pass a rigorous criminal background check. States conduct such checks now, but they tend to be compromised by the state's need to engage simultaneously in related certification paperwork.

Beyond these minimal qualifications, the competitive approach presumes that preparation and training are not only desirable but also essential, as is true in other professions where subtle skills and interpersonal dynamics are essential to effective performance. The questions are where to obtain this training and who should pay for it. Contemporary teacher preparation imposes nearly all of the costs on candidates by forcing them into a system of training that removes key incentives for quality and relevance in teacher preparation. The competitive model instead treats teachers as autonomous professionals able to make informed decisions about developing their skills and expertise. In short, the competitive model would substitute meaningful professional development for what is essentially a guild system funded by levying a significant tuition-based tax on aspiring teachers before permitting them to enter the profession.

The Assumptions of Certification

Over the years, an array of studies has sought to determine whether certified teachers serve students more effectively than uncertified teachers. There are two problems with this line of work. First, the methodological wrangling has often obscured the larger questions and the central assumptions of the certification model. Second, the case for certification is thin whether or not certified teachers boost student achievement more than their uncertified peers. The issue is not whether teacher education improves the performance of graduates, but whether we ought to—as best we are able—bar from teaching those who have not completed an approved preparatory program. Certification systems deny school administrators the ability to take their context or the promise of a particular applicant into account when hiring. Even if certified teachers are generally more effective than uncertified teachers, such a policy only makes sense if we believe that uncertified applicants are uniformly incompetent to teach or that school administrators cannot be trusted to assess their competence.

The allure of certification rests on three implicit assumptions. They are the beliefs that: (1) the training one receives while getting certified is so useful that the uncertified will be relatively ill-prepared; (2) certification weeds out unsuitable candidates; and (3) certification makes teaching more "professional" and therefore a more attractive career. However, each of these presumptions is problematic in the case of teacher certification.

As a general principle, certification is most effective when the licensing body ensures that aspiring professionals have mastered essential skills or knowledge and denies a license to inadequate performers. Licensure is most essential when a professional's tasks are critical and when clients may have trouble assessing a provider's qualifications. For instance, licensure is considered particularly appropriate for engineers, doctors, and attorneys because those who design bridges, tend us when we are ill, or defend our rights all perform tasks essential to our well-being and are frequently charged with aiding us at our most vulnerable. Moreover, it can be difficult for members of the public to know whether a bridge is properly designed, whether a doctor is performing appropriately, or whether an attorney is knowledgeable in the law. Licensing is not an assurance that these professionals are talented practitioners, but it does ensure that they have demonstrated an established degree of professional knowledge.

Educators are also charged with a crucial task. However, the oversight challenge is very different in education, where we have not established a specific, measurable body of skills or knowledge that teachers must master. Educational "experts" themselves argue that teaching is so complex that it can be difficult to judge a good teacher outside of a specific classroom context. This makes it difficult, if not impossible, to determine abstractly which aspirants possess satisfactory "teaching skills." Meanwhile, there is widespread agreement that colleagues, supervisors, and families have at least a proximate ability to gauge whether a teacher is effective. Given these circumstances, it is unclear how standardized licensing helps to safeguard teacher quality.

Such a conclusion does not require refuting the claims of teacher educators or the supporters of certification. It actually follows if one simply accepts their claims. Professional educators themselves have thus far been unable to explain in any concrete sense what makes a teacher competent or what teachers need to know and be able to do.

Consider the widely praised standards that the National Board for Professional Teaching Standards (NBPTS) has painstakingly constructed in twenty-seven distinct fields, standards that certification's proponents have hailed as a breakthrough in quality control. The area where the NBPTS ought to have the easiest time creating straightforward standards is high school math and science teaching, where there is widespread consensus as to what teachers are supposed to do. Even in these areas, however, the NBPTS's "exemplary" standards are so broad and vague as to make concrete judgments of competence nearly impossible. For instance, to receive National Board certification to teach high school math, teachers are to demonstrate mastery of eleven standards, including: commitment to students and their learning, the art of teaching, reflection and growth, and reasoning and thinking mathematically. The board tries to clarify these standards by explaining, for instance, that "commitment" is interpreted as meaning that "accomplished mathematics teachers value and acknowledge the individuality and worth of each student, believe that all students can learn," and so on. Mastering the "art of teaching" is taken to mean that teachers "stimulate and facilitate student learning by using a wide range of formats and procedures." While these are certainly admirable sentiments, nowhere in the National Board's rarified standards is it clear how we are to gauge just what constitutes "competence" in these tasks. The result, unsurprisingly, is that the board has been assailed for the capricious way in which the standards are being interpreted and applied. Despite the best of intentions in the drafting of the INTASC standards, which Mary Diez discusses, a cursory read makes clear that they are plagued by the same ambiguities evident in the NBPTS standards.

For another prominent example, consider education professors Gerald Grant and Christine E. Murray's award-winning 1999 Harvard University Press book, *Teaching in America*. They identify five "essential [teaching] acts" that can be analyzed and taught: listening with care; motivating the student; modeling caring by hearing and responding to the pain of others, and by creating a sense of security in their classrooms; evaluating by clarifying, coaching, advising, and deciding on an appropriate challenge for this boy or that girl; and reflecting and renewing. How one is to teach these five "essential acts," much less determine whether a teacher has satisfactorily mastered them, are questions that Grant and Murray never address.

If clear standards of professional competence do not exist, we typically (and appropriately) hesitate to prohibit some individuals from practicing a profession. This is not to say that we think incompetence is acceptable in such a profession—only that we recognize licensing as an ineffective and potentially pernicious way to control quality. While licensure could protect community members (including children) from exposure to "bad" entrepreneurs or journalists, we do not prohibit some people from seeking to start businesses or work for a newspaper. Instead, we trust that potential investors or employers are the best judges of who ought to be supported or hired. If an aspiring writer or entrepreneur is unsuccessful, we trust that they will eventually be persuaded to find a line of work for which they are better suited. This free-flowing process fosters diversity and ensures that unconventional workers are given a chance to succeed.

Even in professions with clear knowledge- or performance-based benchmarks for certification, as in law or medicine, licensure is useful primarily as a way of establishing minimal competence. A medical or a law license is not imagined to ensure competence in ambiguous, subtle skills like comforting a patient or swaying a jury—skills analogous to the interpersonal relations thought crucial to teaching. Basing certification on such traits is difficult, because we may disagree about what they entail or how they can be assessed devoid of context. The skills that teacher educators deem most important—listening, caring, motivating—are not susceptible to standardized quality control. Emphasis on these qualities is the norm in professions like marketing, journalism, consulting, or policymaking, where a subtle blend of people skills, knowledge, and relevant expertise is required. In professions like these, where there are a number of ways for practitioners to excel but where it is difficult to know in advance how any particular practitioner will perform, the most sensible way to find talent is to allow aspirants to seek work and to permit employers to screen on a variety of criteria—such as education, experience, and references.

A Dubious Screen

While certification can serve to screen out aspirants who fail to meet a minimal performance standard, our current system is not designed to do so. Generally speaking, schools of education are not selective, flunk out few if any students for inadequate performance, and see that many of their teacher education graduates receive teacher licenses. The licensing exams are simple, and standards for passage are generally so low that the Education Trust concluded they exclude only the "weakest of the weak" from classrooms.

More than 1,300 institutions provide the training required for licensure. While defenders of the current approach to certification often focus on the certification programs at elite institutions, the top 25 education schools train less than 5 percent of the roughly 200,000 new graduates that teacher programs produce each year. It is the regional colleges, such as Illinois State University, Cal State–Hayward, and Southwest Texas State University—not the Stanfords and the Ohio States—that train and license the vast majority of teachers. The value of certification turns not on the quality of elite programs but on that of regional colleges.

Teacher-preparation programs neither screen out nor weed out weak candidates. Even at elite schools, such as UCLA or the University of North Carolina, where admissions rates are about 5 percent for medical school and 25 percent for law school, the M.Ed. programs (which include those seeking postgraduate training for teacher certification) accept more than half of their applicants. Moreover, education school officials often make it clear that they do not see their mission as weeding out students during their course of study. Notes one such official, "We're here to develop teachers, not to screen people out. For the most part, everyone who enters the program is going to complete it, unless they decide that teaching's not for them."

The Costs of Certification

Especially for anyone who didn't complete a teacher-training program as an undergraduate, the costs of certification can be significant. It is not unusual for postgraduate teacher-training programs to require a full-time commitment of sixteen or even twenty-four months or a part-time commitment that can stretch to three years or more. The cost of training and the loss of salary due to time spent out of the workforce can easily reduce a teacher's real compensation during her first five years by 25 percent or more.

These barriers make other professions relatively more attractive, so that potentially talented teachers who are unsure about their interest are less likely to try teaching. Whereas candidates can readily try journalism or consulting or marketing for a year, they must make an extensive commitment before they can try public school teaching. The result is that many who might make fine teachers never enter the profession. There is disturbing evidence that certification may especially dissuade accomplished minority candidates—who have a number of attractive career options and who are often less well situated to absorb the costs of teacher preparation—from entering teaching.

This would pose no real problem if we were blessed with a surplus of good teachers. In such a case, we might scoff "good riddance" to those dissuaded from teaching. However, we have a desperate need for competent teachers. Moreover, rather than a lack of commitment to teaching, a reluctance to pursue certification may indicate that individuals have attractive alternatives. It is the most talented and hardest working individuals who have the most career options and who sacrifice the most by entering a profession where compensation is unlinked to performance and where opportunities for advancement are few. They may wish to teach but be unwilling to forgo work for a year, sit through poorly regarded courses, or jump through procedural hurdles. It is candidates with fewer attractive options who will find the tedious but intellectually undemanding requirements of certification less problematic. In fact, by suppressing the supply of teachers, certification provides teachers with enhanced job security. Coupled with a compensation scale that rewards seniority rather than performance, certification may well make the profession more attractive to graduates seeking a less demanding line of work. In this way, certification can actually harm the public's perception of teaching as a profession—the very opposite of what certification proponents wish to do.

Creative Destruction

In a world without certification as we know it, districts and schools would have more flexibility to ensure that their new teachers are prepared, inducted, and supervised in a manner appropriate to the challenges at hand. Because aspiring teachers would no longer have to attend formal teacher-preparation programs in order to teach, they would be free to make professional decisions about training in the same manner as business school or journalism school students. Weaker teacher-preparation programs would likely fall by the wayside. The fact that schools of education could no longer rely on a captive body of aspiring teachers would expose them to the cleansing winds of competition. Schools would have to contribute value—by providing teacher training, services, or research that created demand and attracted support—or face significant cutbacks. Teacher-preparation programs would find it in their own self-interest to ensure that their graduates were knowledgeable and skilled, as this would help graduates to win desirable jobs amid increased competition, making preparatory institutions more attractive.

Under a competitive certification system, little is likely to change in many of our high-performing suburban districts, where officials are inundated with applicants and are unlikely to tamper with a formula that is "working." In such districts, except in rare cases, we would expect that administrators would continue to cherry-pick from the nation's top teacher-education graduates. It is in the less desirable and more troubled systems, the nation's urban and rural school districts, that administrators currently have tremendous difficulty finding sufficient numbers of certified teachers. This is doubly true in the areas of math and science education. It is in these districts and subjects, where critics have fretted about the numbers of long-term substitutes and "burned out" veterans, where the wave of new teachers will most likely be recruited and welcomed. While many of the resultant applicants will no doubt be deemed unprepared or unsuited for the jobs they pursue, there are few urban or rural principals who would not welcome the chance to pick and choose from their ranks.

Critics may fear that the elimination of licensure requirements will mean the end of teacher preparation and professional development. Such concern is unfounded. First, allowing uncertified individuals to become teachers does not mean that they must be viewed as "completed" professionals. Such a mindset is one of the vestiges of our current system, which is erected on a premise that all teachers are certified and therefore competent. Here, a better model might be medicine or law, where entering professionals begin their career with a trial period (serving as a hospital resident or as a junior partner in a law firm, for instance) during which their full panoply of skills is developed and monitored. Beginning teachers might serve on a probationary basis, receiving substantial monitoring and counseling. However, legal and contractual language ought to make it much simpler to terminate ineffective teachers or to mandate that they engage in support activities designed to improve their performance.

Second, moving to competitive certification does not mean doing away with professional teacher-education programs. Many applicants attend journalism school or business school, even though such training is not officially required, because it may make graduates more effective and can help them find better employment more readily. Likewise, aspiring teachers would presumably continue to attend those teacher-training programs thought to enhance their employability. This change would introduce some much-needed market pressure in this area, as schools would be forced to compete for students based on the usefulness of their course offerings.

Giving districts more leeway to hire promising candidates does not mean they will always make good decisions. Some ineffective teachers will inevitably continue to be hired. However, if entry to the profession is eased, it is appropriate that exit be eased as well. If administrators are to have more leeway to make hiring decisions, they also must be given more leeway to fire—and they must be held accountable for both sets of decisions.

At the end of the day, the individuals best equipped to assess the qualifications of prospective teachers are the principals who will be responsible for them. These same principals ought to have the strongest incentive to see that teachers are effective. If we believe that the administrators charged with managing and supervising schools either are unequipped to evaluate prospective teachers or are unwilling to do so, teacher certification will not suffice to protect our children from such profound systemic dysfunction. If we trust administrators, then certification is unnecessary and entails significant costs. If we don't trust administrators, let us address that issue directly and not rely on the hollow promise of flimsy parchment barriers. Regardless, it is past time to fully acknowledge the nuanced, multifaceted, and professional nature of teaching and to move beyond a system that restricts professional entry with procedural barriers characterized by ambiguity that are the result of an inability to clearly define the skills, knowledge, or training essential to good teaching.

FREDERICK M. HESS is a resident scholar at the American Enterprise Institute.

⁓

CHAPTER FOUR

In Defense of Regulation

Mary E. Diez

I recently came across a flyer from the National Private Schools Association offering, among other things, certification for private school teachers. Intrigued, I went to the association's website and discovered these requirements: provide information, all self-reported, on your academic background, teaching experience, and character; obtain a reference from an employer or colleague who will nominate you for certification (although no criteria for such nomination are provided); and pay $50 (your school also must pay an annual fee of $75 for you to be eligible).

While the existing system of licensure for public school teachers is more rigorous than simply rubber-stamping someone's self-report on competence, most thoughtful people agree that the system is in need of a major overhaul. As a result, the processes and institutions that license teachers are changing, and many of the changes promise to ensure that teachers enter the classroom well equipped to work effectively with learners.

The problem with many states' licensure requirements has been that they have not been thoughtfully developed as a coherent picture of what teachers need to know in order to be effective.

Why License Teachers?

Requiring teachers to be licensed seems intuitively appropriate, given their role in society. Society requires many professionals who work directly with the public, including lawyers, psychologists, nurses, and doctors, to be licensed in order to protect the public. These regulations ensure that the professionals working in these fields have the skills and knowledge required to perform their services effectively and ethically. Should the professionals who spend six to eight hours alone in a room with twenty vulnerable children be subject to any less scrutiny? Licensing teachers is a way to assure the public that teachers are competent, are qualified, and will, at the very least, do no harm.

The most basic purpose of licensure is to give the state control over who can teach, preventing those convicted of sexual misconduct, child abuse, or other relevant offenses from becoming or continuing to be school employees. Most states require a criminal background check as a part of licensure. Similarly, states screen with tests of basic skills in literacy and mathematics to ensure that the academic skills of would-be teachers are at least above some minimum threshold.

Like other bureaucratic processes, licensure also serves as a means of enforcing regulations. Most states have prescribed the coursework that candidates for licenses must take, down to the number of credits in specified courses with specified content. In Wisconsin, for example, elementary teachers cannot receive an initial license or renew a current license without proof of having completed coursework in how to teach reading using phonics. For an initial license, that proof comes as part of a twelve-hour concentration in reading and language arts. In many states, teachers must earn additional professional development credits (usually six credits every five years) in order to renew their licenses, but teachers can earn these credits in areas that bear little relationship to their practice. Many teachers select courses based on their convenience and cost instead of their professional value. At a recent Wisconsin Education Association Council's convention, banners over the booth of one out-of-state professional development provider read, "Three credits—five days!" States have written their policies in such a way that the number of credits earned has become more important than the skills learned, in both teacher education and continuing professional development.

The problem with many states' licensure requirements has been that they have not been thoughtfully developed as a coherent picture of what teachers need to know in order to be effective. Rather, they have been piecemeal collections of basic knowledge and skills, coupled with trendy political issues that have been voted into statute. For example, state legislators added the study of environmental education, human relations, and conflict resolution to the licensure requirements in Wisconsin. And if you want to be licensed to teach high school social studies in Wisconsin, state law requires that you study the economics of dairy cooperatives.

Licensure, for the most part, has served its basic purpose of keeping dangerous people out of the classroom, ensuring that teachers are literate and numerate, and enforcing training and coursework requirements. Furthermore, in the past fifteen years, the route to licensure has become less rigid and bureaucratic. In some states, dual systems of licensure—for "regular" and "alternative" routes—have emerged, sparking lively discussion among those who continue to be held to the "regular" requirements. Nevertheless, the process of licensing teachers has come under scrutiny in an increasing number of states, as critics ask whether current licensure practice actually leads to higher student achievement. More and more, the challenge to business as usual in teacher licensure is resulting in a complete overhaul of the process.

A Meaningful License

Reformers have asked three questions in seeking to develop a licensing system that guarantees not only that teachers have met a series of requirements, but also that they are prepared to enter classrooms as effective teachers. They concern:

- Standards: What should teachers know and be able to do in order to work effectively with learners?
- Assessment: What counts as evidence that teachers have learned these skills and knowledge? In other words, how should their performance be measured?
- Training: What are appropriate routes to developing these skills and knowledge?

The standards issue emerged in the mid-1980s, as states began to develop standards for what K–12 students ought to learn at each grade level. This had clear implications for the knowledge and skills that teachers who work with K–12 students need to possess. No less important was the emergence of alternative routes to teacher certification, such as the Troops to Teachers program for retired military personnel. Because licensure in most states had come to mean completing a series of mandated courses, the process wasn't equipped to handle candidates who brought important skills and experiences to the classroom—skills and experiences that would allow them to move more quickly into the classroom if it weren't for the state's bureaucratic requirements. At first, states grappled with what appeared to be inequitable systems—a prescribed system for regular candidates, and a loose system for career changers. Legislators and reformers have addressed this inequity by focusing on standards rather than on requirements. Indeed, the American Association of Colleges for Teacher Education has stated that while all teachers should be held to the same standards, alternative routes to meeting the standards can and must be developed.

The focus on licensing standards got a boost from the work of the National Board for Professional Teaching Standards, even though the National Board was concerned more with certifying accomplished teachers than with state licensure. The National Board's standards of good teaching practice guided the work of the Interstate New Teacher Assessment and Support Consortium (INTASC) as it began to develop a set of prototype standards for teacher licensure. At this writing, thirty-seven states have used those standards in revising their licensure process.

The INTASC standards attempt to richly describe what the role of the teacher demands. They are outlined in three parts—knowledge, dispositions, and performances—making clear that teaching is a complex endeavor. While subject-area knowledge is privileged in the standards—INTASC has developed specific standards for science, mathematics, English language arts, and special education, and will soon release those for the elementary school level, social studies, and foreign language—the standards also make clear that knowledge of child development, learning theory, and teaching approaches is essential. And some attention is being paid to candidates' attitudes toward their subject matter and toward learners in the statements of "dispositions" that are incorporated into each of the standards.

To illustrate, let's examine INTASC's Standard 3, which reads: "The teacher understands how students differ in their approaches to learning and creates instructional opportunities that are adapted to diverse learners." (See pp. 48–49 for full text of the standard.) The knowledge required of teachers to meet this standard builds on the findings of cognitive psychology in stipulating that teachers must understand various learning styles and approaches to learning, as elucidated in Howard Gardner's work on multiple intelligences. It also requires that they know how to handle specific differences that matter in the classroom, like students for whom English is not their first language or students with special needs. Teachers must understand and adapt their instruction to their students' previous experiences, language, culture, and community values.

Dispositions identify the attitudes and values that guide and support the work of the teacher. In the case of Standard 3, the key disposition is respect for the individual learner, as shown in teachers' efforts to connect with their students and to tailor instruction to their students' individual needs. Finally, the performance standards describe the application of teachers' knowledge and disposition in the tasks they undertake in the classroom.

The standards issue, however, is not without controversy. Standards can be just as politicized as the old state codes often were. Special interests may attempt to hijack standards, and they sometimes succeed in using them to promote a particular philosophy or approach, as we saw in the controversy surrounding drafts of the K–12 history standards. Standards cannot, by themselves, force people to rethink teacher education. Indeed, some teacher educators resist moving from the old practice of course-based teacher education and simply overlay a new surface of standards language. The past has perhaps conditioned us to look at courses as separate "bits" that together count as a program. In a standards-based approach, what candidates do in courses contributes to their meeting standards, but the standards provide a framework that cuts across courses. At times, state bureaucrats and teacher educators seem to be attempting to turn the standards into the same kind of check-off approach that counting courses represented. I have visited some programs where one standard is reduced to a single project required in course A and another to a single paper in course B. Given the rich language of INTASC's Standard 3, a single project or paper could not possibly provide evidence of mastery.

Standards represent a major shift, from focusing on inputs to identifying key results. Standards invite all those involved in the endeavor—current teachers, school administrators, teacher educators, and state education officials—to a conversation about the meaning of good teaching and its impact on student learning. Wisconsin's revision of the public instruction code for teacher education is using the meaning of the standards to allow both regular and alternative teacher-education programs to design their own approaches in contrast to the "locked-in" course requirements of the past. Institutions and alternative providers alike must make a case for how they've adhered to the standards.

The first responsibility of the licensure process is thus to make clear, through the development of standards, what the license stands for—indeed, what it guarantees about the knowledge, skills, and dispositions of the teacher who holds it.

The New Standards in Teacher Education

The standards of the Interstate New Teacher Assessment and Support Consortium (INTASC) outline the knowledge, dispositions, and performances necessary for effective teaching. Herewith, INTASC's Standard 3 and the knowledge, attitudes, and skills necessary to meet it.

INTASC Standard 3: *The teacher understands how students differ in their approaches to learning and creates instructional opportunities that are adapted to diverse learners.*

Knowledge

- The teacher understands and can identify differences in approaches to learning and performance, including different learning styles, multiple intelligences, and performance modes, and can design instruction that helps use students' strengths as the basis for growth.
- The teacher understands and can provide adaptations for areas of exceptionality in learning—including learning disabilities, visual and perceptual difficulties, and special physical or mental challenges.
- The teacher knows about the process of second-language acquisition and about strategies to support the learning of students whose first language is not English.
- The teacher understands how students' learning is influenced by individual experiences, talents, and prior learning, as well as language, culture, family, and community values.
- The teacher has a well-grounded framework for understanding cultural and community diversity and knows how to learn about and incorporate students' experiences, cultures, and community resources into instruction.

Dispositions

- The teacher believes that all children can learn at high levels and persists in helping all children achieve success.
- The teacher appreciates and values human diversity, shows respect for students' varied talents and perspectives, and is committed to the pursuit of "individually configured excellence."
- The teacher respects students as individuals with differing personal and family backgrounds and various skills, talents, and interests.

- The teacher is sensitive to community and cultural norms.
- The teacher makes students feel valued for their potential as people, and helps them learn to value each other.

Performances

- The teacher identifies and designs instruction appropriate to students' stages of development, learning styles, strengths, and needs.
- The teacher uses teaching approaches that are sensitive to the multiple experiences of learners and that address different learning and performance modes.
- The teacher makes appropriate provisions (in terms of time and circumstances for work, tasks assigned, communication and response modes) for individual students who have particular learning differences or needs.
- The teacher can identify when and how to access appropriate services or resources to meet exceptional learning needs.
- The teacher can identify when and how to access appropriate resources to meet the needs of students with particular talents.
- The teacher seeks to understand students' families, cultures, and communities, and uses this information as a basis for connecting instruction to students' experiences (e.g., drawing explicit connections between subject matter and community matters, making assignments that can be related to students' experiences and cultures).
- The teacher brings multiple perspectives to the discussion of subject matter, including attention to students' personal, family, and community experiences and cultural norms.

Assessment

The most critical issue for licensure is assessment. What will count as evidence that a candidate is ready to be licensed? What makes the guarantee of the license meaningful?

In the past, most states granted a license if the candidate completed the courses in the approved program of a college or university. Few would seriously argue that completing courses is automatically the same as developing the knowledge, skills, and dispositions required for effective teaching. Yet states and teacher educators alike have accepted—and some continue to accept—the proxy as appropriate.

On many campus visits I've made as part of my work as a member of the board of examiners for the National Council for the Accreditation of Teacher Education, I've asked faculty members about the relationships between the statements in the front of their syllabi and the process of determining grades, outlined at the end of the syllabus. In these syllabi, statements of goals regarding knowledge, skills, and disposition are usually written well. The key is whether students can pass the course without demonstrating that they have met the goals. Rarely are assessments clearly linked to the goals. Too often what passes for assessment is less focused on quality of performance than on issues of format and punctuality—both of which can be important, but are not central. Point systems may give a nod to quality, but they don't often make explicit the criteria for quality. And faculty members often admit that students can earn enough points to pass without demonstrating the aspects of standards intended to be developed in the course.

Assessing whether a candidate has adequately demonstrated an aspect of a standard first requires clear criteria for what would count as such a demonstration. For example, in an Alverno College assessment focused on teaching writing in elementary school, candidates work with samples of actual student papers from a local district. After working with the district's rubric, each candidate is given a sample paper to assess; the task involves first providing the evidence to support the candidate's judgment about the developmental level of the 5th grader's performance. Then, building on that judgment, the candidate develops an instructional plan based on her diagnosis of the learner's strengths and needs.

Criteria for successful completion of this assessment include accurate use of the rubric (compared with the district teacher's ranking of the paper) and effective reasoning based on specific aspects of the student's writing. For the second part of the task—developing an instructional plan—criteria include the designation of two to three appropriate areas that the teacher would work on next with this learner and a clear rationale for the links between the student's needs and the instructional plan.

Some programs simply ask teaching candidates to provide samples of different types of lesson plans, unconnected to school context, as artifacts that go into a portfolio to demonstrate meeting the INTASC standards. Such sample plans, developed in the absence of real learners' needs, do not provide clear evidence that a candidate can "create instructional opportunities that are adapted to diverse learners."

I've argued that a person could conceivably demonstrate some, most, or even all of the standards we require with little or no input from a teacher-education program. Shouldn't we recognize, for example, the understanding of developmental psychology that literate parents have developed through the experiential learning involved in raising a child? And if those parents can transfer the understanding gained through experiential learning to designing developmentally appropriate instruction for learners, shouldn't we be able to validate that knowledge and skill? If we took assessment seriously, we could develop learning experiences and assessment processes to fit the accumulated knowledge of candidates—and not have everyone move lockstep through the same series of courses.

A number of significant problems with assessment as related to licensure continue to dog the credibility of the process. Most important, while the standards describe teaching as a set of highly complex tasks, much of what currently passes for teacher testing follows a reductionist model—looking not so much at what's important but at what's easy to measure. Critical aspects of the standards are ignored because they are difficult to assess. For example, for Standard 3, we want to know how the teacher works with a group of twenty-five students, with a range of needs, and adapts instruction to meet their individual needs. Assessing that kind of instruction is an expensive, complex proposition. It requires documenting what the teacher knows about the learners and how she uses that knowledge in day-to-day work with the range of needs. Less expensive might be a multiple-choice test in which a teacher identifies the names of theorists and links them to their theories, but this does not begin to provide the same level of information. In the current world of teacher licensing, cost is an issue, and so many states let multiple-choice tests stand as proxies for the more complex assessment that would provide evidence of whether candidates meet the standards.

In order to make licensure a mark of quality, assessment needs to document knowledge and performance in practice and over time. In the new Wisconsin requirements, teacher-preparing institutions and alternative providers alike must give evidence of multiple, complex assessments tied to the standards for the initial license. At Alverno, we embed complex assessments in both liberal arts and teacher-education curricula. For example, our students interact with and observe four-year-olds to see how developmental theory is played out in the way children approach the world. They develop and teach lessons in classrooms over five semesters, initially tutoring one or two students and then teaching small groups and whole classes. They learn the expectations of a local district's science curriculum and not only show the ability to assess 6th grade science projects using the district's rubric, but also plan the next steps in designing instruction to meet the students' needs.

Faculty members provide feedback on these assessments, assisting teacher-education candidates as they continue to build their knowledge and skills in preparation for their role with learners. During student teaching, candidates put together a portfolio that illustrates their work with K–12 learners, assessing their work and giving them feedback and showing how their planning addresses the needs of their class. Thus the portfolio includes videotapes of the teacher working with students across a range of lessons, lesson plans, student work samples with teacher feedback, and the teachers' continuing reflections on why they are doing what they do.

Similarly, in Oregon, teacher candidates put together work samples demonstrating the links between teaching and K–12 student performance; they do this during student teaching and again in the first year of practice. A work sample usually includes a description of the class's make-up, with demographic and other data, lesson plans, data from pre-tests and post-tests, and analysis of the learning gains made by students. In Connecticut, the BEST program requires new teachers to put together a portfolio of their performance during their second year that demonstrates their planning, instruction, assessment, and feedback practices. Continued licensure is contingent on meeting the criteria for adequate performance.

The Connecticut BEST portfolio assessment is more expensive than a multiple-choice test, but the evidence it provides is far superior. Teachers who serve as assessors receive rigorous training in the observation and assessment of teacher performance against well-articulated standards. This training of teachers as assessors for the process is also helping to build a different culture of learning, based on the statewide conversation about what constitutes good teaching.

During student teaching, candidates put together a portfolio that illustrates their work with K–12 learners, assessing their work and giving them feedback and showing how their planning addresses the needs of their class.

Training

James W. Fraser argues that it's time to decouple the relationship between teacher education and licensure. I agree that the status quo, in which the state blesses college- and university-based teacher-education programs but never seeks evidence of teachers' performance in real classrooms, must be changed. Just taking courses does not ensure that candidates become quality teachers, just as knowing a subject doesn't guarantee an ability to teach it. The shift toward standards and meaningful assessments opens up more possibilities. Now, whatever route candidates take to licensure, they must demonstrate the knowledge, dispositions, and performances outlined in the standards. Some candidates could prepare outside of a program and still be able to demonstrate the necessary skills—some, but not many.

Two arguments support maintaining a connection between state requirements for licensure and the programs that prepare teachers to stand for licensure, whether those programs are housed in higher-education institutions, in school districts, in other organizations, or in collaboratives involving any combination of groups. First, such a connection can protect the public by identifying programs that have provided evidence of offering legitimate, credible preparation that is linked to the standards to which new teachers will be held. In the past, colleges and universities were assumed to have a lock on legitimacy; I would instead like to see all providers produce evidence of their credibility. Not everyone who wants to put out a shingle to prepare teachers is necessarily qualified to do so.

Second, such a connection can protect the candidates who are seeking a viable route into the classroom by ensuring that programs provide candidates with the opportunity to learn, through both meaningful experiences and effective developmental assessment. Assuming for the moment that some candidates could stand for assessment and be licensed outside of a formal program, I believe that those who choose to go through a program—again, wherever it is provided—should have some assurance that what they get is worth the money they pay for it.

Opening up the range of providers might encourage more cutting-edge approaches. With advances in both assessment and technology, providers of teacher preparation ought to be able to design an almost infinite array of paths to demonstrating performance that meets the standards.

Thus, where Fraser argues for no relationship, I would urge a partnership in which the state encourages the responsible development of a range of program options. In fact, Alverno is involved in two such alternative programs, one with an urban school district and two other colleges, the other with three foundations, a group of independent schools, and another college.

We need to avoid the narrow thinking that says there's one best way to prepare teachers. A few years ago, the Holmes Group argued the necessity of five- and six-year programs. However, the Federal Awards for Excellence in Teacher Preparation, which sought to find programs that have documented impact on K–12 student learning, honored three undergraduate programs

(Alverno, Samford, and Eastern Carolina) and one graduate-level program (Fordham) in 2000. Many approaches may lead to the outcomes that we seek; states should not fall into the trap of specifying only one or a few approaches.

Thus it is the third responsibility of the licensure process to sanction approved routes and programs to obtaining the license, wherever they are established.

The Case for Licensure

Thoughtful critics have suggested that teacher licensure is an unnecessary burden when it is placed on candidates with appropriate content majors and related work experience. Underlying this argument is the notion that knowledge of student development and modes of learning either is best learned on the job or is not relevant.

While it's hard to make the case for licensure when it requires only taking a collection of courses, it's even harder to argue against a standards-based licensure system that ensures that every child will have a well-trained, high-quality teacher. Such a system depends on complex processes of assessment that incorporate basic skills, content knowledge, pedagogical knowledge, and performance in a school setting with real students.

Perhaps another Wisconsin analogy will help focus the case for meaningful licensure. In Wisconsin, a licensed veterinarian has to pass three types of exams: a written standardized test, an oral interview, and a demonstration of surgery on a small animal. Should the requirements be any less stringent for those to whom we entrust our children?

MARY E. DIEZ is professor of education at Alverno College.

CHAPTER FIVE

We Need New Types of Administrators

Frederick M. Hess

In the early 1990s, IBM had fallen on hard times. The leader of the personal-computing revolution was losing billions of dollars a year and looking for a new CEO. Observers were aghast when the board of directors recruited Lou Gerstner, CEO of RJR Nabisco and veteran of the food and tobacco industries. Critics insisted that his lack of experience running a technology concern would leave him at a "huge disadvantage," wrote Doug Garr in a 1999 book about Gerstner's tenure, because the computer business "moved at a faster pace than other industries; competition came from . . . fanatics who thrived in the often quirky and murky world of digital chaos." It was believed that managers in the high-tech field needed both business savvy and technical skills. Gerstner was seen as woefully unprepared.

By the late 1990s, IBM was again a highly profitable technological innovator. Gerstner was hailed for engineering, as the subtitle to Garr's account, *IBM Redux*, put it, "the business turnaround of the decade." Might another CEO, especially one with more experience in technology, have done better? Possibly. Were the concerns about Gerstner's lack of experience valid? Sure. However, the larger lesson is that Gerstner provided what IBM needed—a CEO "who could penetrate the corporate culture and change the company's insular way of thinking and operating."

Likewise, consider Meg Whitman. Formerly a brand manager at Procter & Gamble with an M.B.A. from the Harvard Business School, Whitman was hired in 1998 to lead eBay, the ubiquitous Internet auctioneer. Concerns over Whitman's lack of familiarity with the Internet were initially widespread, but her marketing experience proved invaluable as eBay became one of the few web pioneers to actually turn a profit. Gerstner and Whitman aren't even unusual examples; businesses often turn to leaders from outside their industries.

Recruiting outsiders has become more common in K–12 education, at least at the superintendent level. In recent years, urban school districts from New York City to Seattle have hired candidates from outside education to lead their schools. Nonetheless, the overwhelming majority of superintendents, school district officials, and school principals rise through the ranks the traditional way—first as teachers, then as assistant principals, principals, and then up to the district office. Many of them make fine leaders. But the fact is that the traditional route to K–12 school management is not serving the nation well. The public school system suffers from a lack of effective managers at both the school and the district level. In 2002, Paul Houston, executive director of the American Association of School Administrators, said, "Five years ago, the pool of good superintendents was fairly shallow, and I thought it was as bad as it could get. I was not nearly pessimistic enough. It's gotten worse." In turn, 60 percent of superintendents in a recent Public Agenda survey agreed that they have had to "take what you can get" in hiring a school principal. The problem is not a lack of warm bodies, but an artificial shortage of individuals with the skills, training, and knowledge to lead modern schools and school systems.

The shortage is artificial in the sense that state laws needlessly limit the supply of principals and superintendents. More than forty states require would-be principals or superintendents to acquire a license in school administration in order to apply for a job. Typically, attaining licensure as a principal requires three or more years of K–12 teaching experience, completion of a graduate degree in educational administration, and an internship (see table 5.1). In several states, candidates are also required to pass the School Leaders Licensure Assessment, an exam designed to check whether the applicants hold professionally sanctioned values and attitudes. The licensing of superintendents involves similar requirements (see table 5.2), though states are more likely to issue waivers if a school board requests one. The problem is that these licensure rules constrain the pool of potential applicants when there is no evidence that they produce more effective school managers.

Changing Demands

In today's reform environment, school leaders must be able to leverage technology, devise performance-based evaluation systems, recruit top-notch staff,

Table 5.1. Certification Requirements for Principals

Selected states with medium to high barriers to certification

State	Elementary/Secondary Teaching Experience	Master's Degree	Program Summary	Test
Ohio	Two years of licensed teaching	Yes	Principal preparation program in school of education	State exam
Illinois	Two years of teaching or school service	No	Graduate principal preparation program in school of education	Certification exams
Louisiana	Five years of teaching	Yes	30 graduate semester hours in educational administration and two-year principal internship	Educational administration exam
D.C.	Five years in education, including three as a teacher	Yes	Master's or doctoral degree in education administration/leadership or equivalent degree	Passing score on the Interstate School Leaders Licensure Consortium's standards-based exam

SOURCE: National Center for Education Information, 2003.

Table 5.2. Certification Requirements for Superintendents

Selected states with medium to high barriers to certification

State	Elementary/Secondary Teaching Experience	Prior Administrative Experience	Graduate Degree	Program Summary	Other
California	Three years of public or private school teaching/ services & valid credential	None required	Not required	24 semester units of administrative services program or one-year internship	No additional requirements
Indiana	Two years of teaching and K-12 license	None required	Ed.S., Ed.D., or Ph.D.	Standards-based preparation including internship	Must pass written assessment
Massachusetts	Valid educational license	Three years of administrative experience	Master's or other advanced degree in appropriate field	A passing score on an assessment of leadership, administrative skills, communication, and literacy	Alternate certification methods: administrator internships, apprenticeships, or certification by review panel
Minnesota	Three years of licensed teaching	None required	Minnesota graduate school, doctoral or other specialist program	No specific program requirements	Field experience of 320 hours in 12 continuous months as administrative aide or internship
Pennsylvania	Six years of teaching/ services, including three years with a public school certificate	None required	Graduate specialist program	State-approved, two-year graduate-level program in educational administration	Be recommended by the preparing institution for certification

SOURCE: National Center for Education Information, 2003.

draw upon data and research when making decisions, and motivate their teachers and students to meet state- and federally-mandated goals. If the past performance of traditional school administrators gives any indication, it is unclear that teaching experience or education-school coursework provides candidates with the unique combination of technical and interpersonal skills these tasks demand. Inasmuch as private sector, nonprofit, and governmental managers outside of K–12 schooling face many of these same challenges in their work, there is no reason why talented individuals from these sectors should not also be considered for positions as school principals and district administrators.

It is time to adopt a straightforward, two-point standard for licensing school administrators. Applicants for principalships, superintendencies, and other management positions should be expected to demonstrate the following qualifications:

- A college degree and evidence of personal integrity, including passing a criminal background check.
- Knowledge and skills that are essential to lead schools and school systems, as defined by those selecting the leader.

While schools and school districts might seek candidates with formal qualifications or credentials, such as teaching experience, a graduate degree in educational administration, or even an M.B.A., the lack of such credentials would not prevent someone from applying for a position. School districts would be free to consider a range of candidates, rather than only those with the requisite teaching experience and graduate degree.

This approach is similar to the deregulatory strategy many states are using to solve their shortages of high-quality teachers and to attract more mid-career professionals to teaching. However, school management positions are even more ripe for deregulation than is classroom teaching. Teachers spend most of their time working independently in self-contained classrooms. By contrast, school managers operate as part of a team and hold more amorphous responsibilities. Not every administrator needs to possess the full range of skills required to run a school or school system. While it may be important for some members of the leadership team to know good teaching when they see it, others may bring complementary skills that can be transferred to an educational setting. It is the team taken together that needs to hold the full complement of skills.

Deregulating the recruitment and training of school managers is especially crucial at a time when the K–12 education system is moving toward using standards, testing, accountability, and choice as its chief reform strategies. To thrive in this new environment, school leaders will need a background in fields where accountability for performance is a part of their everyday working lives. The ability to build effective teams, to set goals and motivate individuals toward meeting them, and to create a sense of purpose and mission in the schools is now even more urgent. Given these new demands, it is imperative that school boards not be unduly constrained by state regulations that dictate whom they may consider for school management positions.

Instead of recruiting effective leaders from other fields, public schools opt to pull an enormous share of principals and superintendents from the ranks of the nation's gym teachers. In 1999–2000, 34 percent of the nation's principals had been coaches or athletic directors. What uniquely equips a high school coach rather than a director of a tutoring program to lead an elementary school? It might be that coaches are used to managing and motivating teams in a competitive setting and enforcing basic discipline, but this gives lie to the notion, popular among experts on educational leadership, that principals and superintendents must be "instructional leaders."

Recruiting leaders from other fields would yield a range of benefits—including those for school administrators themselves. Presently, educational leaders enjoy little respect. While high-ranking military personnel and members of urban mayoral administrations often find themselves with plum offers from the private sector when they leave those fields, few school managers are seen as qualified to do much else. Prying open the channels between leadership in education and other fields will help reverse the tendency to ghettoize school administrators. This would force school systems to pay a fair rate for managerial talent and would create new opportunities for administrators to command the support and respect enjoyed by their counterparts in other sectors.

The new crop of managers will also demand the same tools and responsibilities that they enjoyed in other fields. School leaders who are not given the right to hire and fire teachers, reward and sanction personnel, or allocate resources cannot be held fully responsible for the results. The first to benefit from these changes will be the thousands of hard-working principals and superintendents who have grown frustrated with their inability to run their organizations effectively. This new agenda is not an attack on school administrators. It is a commitment to professionalize their chosen field.

Closing the Door to Talent

The burden of proof regarding licensure should rest on those who embrace it. Why? Licensure prohibits those who don't meet the guidelines from applying for work. This makes sense only if we are certain that someone who has not taught and has not completed a university-based program in school administration cannot be an effective principal or superintendent. If we're not certain, if we just believe that former teachers will generally make better principals, then licensure is neither necessary nor desirable. It's not necessary because, if former teachers and graduates of programs in educational administration are more qualified, school districts will hire them ahead of other candidates. It's not desirable because, unless we believe that nontraditional candidates cannot be effective, there will be times and places where the best candidate is not licensed—and districts will nonetheless be barred from hiring her.

Meanwhile, the current approach has fostered a leadership culture that is ill-suited to manage by objective, ill-equipped to implement new technologies, and reluctant to be held accountable for student learning. Of principals surveyed in 2001, 48 percent thought it a "bad idea" to "hold principals accountable for student standardized test scores at the building level." We need principals who welcome responsibility for student learning, whether they came from the classroom or not.

Licensure is a crude device, one best suited to ensuring that the clearly incompetent cannot prey on the public. It is especially well suited to professions like medicine or law, where practitioners are often independent and their quality of work is difficult for clients to gauge. Principals and superintendents, by contrast, work in a highly visible context—within a large public organization where their performance is increasingly monitored by state officials, local activists, businesspeople, journalistic outlets, and others.

The problem with requiring school managers to earn a license is that the work of a school principal or superintendent is typically shaped by that person's immediate context. Job requirements evolve over time and differ from one milieu to the next. Leadership in other lines of work has much the same quality. This is why we cannot imagine licensing business or political leaders, and why the M.B.A. is not a license, but a credential that employers value as they see fit. Even in higher education, where formal credentials are required for an individual to become a professor, additional credentials are not necessary to become a dean or president. In fact, as fundraising and running a multimillion-dollar institution have become the chief responsibilities of an academic presidency, more and more universities are looking to nontraditional candidates.

Three fundamentally flawed assumptions underlie the existing approach to licensure:

Only former teachers can lead, especially at the principal level. This notion begins with the claim that only a former teacher can provide "instructional

leadership." The belief that principals need to have taught rests on two articles of faith: that only former teachers can monitor classroom personnel or
mentor teachers. Both claims are of dubious merit.

The first may have been plausible when administrators could judge a
teacher's effectiveness only by observing classes and monitoring parental complaints. Today, however, there is a wealth of information on achievement, and
entrepreneurial managers are finding ways to gather data on other facets of
teacher performance. In addition, an effective principal can use master teachers to evaluate their peers, as an increasing number of schools are doing.

The claim that principals must be mentors is equally problematic. In very
small schools or systems where no one else is available to work with teachers
on curricular or instructional issues, administrators do play this role. But in
larger schools, where most students are to be found, principals and superintendents lead teams that include a variety of individuals with different
strengths. An administrator who uses her team wisely can provide more useful assistance than an overstretched leader drawing on only her personal
knowledge. In recent years, a number of nonteachers have performed compe-
tently as district superintendents or charter school principals. Doctors,
lawyers, engineers, and other professionals routinely work in organizations
led by individuals from other fields. Are teachers alone so iconoclastic or frag-
ile that they can work only for one of their own?

In fact, the skills that characterize effective teachers may actually hinder
their performance as managers. Though experts in educational leadership
argue that principals and superintendents—especially those in troubled venues—must be proactive risk-takers who engage in "creative insubordination,"
research has found that "teachers tend to be reluctant risk takers." A 2003
Public Agenda survey found that barely one in five teachers thought linking
teachers' salaries to their effectiveness would help motivate teachers or
reward high-performers, while more than 60 percent worried that it would
lead to jealousy. Even though 78 percent of teachers reported that at least a
few teachers at their schools were "simply going through the motions," just 23
percent thought unions should make it easier for administrators "to fire
incompetent teachers."

Even professional managers express profound anxiety about tasks like
delivering negative evaluations and terminating employees. It is not much of
a stretch to suggest that teachers reluctant to link rewards to student performance or unwilling to support steps to purge ineffective teachers may be
ill-suited to some unpleasant but crucial managerial tasks. The years that

principals or superintendents spent as teachers immersed in classroom culture may leave them hesitant to take the harsh steps that performance-based leadership sometimes requires.

Quality control. One argument for licensure is that it screens out incompetent aspirants. But earning a master's or doctorate in educational leadership does no such thing. Even elite programs impose shockingly little quality control. Education schools do not make it possible to examine admissions data specific to their administration and leadership programs, but we can garner a rough idea of selectivity by comparing overall admissions data from colleges of education with those from graduate business schools.

A few examples from the 2004 *U.S. News & World Report* rankings of graduate programs help to illustrate the point. Penn State University's 33rd-ranked business school accepted 24 percent of its applicants; admitted students had a mean GMAT score of 650. Meanwhile, the university's school of education, which housed the nation's 6th-ranked educational administration program, accepted 48 percent of its doctoral applicants, and the admitted students had a mean verbal GRE score of 480. Ohio State University's 19th-ranked business school accepted 25 percent of its applicants, and admitted students had a mean GMAT score of 660, while the university's education school, home to the nation's 2nd-ranked administration program, accepted 44 percent of doctoral applicants, and admitted students had a mean verbal GRE score of 480 (see figure 5.1). The 13th-ranked University of Michigan–Ann Arbor business school accepted 19 percent of its M.B.A. applicants, while the education school (with the 9th-ranked administration program) accepted 37 percent of its doctoral applicants.

Professionalism. Today, due in large part to licensure, educational administration is a subspecialization of the sprawling field of leadership and management. Experts on educational leadership dismiss the existing canon of management theory and practice, instead offering their own "educationally unique" formulations of leadership. Prominent thinkers, such as Thomas Sergiovanni in *Leadership for the Schoolhouse*, argue that "corporate" models of leadership cannot work in education. Such simple-minded dichotomies are mistaken. There is no one style of "corporate" leadership; nor is there a unique "educational leadership."

The result is training that does not expose educators to the body of thought that conventionally trained executives deem essential. Major publishers produce lists of "educational administration" texts that number hundreds of books, though they publish nothing similar on managing pharmaceutical firms, retire-

Figure 5.1. School Administration's Permissive Filter

At Ohio State University, candidates admitted to its 19th-ranked business school scored better than 87 percent of all takers of the GMAT. Meanwhile, doctoral candidates admitted to Ohio State's education school, which houses an educational administration program ranked 2nd in the nation, scored higher on the GRE verbal exam than only 54 percent of test-takers.

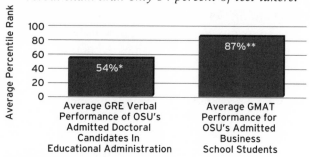

* Reflects an average verbal GRE score of 480.
** Reflects an average combined verbal and math GMAT score of 660.

Note: GMAT scores are a combination of math and verbal scores, and thus scores on the GMAT and GRE do not directly correspond. However, students who take these exams tend, on average, to perform similarly on both.

SOURCE: U.S. News & World Report, 2004; Educational Testing Service; Graduate Management Admissions Council.

ment communities, or fire departments. The absence of cross-pollination leaves school administration a lightly regarded backwater.

Surveying some of the titles prominently advertised in Corwin Press's fall 2002 catalog illustrates the problem. Widely used in administrative training are books like *Leading for Diversity: How School Leaders Promote Positive Interethnic Relations*; *Caring Enough to Lead: How Reflective Thought Leads to Moral Leadership*; and *Leadership and the Force of Love: Six Keys to Motivating with Love*. These volumes never explain why conventional management wisdom and analysis are inappropriate for schooling.

The Costs of the Status Quo

Licensure makes it more costly to seek a management position in education, making other professions relatively more attractive. If the hurdles screened out the incompetent or ill-suited, that would be one thing. However, there is no evidence and little reason to believe that one's willingness to pay tuition for lightly regarded courses during evenings, weekends, and summers says much about one's aptitude or suitability for leadership. Willingness to bear such burdens may reflect a lack of interest in teaching, a lack of attractive alternatives, or hunger for a position of authority just as readily as a commitment to learning.

An Army of Leaders

In about nine months, the U.S. Army turns laypeople
into military officers

Consider the approach of another public organization that also wrestles with leadership preparation: the U.S. Army. After all, while educators hold the fate of innocent children in their hands, nowhere are the consequences for leadership failure as devastating as on the battlefield, where an officer's ineptness can result in the deaths of those entrusted to his care. Clearly, the need to screen out the ill-suited and ensure essential mastery is at least as great as in public education. Moreover, especially after its dramatic successes in Afghanistan and Iraq, the U.S. military is hailed as perhaps the most cohesive, equitable, diverse, and efficient public institution in the world. How does the Army select and train its leaders, and what lessons might it teach our nation's schools?

Recognizing that it never has enough good leaders, the Army provides an array of avenues by which individuals can enter its officer ranks. A handful of aspirants enlist in the Army and then seek promotion, but most apply to West Point out of high school, enroll in ROTC while in college, or apply to Officer Candidate School (OCS) from outside the military. In all cases, the Army actively recruits talent for its officer corps. While school administration programs offer training to just about any teacher who wants it, the Army works to identify and pursue promising candidates and ruthlessly screens out the unqualified. The Army recruits only a tiny percentage of officers from within the enlisted ranks, instead relying on officers selected from a distinct talent pool and trained for different roles. This approach is precisely the opposite of what is followed in schooling.

The West Point model—extensively training hand-picked aspirants from an early age—makes evident sense, as does promoting a handful of select veterans. The most interesting example, however, is OCS. The Army has devoted decades of research to ensuring that it entrusts combatants only to prepared leaders. How long does that training take? For those who enter OCS and demonstrate the required competencies, it is possible, with no previous military experience, to be in the field leading troops after only forty weeks. Nine weeks of basic training, fourteen weeks of OCS, and only four months of specialized preparation suffice to teach all the leadership and technical expertise essential for combat leadership.

In an ideal world, the Army would train OCS personnel for another two to three years. However, the Army recognizes that it cannot afford arbitrary barriers that might cost more in talent than they return in preparation.

It is simply not the case, as proponents of licensure argue, that school management positions are so challenging that nobody wants them. Recent years have witnessed the creation of several programs that train aspiring nontraditional principals and school district officials. In 2002, New Leaders for New Schools received 400 applications for 33 fellowship slots in its cohort of principals-in-training; the Broad Foundation's Urban Superintendents Academy had over 1,300 inquiries and more than 200 applications for 25 slots; and the KIPP (Knowledge Is Power Program) Foundation's principal academy had 410 applicants for 20 slots.

The most motivated candidates may be the least willing to sit through poorly regarded courses or to suffer procedural hurdles. In fact, an extraordinary number of entrepreneurs pursue charter school management positions—despite the obstacles, uncertainty, and reduced compensation—because they are unwilling to wait the requisite years before being permitted to seek a position in a conventional district school.

Tried but Not True

Present reform efforts fall into opposing camps. One is represented by the Interstate School Leaders Licensure Consortium's (ISLLC) efforts to define "standards" for educational administration and to stiffen the requirements for licensure. The idea is to improve the training of potential principals and superintendents—a worthy goal, but one whose effect would be to further narrow the field of candidates.

Formed in the 1990s, ISLLC is a coalition of administrator organizations (like the National Association of Elementary School Principals), education unions, education schools, and other education client groups. In line with what these groups have long advocated, the ISLLC standards assess individual beliefs rather than knowledge or skills. The six standards assert that school administrators should "promote student success" by doing things like "facilitating . . . a vision of learning," "collaborating . . . with community members," and "influencing the larger political . . . legal, and cultural context." These sentiments are pleasing primarily to those who embrace the ISLLC's notion of "diversity," endorse constructivist pedagogy, and believe school leaders ought to wield political and legal levers to advance "social justice."

The problems are made clear by the ISLLC School Leaders Licensure Assessment, which several states now use to assess the competence of candidates for principalships. While the exam's designers claim that it is "grounded in research," the exam does not assess legal, budgetary, management, research, curricular, or pedagogical knowledge—but determines little more than fidelity to ISLLC values. As the ISLLC's chairman, Ohio State University professor Joseph Murphy, concedes, "[The exam] is a statement of values about where the profession should be"—or at least, where it should be according to Murphy and his allies.

Of the sample situations and questions in the on-line preparation materials, not one asks a candidate to exhibit an understanding of scholarly research, legal statute, or budgetary concepts. One sample vignette asks candidates to determine what is "in the best interest of the particular student" in a case where a high school senior failing a class asks the principal if he can drop the class, even though permitting the student to do so is "contrary to school policy." In the example, the principal permits the student to drop the class, and test-takers are then asked to explain whether this decision served the student's "best interest." Endorsing the principal's action earns the test-taker a perfect score while those who recommend denying the request are marked down. ISLLC's public materials indicate that graders would give a score of zero to the following candidate response: "The principal's action is wrong. . . . Much more is learned in high school than academics. Students must learn that there are consequences for their actions. . . . If this student is allowed to graduate, the lesson he will learn is that he does not have to accept the consequences of his actions."

The other reform strategy pursued in recent years, by large urban districts from New York to San Diego, is to recruit celebrity superintendents from other professions, such as Joel Klein, the Clinton administration's antitrust official, who is now serving as chancellor of the New York City schools. There is nothing wrong with pursuing high-profile nontraditional superintendents. Such hires have imported a number of promising executives into the schools and challenged shopworn assumptions. However, searches for nontraditional leaders too often devolve into a quixotic quest for "white knights."

Most nontraditional superintendents were hired not on the basis of a reasoned assessment of their skills but because they were considered forceful individuals. The fascination with "leadership" that can be readily transferred from one field to the next has sometimes been shockingly simplistic, as with the presumption that military generals would make good superintendents because they run taut organizations or that attorneys would because they're familiar with law and politics.

American education doesn't need a few dozen superintendents gamely swimming against the tide, but tens of thousands of competent superintendents, principals, and administrators working in tandem. The problem with today's efforts is that they are not part of larger efforts to recruit thoughtfully out of an expanded candidate pool, to build and support teams, and to rethink management. Instead, they are too often one-shot prayers in which the district hopes that charisma and personal credibility can jumpstart their moribund institutions.

In the years immediately following World War II, business administration was a minor profession, and business schools were institutions of modest repute, viewed as intellectually suspect step-cousins to university economics departments. As management became more crucial to the postwar economy, the quality of executives improved, and business schools responded to competitive forces. Businesses were forced to discipline their hiring through a new reliance on the bottom line, and business schools became increasingly selective and focused on teaching critical economic, accounting, and quantitative content in a useful and relevant fashion. Today, America's executive workforce is admired across the globe, and its business schools are among the nation's most prestigious educational units. This all transpired without formal licensing; neither business schools nor America are any the worse off because Bill Gates and Michael Dell never obtained an M.B.A. The world of educational leadership is ripe for a similar revolution.

FREDERICK M. HESS is a resident scholar at the American Enterprise Institute.

CHAPTER SIX

New Leaders:
Will Public Schools Hire Them?

Alexander Russo

On the first Monday of the 2003–2004 school year, Pablo Sierra was not where he hoped to be. Instead of greeting students as the new principal of a Chicago public school, Sierra was driving downtown for another round of meetings with district officials, trying to keep his spirits up and hoping that a position would open soon.

As a newly minted graduate of the widely heralded New Leaders for New Schools training program for aspiring principals, Sierra (and the developers of New Leaders) had understandably expected to find a slew of opportunities awaiting him. He thought that his prestigious M.B.A., private-sector experience, and nine years as a classroom teacher would distinguish him from more traditional applicants for the principalship. The intense yearlong "residency" program developed by New Leaders would make up for his lack of traditional administrative experience.

As of September, however, Sierra had all but given up on his first choice: being tapped to run a neighborhood school. He had started looking for a start-up or charter school opportunity and was hoping to avoid taking a job as an assistant principal. The silver lining is that Sierra was eventually able to secure a job as the assistant principal of a charter school and is now set to head a new charter school opening next year.

Sierra's situation was not unique among his New Leaders peers. Of his graduating class at the program's Chicago location, less than half had found jobs by late June. Those without preexisting connections to the community or to the school bureaucracy were struggling even to get interviews. Surprisingly, Sierra's private-sector training and experience were "not being perceived as positive," he said. "All the positions are going to experienced [assistant principals]."

Since its founding four years ago, New Leaders has shown that there is no shortage of accomplished individuals like Sierra who want to be principals. The program continues to expand each year and has become a national voice for the reform of principal training. The remaining questions are whether school districts will let New Leaders run their own neighborhood schools—and are the New Leaders fellows really ready for the job?

New Blood

New Leaders for New Schools is the brainchild of a group of graduates from Harvard's business and education schools including CEO Jonathan Schnur, a former Clinton administration official. The New Leaders idea is to recruit accomplished individuals from both the private and public sectors, including public education, and provide them with the leadership training necessary to take on significant school management roles. "We're looking for the best people, wherever we can find them," says Schnur.

The motivation behind New Leaders was to supply new blood to cities that were reportedly facing shortages of qualified principals ready to turn around dysfunctional schools. New Leaders fellows would also receive the kind of leadership and management training that principals hired through traditional routes seldom enjoy. Each cohort of "new leaders" is chosen through a highly competitive application process. Those selected take courses during the summer, then spend a year in full-time "residency" at a school under the guidance of a mentor principal.

While securing principalships for the program's trainees has been challenging, finding accomplished aspirants has not. In 2003 the program received more than 1,000 completed applications for just 55 spots. Overall, roughly half the applications—and half of those accepted into the program—have come from nontraditional candidates, meaning that they were coming to the program from outside education or from another part of the country. Even those with traditional education backgrounds have flocked to New Leaders, seeking a program that is more hands-on and collegial than many of the principal-training programs based at schools of education.

As a result, the pool of New Leaders includes a concentration of individuals with backgrounds not often found among public school principals. For instance, Danny Kramer was a VISTA coordinator, a member of an Internet start-up, and a website designer for Oprah Winfrey. Drema Brown graduated from Yale Law School and ran a children's program in New Haven, Connecticut. And Cindy Moeller, a member of the current cohort of fellows, entered the program after earning her M.B.A. at Northwestern and serving as a vice president for human resources at Baldwin Pianos. New Leaders usually requires its applicants to have two years of classroom experience in order to meet guidelines for certification as a public schools administrator. The program also works in partnership with local universities to secure formal certification for its graduates.

The current fellows range in age from their late twenties to their mid-fifties. Two-thirds are African American, Hispanic, or Asian American, and two-thirds are women. Most important, they are among the most confident, determined, and accomplished school leadership candidates you can imagine.

What Shortages?

Despite their accomplishments and passion, New Leaders fellows have had a hard time breaking into traditional public schools, especially those fellows who lack contacts or extensive experience in education. It's not that New Leaders can't get work; nearly all of the New Leaders have secured education-related jobs. But just 5 of the first 15 graduates and just over half of the 32 graduates in 2003 found positions running schools of any type.

Of course a 50 percent placement rate for aspiring principals is no small accomplishment, and there has been undeniable progress in getting fellows hired at neighborhood schools. Patrick Baccellieri, a graduate of the program's first year in Chicago who had previously run a nonprofit, was hired to run a traditional school, as was second-year graduate Jarvis Sanford, a former diversity consultant for the Anti-Defamation League who holds an M.B.A. and a Ph.D. Drema Brown is currently running a traditional public school in the Bronx, New York. Carleton Gordon, a longtime financial services executive, was named the principal at a tough school in Brooklyn in the fall of 2003. And after just a short time, some New Leaders have moved from assistant principal to the leadership spot in their schools.

However, these are the exceptions. Only seven (out of forty-seven) New Leaders have been hired to run traditional neighborhood schools. One problem is that, as it turns out, there isn't really that much of a numerical shortage of principals in the four cities—Chicago, New York, Washington, and the Bay Area—where New Leaders currently operates training programs. Principalships don't open up all that often. And when they do, these school districts receive tons of applications from insiders with more experience in education.

For instance, New York City may need to fill 150 open slots each year in a system with more than 1,200 schools. Program founder Schnur estimates that there are well over a thousand qualified candidates. Schnur says that there were only 60 to 70 genuine openings in Chicago this year, with about 65 applications for each position.

It is not just a numbers game though. The fact is that school district administrators and teachers have not wholly embraced the New Leaders concept. They tend to believe that the principal is also the instructional leader and should therefore have significant classroom experience. "Certainly, experience in other professions brings a perspective that could be a plus," says Deborah Lynch, president of the Chicago teacher union. "But so little teaching experience really makes me wonder if that's enough for a person to really get to know instructional improvement and school leadership."

Even the New Leaders candidates agree that this is somewhat of a disadvantage. "I might have wanted a few more years in the classroom from the curriculum side," says Kelly Wilson, a New Leaders graduate who holds an M.B.A. and has a background in TV production. "We're being developed as curriculum leaders, but I probably needed more exposure to that."

The New Leaders training, while intense, will not make them curriculum experts. They get enough training and experience to talk the talk and are expected to learn along the way. And so, despite the widely acknowledged need for better-trained principals, reports of shortages, and waves of retirees, New Leaders candidates can end up seeming green. "Everybody just wants experience," says one Chicago school administrator who has observed several of the principal searches where New Leaders fellows were interviewed. "The bottom line is that schools want someone to run the school, not just theories."

There are also cultural and stylistic conflicts that can complicate the relationship between nontraditional principals and career educators. Winning trust at a new school—what New Leaders tend to call "gaining entry"—is a key challenge, especially for those who have spent most of their careers outside of schools.

Danny Kramer, for example, had a few run-ins with other teachers during his residency year that a more experienced administrator might have avoided. "Danny started with us before the school year started and stayed with us the whole year," says Armstrong Elementary principal Arline Hersh. "He put his foot into it occasionally and learned that way," she says. "But that's part of the process, learning how to extricate yourself gracefully."

There are also those who, threatened and offended by the notion of programs like New Leaders, question the fundamental legitimacy of bringing in outsiders. "Why should we think someone would be an effective principal just because they were once a student?" asked Jill Levy, president of the 5,500-member Council of School Supervisors and Administrators in New York, last year. Her organization has vociferously opposed Chancellor Joel Klein's efforts to revamp principal training in New York City.

Conservative Hiring

New York is actually a bright spot in the New Leaders portfolio. Three quarters of the 2003 graduates of the New York program were selected to lead schools—a big increase from the previous year, when just two of eight became principals. Chicago has been more difficult to break into. In the program's first year, just one New Leaders graduate was tapped to run a school; two more have moved up to the top job since then. The share remains below 50 percent for the 2003 crop of New Leaders.

The disparity at least partly reflects the sheer size of the New York school district and thus the greater number of openings it has to fill. But the actual mechanisms for hiring principals in each city may provide a more likely explanation.

In New York it is largely up to district administrators to hire and assign principals. By contrast, in Chicago each individual local school council makes its own hiring decision. These councils, made up of parents, teachers, and community members, can be advised by the district. But the decision is, in the main, the council's to make.

Making the situation more difficult, roughly three out of four New Leaders in Chicago come from outside education—reflecting a priority expressed by the Chicago board of education, says Schnur.

The effects on the hiring process in Chicago are many. Local councils may not be familiar with the still-new New Leaders program, creating an enormous marketing challenge. With their strong ties to the community, local councils may also be more inclined to hire an inside person—an assistant principal, interim principal, or someone else from the community. And the principal contracts, set at terms of four years, make it very hard to remove someone if a decision goes awry.

"It is hard to get these people hired," says John Ayers, executive director of Leadership for Quality Education, a Chicago education reform group that has worked with New Leaders and supports its efforts. "Local school councils tend to be surprisingly conservative."

Bernard Lacour, a longtime school reformer who works with local school councils and consults with New Leaders on placement issues, believes that the obstacles thrown up by council dynamics and the predisposition for experience may be exacerbated by system politics, the advantages of incumbency, and fear among local councils that their candidates will be challenged by the board of education and their authority taken away from them.

Lacour notes that candidates who have not been administrators or who come from outside education frequently make it to the interview stage but rarely get hired or placed in the Chicago system. Only in rare cases is someone's newness and lack of strong affiliation with the school system a real advantage. Sometimes council members don't even know who has applied for the job, he says. "What we need is a process that is less daunting and procedural."

Heading Charters

Not surprisingly, one result is that a substantial number of New Leaders end up running charter schools, small schools, start-ups, or education organizations rather than traditional schools, especially in Chicago.

Take Kelly Wilson. She was the second New Leader to do her residency at a small but well-known school, Ariel Community Academy, located on the south side of Chicago. Her predecessor had been hired as an assistant principal at Ariel, but before the year was even over, Wilson became executive director of a school-based teacher-training program in Chicago. She was the second New Leader to hold this position.

Opinions vary about whether this is a good outcome for graduates of New Leaders. Wilson and others say that having effective leadership in urban school systems is important, regardless of where that leadership is located. But sending too many New Leaders into alternative schools could easily create the impression that the program is not well suited for mainstream schools or that the school system is not ready and willing to hire even the most capable candidates if they enter through alternative routes. After all, imagine what would have happened if Teach for America, the storied program that places talented college graduates into low-income schools, had sent many of its members into charter schools.

In fact, many New Leaders would rather work in a traditional environment. "I'd love to work in a traditional school," says Kramer, who is now serving as an assistant principal at Clinton Elementary School. "But that's a hard nut to crack, to get the [school councils] to interview you."

Despite these difficulties, New Leaders already seems to be making an impact, both directly and indirectly. Evidence from the 2002–2003 school year, while minimal, suggests that schools with New Leaders fellows at the helm outperformed other schools with first-year principals in reading and math improvements and in reduced percentages of failing students.

At the same time, there has been an enormous increase in attention toward new ways of recruiting, training, and placing principals, at least some of which can fairly be attributed indirectly to New Leaders. New Leaders has fifty-five residents in training this year, has expanded to Washington, D.C., and will be expanding to Memphis, Tennessee, this summer. Moreover, the organization was recently named one of the top twenty organizations that are changing the world by Fast Company magazine. In the meantime, other efforts to set up fast-track principal training programs dot the nation, and in-depth residency components are increasingly common. The New York, Chicago, and Boston school systems have all initiated or adapted school leadership programs that have key elements in common with New Leaders.

Befriending the System

Nevertheless, New Leaders will need to find more success in placing its graduates if it is to remain a viable model for improving the management of regular public schools. This presents no small challenge. In the end, hiring a nontraditional principal may be considered more of a risk than hiring teachers or superintendents with nontraditional backgrounds—two related trends that have swept the nation over the past decade.

For starters, compared with the principal, a teacher has an important but relatively small role in the overall well-being of a school. Principals and administrators may be more willing to "take a chance" with a single 4th-grade class than risk the health of an entire school on a candidate with little experience in education. Furthermore, with the proliferation of alternative certification and programs like Teach for America, the practice of hiring teachers without formal degrees in education or classroom experience is fairly well established. Teaching, unlike the principalship, is also often an entry-level job that requires little previous experience aside from student teaching. The only real difference between a Teach for America teacher and a regular teacher is the nature of their training.

Similarly, the trend toward bringing in outsiders to run school districts is now at least a decade old. Superintendents with backgrounds in business, the military, or government are hired more for their forceful personalities and management skills than for their knowledge of instruction. They can arguably rely on the veteran educators within their systems to provide instructional leadership, while school principals need to be involved more directly in the process of upgrading the curriculum and monitoring the performance of teachers. By contrast, entering a role that involves directly managing professionals, like teachers, is tough to nearly impossible in any field where a candidate does not have significant experience. After all, how many newspaper editors did not do significant time in the reporting trenches? How many law firms' managing partners were not once first-year associates?

The lessons from the Chicago experience are clear and are already being implemented, according to Schnur. "We need to become more aggressive earlier in the year about helping nontraditional candidates access networks that can help them and in helping them understand the climate of the school system," he says. Last year, "We didn't invest enough time and energy into this part of the process early enough." This year the program has started networking earlier in the process and beefed up efforts to make sure that, when the time comes, New Leaders fellows are not just ready to take leadership positions, but are also welcomed by the school system.

ALEXANDER RUSSO is an education writer.

Making Teacher Pay
More Competitive

CHAPTER SEVEN

_✐_

Fringe Benefits: AFT and NEA Teacher Salary Surveys

Michael Podgursky

Each year, the two national teacher unions, the American Federation of Teachers (AFT) and the National Education Association (NEA), release their surveys of public school teacher salaries across the nation. And each year, they take advantage of this opportunity to bemoan the condition of teacher pay. On the April 2002 release of the NEA's data, then NEA president Bob Chase complained, "It's hard to convince someone to stay in the classroom when the salary is so low." Likewise, the AFT decried the fact that the "average teacher salary continues to fall well below the average wages of other white-collar occupations." The average teacher, according to the AFT, earned $43,250 during the 2000–2001 school year, compared with an average of $52,664 for mid-level accountants; $71,155 for computer system analysts; $74,920 for engineers; and $82,712 for attorneys.

Of course, the AFT has chosen the comparison groups to make its best case. Where, one wonders, are the comparisons with journalists, registered nurses, assistant district attorneys, FBI agents, military officers, and other not-so-highly compensated professionals and public-sector employees? Shouldn't the average pay of a high school English teacher be compared with that of writers and editors? One could make a case that the salaries of high school physics or calculus teachers should bear some resemblance to those of computer system analysts, but does the AFT believe that the appropriate compensation benchmarks for 3rd grade teachers are the salaries of engineers or attorneys?

Nevertheless, data from the NEA and AFT are highly influential. Indeed, the U.S. Department of Education collects few data of its own on this matter.

For the most part it simply recycles these union data in publications like the *Digest of Education Statistics* 2001, a standard reference in which five of the six tables on teacher pay are based on union figures. On the whole, such data present a fairly accurate picture of teacher salaries at the national level and have some value for state-to-state comparisons. Yet they suffer from severe limitations when interest groups, policymakers, and pundits use them to make a point about how the nation values public school teachers.

Summers Off

One facet of teaching that the NEA and AFT, in their data and in their public pronouncements, routinely fail to account for is the shorter workday and work year. In public schools, the median number of school days is 180 per year. Add half-a-dozen or so workdays for parent conferences, professional development, and planning, and the annual work year for most teachers is still shorter than 190 days. By comparison, an accountant or lawyer with two weeks of paid vacation and ten holidays or personal days will work 240 days annually—nearly 30 percent more days per year than public school teachers.

The typical teacher also has a shorter on-site workday than most other professionals. On average, teachers report being in school for fewer than 38 hours per week. This number rises to 40 hours if largely voluntary after-school activities such as coaching or club sponsorship are included. In fact, language limiting the number of hours that teachers are required to be in school is common in their collective-bargaining agreements, particularly in urban school districts. In the just-expired New York City teachers' contract, the contractual workday was just 6 hours and 20 minutes (including a 50-minute duty-free lunch). The new contract extends the workday by 20 minutes. In Chicago, the limit is 6 hours and 45 minutes, including a 45-minute duty-free lunch.

Of course, many teachers put in nights and weekends at home grading papers and planning for the next week. However, a job that permits relatively more work at home is typically more attractive (particularly to women with children) than one that requires a similar amount of work time on site. And many other professionals bring their work home as well.

The combination of a shorter workday and work year means that the annual hours on the job for teachers are much shorter than in comparable professions. Consider Figure 7.1, which shows hourly rates of pay computed by the Bureau of Labor Statistics for a variety of occupations. By these calculations, only engineers, architects, and surveyors in private practice and attorneys earn more than teachers on an hourly basis.

Figure 7.1. Solidly Middle Class

Because of their shorter work year and workday, teachers actually earn more than many other educated professionals on an hourly basis.

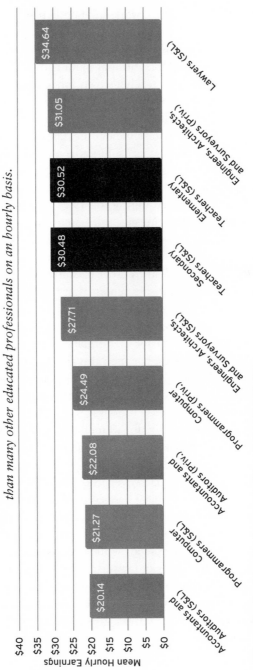

* S&L = employed by state and local governments; Priv. = employed by private firm

SOURCE: Bureau of Labor Statistics.

The shorter workdays and work year make teaching an attractive occupation to those who wish to balance work and family needs. The shorter hours are especially helpful to women who want both a rewarding career and children, which helps to explain why roughly 75 percent of teachers are women and the share is increasing. An additional plum is that the on-site teaching hours match the schedule of a teacher's own school-age children. In short, when the kids are at home, so is mom (or dad).

Consider the "sick kid" challenge. In many professions it is very difficult to take unscheduled time off for a sick child or other family emergencies. In teaching, however, the "substitute teacher" solution is a routine part of school life. Indeed, in collective-bargaining negotiations, school administrators frequently complain of excessive absences among teachers. According to a recent U.S. Department of Education survey, during the 1999–2000 school year, 5.2 percent of teachers were absent on any given day on average. That translates into 9.4 days out of a 180-day school year. During the 2000–2001 school year in New York City, the annual rate of absences reached 11.3 days per teacher. These rates are much higher than in other executive or professional employment. The Bureau of Labor Statistics reports that the absentee rate for managerial and professional employees is just 1.7 percent of annual hours.

Teaching is also family friendly in the sense that little or no out-of-town travel is required for successful job performance. Teachers may choose to attend out-of-town conferences, but such travel is unusual and not a condition of employment. Although I am not aware of any systematic data collected on this topic, out-of-town travel seems to be commonplace for many young professionals.

The expansion of opportunities for women during the past half-century is supposed to have lessened the attraction of teaching. And yes, the earnings of college-educated women in other fields have grown faster than the earnings of teachers in recent decades. However, the mix of nonteaching jobs that college-educated women hold has changed as well. In 1960, 58 percent of college-educated women not employed as teachers worked as secretaries or other clerical workers, and only 13 percent were "managers." By 1990 the clerical share had fallen to 30 percent while the share of managers increased to 35 percent (as did the shares of lawyers, accountants, and doctors). This shift from clerical to managerial and professional employment resulted in an increase in nonteaching earnings, but it also meant longer workdays and work weeks, greater responsibility (and stress), and, probably, less flexibility compared with teaching.

The bottom line is that teaching remains a job that makes it easier for parents to reconcile a career and family. Consequently we would expect female teachers to have more children—which is exactly what we see: among college-educated women aged 40 and younger, the average teacher had 2.1 children, versus 1.7 for other occupations. Of course, some of this difference may simply reflect the fact that teaching attracts women who like children and who would have been predisposed to have more children anyway. However, the fact remains that teaching is a profession that makes it less costly for these women to act on their preferences.

Starting Salaries

The most reliable data on pay and benefits for nonteachers are collected by the Bureau of Labor Statistics. Its economists and statisticians have a well-deserved reputation for maintaining very high standards for accurate and objective data collection on wages, benefits, labor force, and other economic data. Yet the AFT also presents tables and charts on earnings for new college graduates that rely on data collected by a private organization, the National Association of Colleges and Employers (NACE). Several times a year, NACE solicits reports on salary offers (not earnings) to graduating students. The AFT compares data from these NACE reports with scheduled starting salaries for teachers. In releasing the 2002 report, the AFT made much of the fact that "for new teachers, the $28,986 average beginning salary lagged far behind starting salary offers in other fields for new college graduates." By comparison, the AFT says, accounting graduates were offered an average starting salary of $40,779; sales/marketing majors, $40,033; computer science majors, $49,749; and engineers, $50,033 (see figure 7.2).

While these NACE data apparently have some value to placement officers on college campuses (who pay the hefty subscription fee), they almost certainly overestimate the earnings of nonteachers. First, these data represent salary offers to a very small sample of the total number of college graduates. The 2001–2002 report, for example, was based on only 2,600 offers to students in fewer than 120 higher-education institutions. More important, this sample of offers is likely to result in a misleading estimate of the earnings of all college graduates, since only large businesses or employers are likely to send recruiting teams to campus. Most small colleges do not submit reports to NACE. At a large state flagship institution such as mine, the University of Missouri–Columbia, only the business and engineering schools report job

Figure 7.2. Starting Salaries from American Federation of Teachers Survey

The American Federation of Teachers uses data from the National Association of Colleges and Employers (NACE) to compare the starting salaries of teachers with those in other professions. However, the NACE data dramatically overstate the starting pay of college graduates. Data from the Bureau of Labor Statistics show a gap of only $3,000 in the median pay of teachers and other college graduates under the age of 30—a gap that is readily explained by the shorter workday and work year in teaching.

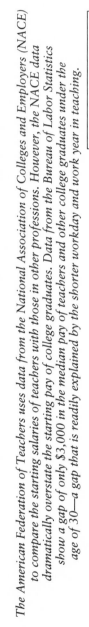

*Rounded to nearest thousand

SOURCE: American Federation of Teachers, 2001, using data on starting pay of college graduates from National Association of Colleges and Employers (NACE).

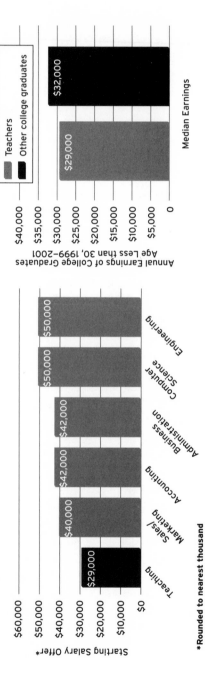

SOURCE: March Current Population Survey, 1999–2001.

offers to NACE. Moreover, for the Missouri business school, the number of graduates far exceeds the number of job offers reported by the placement office.

The AFT's data on starting pay for teachers must also be treated with some caution. Not all states collect such data, in which case the AFT estimates teachers' starting pay. In the most recent report, the AFT had to estimate the starting salary in seventeen states. However, researchers have no way of judging the accuracy of the AFT's estimates, because they failed to document their methods.

A much more accurate picture of the relative pay of recent college graduates can be gleaned from Bureau of Labor Statistics national survey data on annual earnings. I pooled three years (1999 through 2001) of March Current Population Survey data and computed full-time annual earnings for college graduates under 30 years of age whose highest degree is a bachelor's or master's degree. I made no adjustments for hours or weeks of work. Not surprisingly, nonteachers earn more than teachers (see figure 7.2): on average, 32 percent more (nonteachers earned $36,996, versus $28,156 for teachers). However, the pool of nonteachers has many more very high earners than the pool of teachers, which pulls the average up. Thus a more representative indicator of the typical teacher and nonteacher is median earnings. In this case, the gap in earnings between nonteachers and teachers falls to just 10 percent ($32,000 versus $29,000). The latter gap is readily explained by the shorter workday and work year for teachers.

Fringe Benefits

Neither the AFT nor the NEA makes any adjustments for the fringe benefits associated with teaching in a public school, thus masking an important part of total compensation. Unfortunately, published data do not permit precise comparisons of fringe (nonsalary) benefits for teachers and other professionals. For example, the Bureau of Labor Statistics reports fringe benefits for other professions, which include paid vacations. But nearly all teachers are on nine- or ten-month contracts and thus do not receive paid vacations. In addition, due to idiosyncrasies in the federal Social Security law, in some states teachers are included in state pension plans as well as Social Security, while in others they are not. Published Bureau of Labor Statistics data on benefits for "teachers" employed by state and local governments also combine full-time postsecondary teachers with K–12 teachers. This makes the comparison more difficult, but since public K–12 teachers account for more than 80 percent of the combined total, the data still provide some insight into the comparative benefits of teachers.

Employers' largest fringe benefit cost is retirement plans. Virtually all public school teachers are included in traditional defined-benefit plans in which teachers receive pension payments according to a defined schedule on retirement. These differ from defined-contribution plans, like the TIAA-CREF plans in most public and private colleges, in which the retirement benefits depend on investment earnings and saving rates and may vary from employee to employee. Public school teachers become eligible for pension benefits (or "vest") in these plans after five to seven years of employment. The contributions to these systems made by school districts or states are substantial. And because of the high turnover rates of teachers in their early years, these defined benefit plans in practice transfer wealth from young to more senior teachers.

The result is a system that permits teachers to retire earlier than they would if they were covered by Social Security or a conventional pension plan. For example, in the Missouri teacher pension system, a teacher who began teaching at age 22 and served continuously could retire at age 55 with 84 percent of her annual salary. In addition, her pension payments would be adjusted for inflation on an annual basis. Regular cost-of-living adjustments are unusual in private-sector defined-benefit programs. This teacher could also take employment in a new job and still collect her full pension benefits as long as the new employer was not a Missouri public school district.

National data show a similar pattern. In the 1994–1995 Schools and Staffing Surveys, both male and female teachers who retired by the next school year averaged 59 years of age at retirement. By comparison, new retirees collecting Social Security retirement benefits have average retirement ages of 63.7 (men) and 63.6 (women).

The second largest fringe benefit cost (as a percentage of payroll) is health insurance. Health insurance coverage for public school teachers is nearly universal (more than 99 percent). The Bureau of Labor Statistics reports that health insurance benefits amount to 7.1 percent of hourly compensation costs for teachers (including postsecondary), but only 5.1 percent for professionals in private business. These same data suggest that the benefits provided to teachers are attractive relative to the private sector. For example, for individual policies, only 20 percent of health insurance plans for professional or managerial employees in medium and large private-sector firms are fully paid by the employer. The comparable share for teachers is 51 percent. Only 10 percent of medium and large private firms pay the full premium for family policies, compared with 29 percent in public school systems.

Private-Sector Teachers

Understandably enough, in comparing the salaries of public school teachers with those of other professionals, the AFT does not make what may be the most relevant comparison: between public and private school teachers. Perhaps this is why the levels of pay in private schools play such a small role in discussions of compensation in public schools. In areas other than K–12 education, personnel managers routinely use pay and benefits in the private sector as a benchmark in setting government rates. This holds for professional jobs such as lawyers, accountants, and nurses. Indeed, one important function of the compensation data collected by the Bureau of Labor Statistics is to provide private-sector as well as state and local benchmark data for federal wage setting. Public higher education administrators are well aware of the level and structure of compensation for faculty in private institutions.

But public school districts rarely consult private school data in making their compensation decisions, even though 12 percent of teachers are employed in private schools and the two sectors compete for teachers. Mobility between the two sectors is extensive: 36 percent of full-time private and 13 percent of full-time public school teachers report some teaching experience in the other sector.

There are, however, some legitimate objections to public–private comparisons. First, many private schools have a religious orientation and are staffed by teachers of the same religious denomination. To the extent that such schools are advancing a religious mission, their teachers may be willing to work for less out of a religious commitment. Second, private schools are generally more selective in admissions than public schools, and, on average, their students are from households with higher socioeconomic status. To the extent that this results in better-behaved and more academically motivated students, it makes for a more attractive teaching environment in private schools.

Figure 7.3 compares public and private teacher salaries in a manner that attempts to address these concerns. First, I included earnings data only for teachers in nonsectarian private schools. In addition, I excluded private schools that have a special emphasis (special education, Montessori, Waldorf) and focused on schools that most closely resemble traditional public schools in mission. I also controlled for teachers' experience, gender, education level, region, and urban or rural status. As the graph shows, teacher pay in these private schools is consistently below that of public school teachers. Starting pay in private schools begins at 78 percent that of public schools,

Figure 7.3. Nonsectarian Private School Pay as a Percentage of Public School Pay

Public school teachers fare much better than their colleagues in private schools. Salaries in nonsectarian private schools start at just 78 percent of those in public schools; climb as high as 92 percent of public school salaries in a teacher's 12th year; and decline thereafter. Private school salaries are even lower when compared with public school salaries in suburban, low-poverty settings.

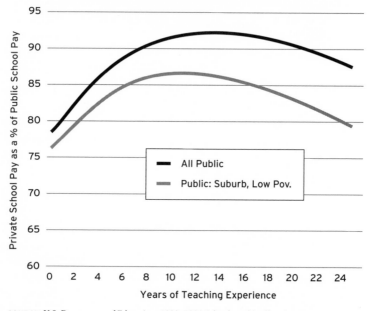

SOURCE: U.S. Department of Education, 1999–2000 Schools and Staffing Surveys.

rises to 92 percent of public school pay by a teacher's 12th year, and declines thereafter.

Even with the above adjustments, a critic might argue that private school teaching is not comparable with public school teaching since the socioeconomic status of private school students is higher. In order to make the public schools more comparable with private, I excluded more than 90 percent of the sample of public school teachers and retained only public school teachers in suburban schools with little poverty (fewer than 5 percent eligible for free and reduced-price lunch). With these new criteria in place, the results look quite different. Interestingly, the shape of the pay function remains the same, but simply shifts down. Private school teachers now start at salaries that are

76 percent of their public school counterparts. This increases to 87 percent by their 12th year and declines thereafter. These results suggest that compared with the private sector, public schools over-reward high levels of experience. Why do they do this? In a recent study, Dale Ballou and I found that public school districts that are unionized and have a large share of high-seniority teachers are more likely to "backload" salary increases by adding additional steps to salary schedules or raising the rewards for seniority.

Benefits are lower in private schools as well. The median nonsectarian private school reports fringe costs (including Social Security) as 18 percent of payroll, while the comparable figure for public schools is 21.5 percent.

Salary Trends

Computing the change in mean teacher salaries from year to year can paint a misleading picture of the average teacher's situation. The reason is that public school salaries are set by schedules laid out in the teachers' contract. These pay schedules, which apply to all the teachers in a school district, base salaries on a teacher's years of experience and number of hours of graduate credits or graduate degrees. (See table 7.1 for a typical salary schedule, from the Chicago Public Schools.)

When school districts raise the pay of teachers, they typically increase all the cells of these schedules by a fixed percentage, say 2 percent. Thus, if the education and experience of the average teacher in the district did not change from one year to the next, then average teacher pay would increase by 2 percent as well. However, that does not mean a typical teacher experienced a 2 percent pay increase between the two years. In fact, most teachers (except those who have "topped out" on the schedule) will receive a pay increase that is larger than 2 percent.

For example, a new teacher with a bachelor's degree hired in Chicago in the fall of 1999 earned $32,561. Between the fall of 1999 and the fall of 2002, the average starting pay for Chicago teachers rose a modest 6.1 percent. However, by the fall of 2002, that teacher hired in 1999 is now in her fourth year of teaching and her pay will have increased to $40, 071, or 23.1 percent in three years. If the 2003–2004 salary schedule again rises by 2 percent, as it has over the past several years, then at the start of the 2003 school year her salary will have grown by 31.1 percent. If she earns a master's by that time, as many teachers do, her pay will have increased by 38.6 percent in four years— an average annual growth rate of 8.5 percent.

Table 7.1. Chicago Public Schools Salary Schedule, 2002–2003 School Year

Schedule of annual salaries based upon a six-hour day during the school term of 40 weeks for regularly appointed members of the teaching staff.

LANE I: BACHELOR'S DEGREE

Step	Annual Salary	Pension Contribution	Total Compensation
1	$34,540	$2,420	$36,960
2	36,330	2,540	38,880
3	38,280	2,680	40,960
4	40,070	2,810	42,880
5	41,860	2,930	44,790
6	43,660	3,060	46,720
7	45,150	3,160	48,310
8	46,950	3,290	50,240
9	48,740	3,410	52,150
10	50,540	3,540	54,070
11	52,480	3,670	56,150
12	54,270	3,800	58,070
MAX	$55,890	$3,910	$59,800

LANE II: MASTER'S DEGREE

Step	Annual Salary	Pension Contribution	Total Compensation
1	$36,930	$2,590	$39,520
2	38,730	2,710	41,440
3	40,670	2,850	43,520
4	42,460	2,970	45,440
5	44,260	3,100	47,350
6	46,050	3,220	49,280
7	47,550	3,330	50,870
8	49,340	3,450	52,790
9	51,130	3,580	54,710
10	52,930	3,710	56,630
11	54,870	3,840	58,710
12	56,670	3,970	60,630
MAX	$58,350	$4,080	$62,430

SOURCE: Chicago Public Schools.

Given the steep tilt of salary schedules, changes in the experience mix of the workforce can be an important factor affecting changes in average teacher pay from one year to the next. This experience-composition problem also arises in analyzing national trends in average teacher pay, since many school districts are hiring more inexperienced teachers in response to rising enrollments, falling class sizes, and the retirement of older, more highly compensated teachers. According to U.S. Department of Education data, the median number of years of full-time teaching experience for public school teachers fell from 14 during the 1994–1995 school year to 12 in 1999–2000. Such a decline in the seniority mix of teachers tends to artificially mask the growth of average teacher pay and to bias comparisons of growth in teacher pay with pay in other professions, where the workforce is typically aging. It also makes simple cross-section comparisons of average pay between school districts or states problematic. We cannot be sure whether average pay is 10 percent higher in state A than in state B because salary schedules are higher in A or the teachers are older.

Trends in teachers' salaries will also understate trends in teachers' compensation if the costs of fringe benefits are increasing faster than salaries. Health insurance is an obvious example. Bureau of Labor Statistics data show that insurance costs (primarily health) represent 5 percent of hourly compensation costs for private-sector professional specialty occupations and managers, whereas for teachers they represent 7 percent of compensation costs.

Between 1980 and 1998 private-sector wage and salary costs grew by 104 percent, whereas costs for health insurance grew by 337 percent (even after widely publicized efforts by private-sector employers to restrain costs by introducing copayments and joining HMOs). Unfortunately there are no comparable data on the rise in insurance costs for public school districts. However, even assuming that public school districts made equally strenuous efforts at cost containment and held their health insurance cost increases to 337 percent, to the extent that health insurance is a larger share of payroll costs for public schools than for other private-sector workers, the relative compensation of teachers has increased. In short, in comparing the earnings of teachers and nonteachers, one cannot examine only trends in salary and assume that fringe benefits have been constant.

As states and districts attempt to meet the "highly qualified" teacher requirements of the No Child Left Behind Act, it will become increasingly important to gather more complete and accurate data on the relative pay and benefits of teachers. These data should also be disaggregated to reflect the fact that teacher labor markets are local or regional, and not national in scope. Attention should also be paid to differences in the opportunities that teachers face in the world outside teaching: a high school physics teacher's potential earnings are not the same as an elementary school teacher's. Policy discussions in this area have relied almost exclusively on the salary data collected by the teacher unions. A valuable step forward would be for the National Center for Education Statistics, in collaboration with the Bureau of Labor Statistics, to expand data collection on the relative pay and benefits of public school teachers so that states and school districts can have objective, arms-length data on this important issue.

MICHAEL PODGURSKY is Middlebush Professor of Economics at the University of Missouri–Columbia.

CHAPTER EIGHT

Low Pay, Low Quality

Peter Temin

Are teachers underpaid? As an economist, I find it difficult to question market outcomes. Goods and services generally cost the market price. Only in the event of some kind of "market failure" do we say that goods or services are either over- or underpriced—meaning that they cost more or less than the price would have been in a fluid, competitive market.

At first glance, it is hard to see how the market for teachers could fail. True, most teachers' salaries are set by governments in a noncompetitive environment. But candidates choose freely whether to become teachers, in full knowledge of what salaries they will receive. In this sense, the people who choose to become teachers are paid a salary commensurate with their skills, preferences, and working conditions. These teachers are not underpaid relative to what they could earn in other occupations.

But what if we wanted to draw a higher-quality pool of candidates to teaching? Are we paying too low a price to accomplish that? I argue that the market for teaching has failed—in the sense that we are paying low salaries for low-quality teachers when we would prefer high-quality teachers. This is the result of two main flaws in the market: the difficulty of identifying who will be a good teacher and the reliance on an obsolete conception of the pool of potential teachers.

Squeezing the Lemons

Nobel Laureate George Akerlof's "lemons model" of market failure helps to explain why schools may not be willing to pay the market price for good teachers. Consider the market for used cars. Buyers want to purchase good cars, but they wonder if only "lemons" are put up for sale. And they have no easy way of evaluating whether a particular car is a lemon. They can look under the hood, take it for a test drive, even ask for the owner's service records, but none of those will guarantee a vehicle's integrity. The buyer's concern for quality without a corresponding ability to evaluate that quality can cause markets to fail. Buyers may not be willing to pay the price necessary to draw high-quality cars into the market, thus ensuring that the proportion of lemons in the market will be higher than if the market were functioning well.

Likewise, schools are deeply concerned with the quality of their teachers, but quality is difficult to discern when hiring a new teacher. Studies have found that graduating from a good college and achieving high scores on tests of verbal aptitude are reasonable, though highly imperfect, indicators of teacher quality. In addition, licensing and certification rules attempt to ensure that teachers possess a certain level of skills. Nevertheless, many of the attributes that make for a good teacher are outside the bounds of a regime for testing or licensing teachers. A high-quality teacher is one who can energize and motivate students in addition to imparting information—qualities that are hard to recognize at the hiring stage. Teachers themselves may know how good they are, but the principals and school boards who hire them have far less information, as in the lemons model. They might desire a higher level of quality, but they are reluctant to pay the salaries necessary to obtain it because of the difficulty of choosing quality teachers.

Teachers are thus underpaid in the sense that we are paying low salaries for low-quality teachers. If we wanted, we could reach a different point in the market, where we would pay high salaries for high-quality teachers. As with used cars, a small salary increase would not change the quality of aspiring teachers; only a dramatic increase would attract a different pool of candidates and prove sustainable. It has been hard to make this kind of radical change because of historical patterns in the workforce that once allowed schools to educate on the cheap.

Women's Work

Women once considered teaching a highly attractive profession because their opportunities were tightly circumscribed. Despite the low wages, teaching was a far better line of work than slaving away in a textile mill. However, the past half-century opened a vast new world of opportunities to educated women. The nation's failure to accommodate these recent changes has kept teachers' salaries artificially low.

In Massachusetts the proportion of teachers who were women rose from half to more than 85 percent during the nineteenth century. By the 1920s almost all elementary school teachers in the United States were women. They never were a large proportion of employed people in New England or even of employed women, but on average teachers taught longer than women worked in other occupations. The pool of female teachers comprised two quite different groups. Those who got married after starting out as teachers taught for about four years on average. But a large proportion of teachers did not marry. Thirty percent of teachers remained single, compared with 15 percent of New England women, after the Civil War. These single teachers taught an average of twelve years, raising the average tenure of teachers.

At the time, teaching was an unusually attractive career for women, compared with the alternatives. Almost two-thirds of Massachusetts women who earned wages in 1837 worked in their homes, producing goods such as palm-leaf hats, straw bonnets, and shoes and boots. The next most important employers of Massachusetts women in the 1830s were the cotton mills. As the century progressed, domestic service replaced braiding hats, but roughly half of employed women continued to work in textiles and the needle trades. This pattern began to erode during the early twentieth century. As store-bought goods and services increasingly replaced those made in homes, women were increasingly demanded for work outside the home. Firms began to hire women to perform the market equivalent of homemaking: cleaning, cooking, and caring for the sick. The increasing need for clerical workers and the invention of the typewriter also afforded better jobs for women.

The participation of women in the labor force grew rapidly during the twentieth century, from less than 20 percent of women in 1890 to well over 50 percent today. But women continued to have a narrow range of job choices for the first two-thirds of the twentieth century. While the choices were not as restricted as in the nineteenth century, it should not be surprising that as late as 1960 many jobs held by women were still in cotton goods, clothing, and boots and shoes.

Only in the current generation have opportunities for women opened up. Previously, school boards hired female teachers in a context of little competition. Even in the mid-twentieth century, with opportunities still limited, teaching remained a good job, one that was considerably more interesting and probably more attractive than the alternatives. Schools didn't need to pay high wages in order to attract high-caliber individuals. High-quality women went into teaching anyway.

Then the market for teachers changed. The opportunities for women have expanded considerably, and their ability to get professional education has increased. In this new world, the brightest women go toward the best jobs. These jobs increasingly are not in teaching. In this kind of market, a higher salary is necessary to compete for higher-quality candidates, who now have other interesting career choices.

Harvard professor of education Richard Murnane argued a decade ago that there were many reasons why good candidates did not go into teaching, and salary was high on the list. In 1988, when the average starting salary for teachers was $19,600, business and industry offered average starting salaries of $28,900 for physics majors, $25,900 for chemistry majors, and $21,000 for humanities majors. The large salary gap for science majors surely discouraged them from entering teaching. Dedicated individuals and poor students who did not anticipate doing well in business still went into teaching, but low salaries discouraged many bright and vigorous students.

Using data on teachers' test scores from North Carolina, Murnane found that teachers with high test scores left teaching sooner than those who did less well. This is not surprising; we may presume that high-scoring teachers had access to better jobs than low scorers. Murnane also found that teachers who were paid more stayed in teaching longer. Taken together, these results showed that low salaries not only discouraged good students from becoming teachers, but they also discouraged good students from remaining teachers. The results of recruitment and retention are consistent; low salaries were associated with low-quality teachers.

New York University economist Frederick Flyer and the late University of Chicago economist Sherwin Rosen standardized teacher salaries for the demographic composition of teachers. They found that what they called the true real wage of teachers has declined relative to wages for other college graduates and has declined even more relative to female college graduates, especially for teachers in elementary schools. Most of this decline took place during the 1970s, when school enrollments fell, but relative wages have not recovered as enrollments have risen more recently.

To see what happened in the 1990s, I examined the relationship between average teacher salaries and women aged 35 to 44 with some graduate education. I compared teachers with women who had some graduate education to capture the comparison between teachers and women who have gone on to get degrees in subjects other than education (see the top line in figure 8.1).

Figure 8.1. Pulling Away

Women with graduate education in other professions now earn 40 percent more than female teachers, reflecting the expansion of employment opportunities for women during the past few decades. Even women with just a college education now earn about 10 percent more than female teachers.

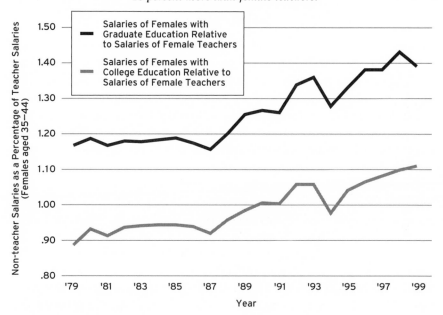

SOURCE: Current Publication Survey.

Highly educated women who were not teachers earned more than teachers throughout the past twenty years. The wage premium stayed under 20 percent until around 1987, and it has risen steadily and strongly since then. The wage premium for women who have some graduate education and are not teachers is now 40 percent. This trend shows that teachers' salaries are falling behind those of highly educated women in other fields at a rapid rate.

Now, many high school teachers have master's degrees, but most elementary teachers do not. Therefore, this comparison may not be accurate for teachers of lower grades; I may have compared them with women who have more education than they do. I cannot distinguish teachers by grade, but I can compare teachers' salaries with women who have only college degrees. This comparison is also shown in the bottom line in figure 8.1. The trends are very much the same, although the divergence of wages is less strong in the bottom trend line than in the top line. Women with just a college degree earn an average of only about 10 percent more than teachers. Relative wages for elementary teachers fell in the 1970s and declined again in the 1990s.

Quality Control

The earnings comparisons tell only part of the story. The career choices open to women have expanded greatly in the past generation. This, coupled with the appearance of women with extensive experience in the workforce, has resulted in rising earnings for professional women. In addition, it has opened up jobs that are more interesting and challenging, careers that are more fulfilling. If there were a way to adjust for the expanding choices for educated women, the gap between teachers' earnings and alternative "earnings" would be larger than those shown here.

There also may be a sample-selection problem in the college-only comparison. If the brightest of women seek education after college, then the control group in the bottom trend line of figure 8.1—women with only four years of postsecondary education—is self-selected to be of lower quality. The comparison in the figure reveals that teachers earn less than even those women who choose not to pursue their education beyond an undergraduate degree.

Finding themselves with lower-quality teachers, school districts have imposed work standards on teachers to make sure they are doing their jobs. These restrictions on teachers' creativity have made teaching an even less desirable job than is indicated by the salary. This is revealed most vividly in the relations between teachers and administrators. The latter feel obliged to keep tight control over teachers, and they set tasks for them to maintain minimum standards. Lesson plans and other reports increase the workload of teachers and force them into a uniform pattern. Of course, these work rules also discourage the most adventurous and creative teachers.

In some urban schools, principals feel free to discipline teachers in front of their students. This process humiliates the teachers and undermines their authority. Teachers are publicly criticized for not keeping their lines straight, for not being in "homeroom circle" properly, and for other minor infractions of classroom neatness. A Boston middle school teacher told me that her principal yelled at her for forsaking her lunch duty place briefly to get food for a student whose lunch she had had to confiscate earlier. This is the kind of discipline that is designed to discourage all but the most dedicated of creative teachers.

Standardized tests, the cornerstone of the federal No Child Left Behind Act, are another way of monitoring teacher performance. The new purpose of the tests is to evaluate the schools and the teachers within it. Tests previously were used to evaluate students, but annual testing was unnecessary for this purpose. The new policies are meant to keep a tight rein on teachers rather than students.

Tests, like excessive paperwork and humiliating disciplinary actions, make life miserable for teachers. They force teachers to teach to the tests, reducing the scope of their teaching. They direct attention to skills that can be measured on annual objective tests and away from learning that is more subtle or long-term. For example, we charge the public schools with promoting civic responsibility. It is not clear how one would test this by multiple choice or if one would look for steady year-to-year increases in this set of attitudes. Less tangible and more creative parts of teaching are discounted relative to the basic mechanics of teaching. If low salaries do not drive creative teachers away, excessive discipline and annual tests should do so.

I do not mean to throw the baby out with the bathwater. Any dramatic increase in salaries will have to be accompanied by an increase in accountability. Inevitably, teachers' performance will have to be measured by some sort of tests. But the current crop of tests appears to be aimed only at evaluating minimum competence. Such tests tend to stultify the most creative teachers even as they, at least in theory, help the worst students.

Principals also may be more a part of the problem than the solution. They are recruited from the pool of teachers, and their quality has also suffered a decline. In the past, the demands on principals—to preserve order and maintain the school building—were consistent with their abilities. But if we wish to move to a point where good teachers will be rewarded for excellence and all teachers will be held accountable for their performance, it is far from clear that the current stock of principals will be adequate. To make tests an effective device for monitoring and rewarding quality, school administration as well as the tests themselves will have to be improved almost beyond recognition.

Higher Aspirations

For most of U.S. history, the nation has been able to operate schools at low cost by exploiting the trapped labor force of educated women who had few other opportunities. Now schools must compete with other mentally and financially rewarding occupations as they recruit teachers. Surely it is immoral for us to shortchange our schools because we cannot bring ourselves to pay enough to attract good teachers.

The underpayment of teachers is likely to have important implications for the future of the American economy. The economy's success during the twentieth century was due to many factors, of which the broad sweep of American education was an important one. The United States led the world in spreading education to the masses. The American economy grew consistently during the twentieth century because we constantly upgraded the quantity and quality of our human capital. The United States has been successful both politically and economically because people have been able to transcend their origins and reach heights undreamed of in earlier times and other places. Education has been one of the primary paths through which extraordinary individuals have found an outlet for their gifts. We should try our best to preserve this commendable quality of American life.

Further education reforms will be hampered by low teacher quality as long as the salaries of teachers do not rise to a competitive level—the level that would attract many high-quality applicants. The current reforms of school administration and evaluation take the quality of teachers as given; they simply rearrange the existing educational assets, and as a result have little or no effect. Only when we break out of the current mix of pay and quality will education in the United States show a marked improvement.

Raising teacher salaries across the board would be very expensive. It also might take decades for higher pay to attract enough bright new teachers to make a big difference in the composition of the teaching staff. In the meantime, today's teachers would be paid more, with little likelihood that they would perform any better than they already do.

A more practical plan of action might be to couple increases in teacher salaries with tougher accountability. In an ideal scenario, only those teachers who were effective or who agreed to work harder to attain this standard would be retained. The pay hike then would not be as expensive, and if better teachers could handle larger classes, expenditures on teachers might not increase much at all.

How would we know which teachers are effective? Tests are imperfect at this stage, and they tend to measure achievement only on basic skills. It is easier to discover whether Mary can add than it is to find out if John is thoughtful and learns from his mistakes. Leaving the judgment up to principals is equally problematic, since they are part of the problem. While accountability is good, the nation's ability to implement it is imperfect. We need to find either a way to anticipate whether teachers will be effective or an acceptable method of evaluating their performance after the fact before we can implement a national program.

This all calls for experimentation. If teachers and their unions can agree, perhaps policymakers can institute bundles of pay raises and accountability in different forms in a variety of school districts. As the results of these pilot programs became known, they could be the basis for a more comprehensive call to action. Evolution may be more attainable and perhaps even more desirable than revolution.

PETER TEMIN is Elisha Gray II Professor, Economic History and Applied Economics at MIT.

CHAPTER NINE

The Case for Merit Pay

Lewis C. Solmon

For more than a century, public education has worked under a single salary schedule that compensates teachers for college credits, education degrees, and years of experience, but not for their effectiveness in the classroom. (See figure 9.1.)

In fact, research shows that the degrees, courses, and experience that teachers have, beyond the first few years of teaching, are unrelated to how much their students achieve. Furthermore, the current salary schedule does not normally take into account the fact that teachers work in schools offering different levels of nonmonetary benefits, such as a safe, pleasing environment. Nor does it recognize that students come to class with different levels of preparation and home support.

Paying all teachers with the same experience and credits the same salary also ignores the fact that graduates of different fields have vastly different alternative career options; think of a physicist compared with someone having a bachelor's degree in elementary education. School administrators report that it is very difficult or impossible to fill elementary teaching positions about 6 percent of the time, while positions in math, physical sciences, and special education are difficult or impossible to fill more than 30 percent of the time. According to the American Federation of Teachers, the estimated starting salary for teachers with a B.A., in 2003–2004, regardless of discipline, was $30,496. The National Association of Colleges and Employers tells us that the average starting salary for accountants that year was $41,110, and for graduates in computer science, $49,691. (See figure 9.2.) Starting salaries for mathe-

Figure 9.1. Patience as a Virtue

Under the rigid salary structure of many public school systems, teachers must work for more than 20 years before they can earn a $50,000 annual salary.

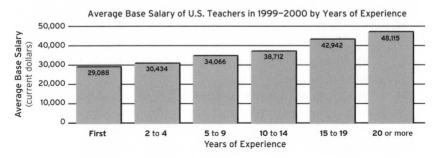

Average Base Salary of U.S. Teachers in 1999–2000 by Years of Experience

SOURCE: National Center for Education Statistics.

Figure 9.2. Compared to the Private Sector

Starting salaries for teachers are competitive when compared to college graduates with a degree in English, but less so for those graduates who specialized in a field that requires mathematical skills, such as accounting or computer science. (Salary figures do not include benefits.)

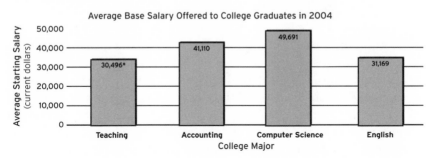

Average Base Salary Offered to College Graduates in 2004

*This is the estimated beginning salary for the 2003–2004 year as provided in the AFT 2003 Survey and Analysis of Teacher Salary trends.

SOURCES: National Association of Colleges and Employers, American Federation of Teachers.

maticians with a B.A., the year before, averaged $40,512; for physicists with a B.A. in 2002, according to the American Institute of Physics, $78,000. Is it any wonder that it is so difficult to hire and retain math and science teachers?

Extra pay for those in hard-to-staff fields would acknowledge the laws of supply and demand—greater opportunities for math or science majors bid up their earnings in other careers, so getting them into teaching requires competitive salaries. It would not mean that physics teachers are more important than elementary teachers.

In the current system, an increase for one teacher requires increases for all. If, for instance, we decided that our teachers are underpaid, as state officials from all parts of the country tell me, current practice would make a meaningful pay increase prohibitive. Just to bring the salaries in the below-average states to the national average would cost $8.5 billion—an amount that is fiscally irrational. It may seem like a meaningless argument, except that such an amount is dictated by the current uniform salary schedule, which requires those below-average states to raise each teacher's salary. It would be much cheaper—not to mention more educationally effective—to raise the salaries of just the most-effective teachers, those deserving of the increase, rather than all teachers. Then there would be money available to give larger raises to the very best teachers.

It would be similarly impossible to bring all teachers' salaries up to the average level of other professions. Why would we want to pay more to the least-effective teachers anyway? What we end up with, then, are paltry average annual increases (as teachers gain experience and course credits), ranging from the high of a $1,498 average increase in California to a meager $503 at the low end in South Dakota.

In the Madison School District in Arizona, the lowest salary for a new teacher with only a bachelor's degree is $31,304 and the highest salary after many years and 72 post-baccalaureate credits is $57,251, an 82 percent increase over a career! Compare that with the legal profession, where the lowest-paid 10 percent earn less than $44,490 and the highest 10 percent earned more than $145,600—a 227 percent difference! The flat salary schedule for teachers is a good reason for those in Madison to welcome the stipends of $6,250 that the district offers to its "master" teachers, who take a leadership role among the faculty, and the bonuses averaging $3,400 to teachers who exhibit outstanding classroom performance and student achievement.

The Teacher Advancement Program

For the past four years, the Milken Family Foundation, founded in 1982 and based in Santa Monica, California, has been working through its Teacher Advancement Program (TAP) in Madison and in more than sixty other schools—mostly elementary and middle schools and a few high schools—around the nation to change the way teachers are evaluated, helped to grow professionally, and compensated.

The TAP is a systemic reform of public schools intended to attract, motivate, develop, and retain high-quality talent in the teaching profession. It has four key elements:

- Multiple career paths allow teachers to pursue a variety of positions throughout their careers—career, mentor, and master teacher—depending on their interests, abilities, and accomplishments. As they move up the ranks, their qualifications, roles, and responsibilities increase—and so does their compensation. When teachers take on more responsibilities, they should receive more pay. The old career ladder programs failed because the best teachers were honored with new titles and more work, but with meager, if any, extra pay.
- Performance-based accountability evaluates teachers' effectiveness through a comprehensive, research-based system that combines such criteria as position responsibilities, classroom observations, and students' gains in test scores.
- Ongoing applied professional growth requires a change in the school schedule that allows time during the regular school day for teachers to learn, plan, mentor, and share with other teachers so they can constantly improve the quality of their instruction.
- Market-driven compensation allows schools to compensate teachers on the basis of their performance and the performance of their students.

Attracting—and Keeping—Effective Teachers

One of the things we all seem to know is that there are few careers, except teaching, in which professionals are not held accountable for their failures and rewarded for their accomplishments. So why, political constraints aside, do we insist on giving raises to reward a teacher's longevity instead of his or her job performance?

For the past seventeen years the Milken Foundation has worked with state superintendents to recognize and reward K–12 educators with a $25,000 gift—no strings attached—for outstanding and effective performance. Of the 1,977 recipients of the Milken award, we know that 1,653 of them are still working. Of these, 281, or 17 percent, have left their school buildings to take jobs at a district office (154), a nonprofit organization (47), a university (41), a federal or state government office (24), or a private company (15).

Unfortunately, we do not know whether this 17 percent turnover among Milken award recipients is better or worse than among those equally experienced and outstanding teachers who do not receive the awards. But we do know that 46 percent of all teachers leave the profession in the first five years and that, anecdotally, the Milken awards have created an aura of excellence about the profession that enhances the environment that our TAP research shows is so important to teacher retention. The very fact that these teachers have opportunities beyond the classroom increases the attractiveness of the profession as a whole.

However, when no compensating salary is awarded for teaching in difficult or undesirable schools, it is easy to understand why the best teachers may choose to teach in the most rewarding and pleasant environment available, moving from low to high socioeconomic status schools when the opportunity arises. Extra compensation is thus needed for those teaching in hard-to-staff schools where conditions are difficult, dangerous, or unpleasant. Defying that pattern, however, some very talented teachers in Arizona are moving from socioeconomically advantaged schools that are not using the TAP to schools of low socioeconomic status that are. Over the past three years, 61 teachers have started working at the two schools of lowest socioeconomic status in the Madison school district, both of which are using the TAP. Of these teachers, 13 (21 percent) have come from schools in high socioeconomic areas in Madison or nearby districts, and they are among the best teachers from the area. They are attracted by the more interesting professional development, the enhanced collegiality, and the opportunity to earn more by being effective.

We want teachers who love kids and want to help them learn, but that does not mean they cannot be interested in compensation as well. Physicians seek to prevent or cure diseases, and some lawyers seek to dispense justice, but that does not bar the best of them—but not all of them—from earning large incomes as well.

Student Outcomes Count

Teachers should be rewarded for producing useful student outcomes, most notably, student learning gains, measured by value-added standards (i.e., improvement) rather than by levels of achievement at the end of a course. This method takes into account differences in where students start as well as differences in out-of-school factors that teachers cannot control. Looking at gains rather than levels of achievement also adjusts for the fear that performance pay will make all teachers want to teach the highest-achieving kids. When student improvement is rewarded, there may be financial benefits to teaching students who have the longest way to go—it may be easier to get a

25 percentile gain from someone starting at the 30th percentile than a 15 percentile gain at the 80th percentile. Providing incentives for teachers to make their students learn more may encourage teachers to do so, but, perhaps more importantly, it will compensate them for the extra effort required to improve the skills that will help their students achieve.

Another issue involves incorporating a school's nonacademic goals into a merit pay system. As we know, schools are expected to develop students' social behavior, career preparation, and positive attitudes. The most hackneyed of these has been enhanced student self-esteem, which sometimes is used as a reason for not failing students who deserve to fail. Let it simply be said that a great way to enhance a student's self-esteem is to have her achieve something academically. Holding teachers accountable for students' academic achievement gains is not inconsistent with students' accomplishing other things in school.

Standards without a Straitjacket

Despite the need to keep the focus on academic achievement, the Teacher Advancement Program acknowledges that research has identified pedagogical methods that help students learn, so it includes evaluation of classroom skills as part of its teacher compensation system. This allows teachers to be rewarded if they do everything right, even if their students' scores do not increase.

A key to this part of the performance evaluation, of course, is developing clear criteria for measuring those classroom skills. Multiple evaluations are conducted by certified evaluators. This helps overcome teachers' fears of bias and nepotism in their evaluations. Moreover, by including principals in the school-wide performance bonus system, they too will have an incentive to ensure that the most-effective teachers are rewarded.

Will such rubrics reduce teachers' opportunities to be creative in their teaching, to try new approaches, to teach as they like? Probably not, because the other test of teacher competence is better student outcomes. Thus the rubric gives credit for the skillful exercise of proven teaching methods, regardless of student outcomes, as well as rewards for student success, regardless of teaching method.

Fix the Whole System

The initial success of these performance- and responsibility-based compensation systems suggests that there are alternatives to the traditional "step-and-column" pay in which no one will earn less than in the traditional system. All teachers who reach certain goals get a bonus; but 50 percent of that bonus is awarded for teaching skills (a classroom-based evaluation) that are not tied to student outcomes and 50 percent for student achievement gains that are not part of the teaching skills evaluation. Furthermore, half of the student outcome bonus is based on school-wide gains and half on gains by an individual teacher's students.

In the three years that we have been using the TAP system, we have found that the school-wide rewards part of the bonus encourages teachers to work together to make everyone more effective. There is the possibility of the "free rider," of course: ineffective teachers reaping benefits from the achievements of their more-effective colleagues. Thus we expect part of the bonus to be based on individual teacher results. All bonuses must be significant or the extra work involved in implementing such a system will not be deemed worthwhile. That means, for instance, that a master teacher in Madison, Arizona, could get a bonus worth as much as 17 percent of his or her salary compared with the 2–3 percent bonus that current salary structures usually set as a cap for such expert teachers.

We have learned that performance pay alone is not enough. It must be supported by a strong, transparent, and fair evaluation system, and by a professional development plan that helps teachers to deal with revealed deficiencies and to improve. Teachers may resist evaluation not because they are unwilling to be held accountable, but instead because they fear they do not know what to do to improve student achievement. If professional growth opportunities are available to help teachers improve, the resistance to being evaluated fades.

A professional development program should use student data to identify areas where teachers need help. It should then have teachers help other teachers improve their teaching and student learning. This fosters collaboration and reduces the competitive attitudes that some fear are engendered by performance pay. Indeed, as long as my receiving a bonus does not preclude anyone else's getting one also, fears of competition and failing to collaborate go away. At schools using the TAP, striving for the annual performance awards improves teaching and enhances collegiality and morale.

One cautionary note: Most school districts are constantly trying to get more money for their teachers. So some will agree to a performance pay plan, but then transform it into an across-the-board salary hike: defining high performance as things everyone does (taking classes toward an advanced degree), setting standards so low that everyone gets the maximum award, or giving all teachers the same evaluation. Districts must guard against such behaviors.

Can It Last?

Merit pay plans are expensive, especially if the performance awards are added to the salary schedule, so there are questions about whether the extra funds will continue to be available during the next economic downturn. What if the superintendent or school board turns over? Will results be demanded too quickly, and will the program be discontinued if test scores do not rise in a year or so?

Establishment of a dedicated funding source, such as an increase in the property tax levy or sales tax, could ensure sustainability. The former has been accomplished in Eagle County, Colorado, and the latter has the potential to support performance pay in the state of Arizona, where voters passed a law in 2000 to raise the sales tax by $0.006 and dedicated 40 percent of the proceeds to performance pay. In fact, most districts in Arizona ended up defining performance pay in ways that gave all teachers the same increases (for example, by allowing more course credits to fill the requirements for meritorious work). The district using the TAP was one of the few that actually used the money for real performance pay. The bottom line, though, is that support and advocacy by teachers is key to sustainability.

Although many teachers initially view performance pay and accountability as contentious issues in reform, absolute levels of acceptance for all the principles embodied in the TAP are high. Since the inception of the TAP, surveys of teachers' attitudes toward the elements of the program show that collegiality and teachers' satisfaction have remained strong in the schools using the TAP. This finding refutes many who argue that pay for performance leads to increased competition and divisiveness. These attitudinal results reflect the holistic approach of the TAP, which combines an accountability system having clear rewards and a professional development system to support all teachers (veteran and novice) in improving their classroom instruction.

Another important way to ensure sustainability is to show that the program is working. There is always the fear that results will be demanded too soon, and then the program will be discontinued if test scores do not rise in a year or so. We now have three years of results from TAP schools in Arizona and two years from TAP schools in South Carolina. We compared 25 year-to-year changes in student achievement in TAP schools to control schools. In

17 of these cases, or 68 percent of the time, the TAP schools outperformed their controls. This compares favorably with the results of a RAND evaluation of schools that have initiated other comprehensive school reform programs. RAND concluded that 50 percent of the schools with these reforms outperformed the control schools in math and 47 percent outperformed the control in reading, although these schools had been operating for a substantially longer period of time than the schools using the TAP. One important anecdotal explanation for the success of the TAP is that teachers in schools using the program improve significantly because their performance evaluations are related directly to TAP teaching rubrics.

Any pay-for-performance plan in K–12 education will succeed only if teachers buy into it from the start, if it is fair, and if it is embedded in a systemic reform that supports all aspects of performance reward, especially those that encourage teachers to become better at their craft. Such a pay plan will be revolutionary, but will not become obsolete in any sense of the word.

LEWIS C. SOLMON is president of the Teacher Advancement Program Foundation.

CHAPTER TEN

Wage Compression and the Decline in Teacher Quality

Caroline M. Hoxby and Andrew Leigh

Though exceptions undoubtedly exist, women with higher aptitudes can ordinarily be expected to be more effective classroom teachers than those with lower aptitudes. It is therefore troubling to think that in the United States those entering the teaching profession in recent years have, on average, lower measured aptitudes than their predecessors.

That able women are no longer entering the teaching profession at anywhere near the same rate as in the past is of special concern, since women compose approximately 75 percent of all elementary and secondary school teachers, almost the same percentage as forty years ago.

Yet a decline in female teacher quality is just what the evidence—most notably a recent study by three University of Maryland economists—indisputably shows (see figure 10.1). According to their findings, the likelihood that a highly talented female (one ranked among the top 10 percent of all high schoolers) will become a teacher fell from roughly 20 percent in 1964 to just over 11 percent in 2000.

The study gives weight to other signs that the teaching profession no longer attracts exceptional teachers. Dr. Leo Klagholz, a commissioner of education in New Jersey in the 1990s, surveyed his state's teacher colleges in the 1980s and found that, for prospective teachers, the verbal and math SAT scores, when combined, were lower than 800 out of a possible score of 1,600. Similarly, the Educational Testing Service in 1990 found that those expressing an intention to become a teacher scored near the bottom among those taking the test. In 1998, Eugene Hickok, then Pennsylvania's secretary of

Figure 10.1. Losing Talented Teachers

As is evident from the percentage of new teachers who scored very well on a high school achievement test, far fewer high-aptitude females are entering the teaching profession.

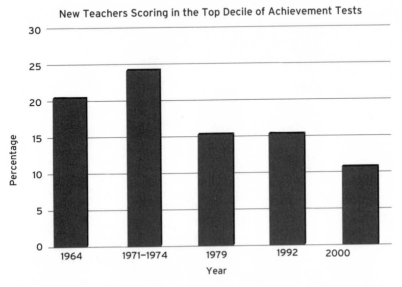

New Teachers Scoring in the Top Decile of Achievement Tests

education, revealed that his state's teacher preparation system provided "limited assurances of competence and quality," leaving "the doors . . . open for C-plus students (or worse) to become teachers."

The icing on the anecdotal cake came in the summer of 2003 with news that a Massachusetts superintendent of education, Wilfredo Laboy, had failed—for the third year in a row—a literacy test that the state's high school seniors needed to pass in order to graduate. The exam Laboy failed has been part of a series of tests required of new Massachusetts teachers since 1998. It was also big news when aspiring teachers took the tests for the first time: almost 60 percent of them flunked. Paul Reville, director of the Rennie Center for Education Research & Policy at MassINC, a nonpartisan think tank in Boston, reviewed many of the written responses from those who failed and bemoaned the high number of the commonwealth's teachers "who were college graduates and yet couldn't string a sentence together."

What Accounts for the Decline in Teacher Quality?

The factors contributing to the reduced likelihood that women of high aptitude will enter the teaching profession appear to come from both within and outside the teaching profession. We focus on two that can be expected to be of critical significance.

First, within the teaching profession, the pay scale of public school teachers has become increasingly compressed since the 1960s. The salary distribution has narrowed so that those with the highest aptitude earn no more than those with the lowest. This may have pushed able women out of the field of education.

Second, outside of teaching, college-educated women have achieved greater parity in their pay vis-à-vis male workers, luring more able women to alternative professions. High-aptitude women may have pulled away from education in order to take special advantage of the new opportunities.

While there could be other explanations outside our investigation, conventional wisdom has long pointed to new opportunities for college-educated women as the primary explanation for the change in teacher quality that many have sensed. We were inclined to accept the conventional wisdom when we began this project, but, after systematically comparing the relative importance of the two factors, we found, surprisingly enough, that pay compression within the teaching profession, induced by the introduction of collective bargaining, has had by far the greater effect.

On further reflection, we were not quite so surprised by the results. For one thing, the overall timing of the decline in teacher quality corresponds to the rise of collective bargaining within education. Teacher unions won collective bargaining rights in key cities and states during the 1960s. Over the next twenty years, collective bargaining spread from state to state across the country.

As a result of union action, the average salary for teachers increased modestly. But as the average was edging upward, the range of the scale narrowed sharply, so much so that able young women were bound to take notice. Moreover, collectively bargained contracts placed a premium on characteristics such as seniority and credentials rather than performance, further depressing the opportunities for the high-aptitude teacher.

Our Approach

Women may enter teaching for any number of reasons, some of which are obviously intangible. We began our study by making the standard economic assumption that a woman's decision to teach is influenced in part by her expected pay within teaching and her expected pay in other occupations. We then subdivided each of these expectations, developing four components that affect the occupational choices of female college graduates:

1. the average pay of all teachers;
2. the differences between the average pay of all teachers and those having a particular aptitude (a measure of pay compression);
3. for all other occupations, the average pay for men with particular aptitudes (what might be considered the base pay for that occupation);
4. for all other occupations, the difference between this base pay for men with a particular aptitude and the pay received by women with comparable aptitudes (pay parity).

Although compression of pay within teaching and improved parity with pay for women in other occupations occurred simultaneously over the past forty years, we were able to distinguish their independent effects, because the timing of their impact varied considerably from one state to the next. For example, parity of pay for women improved sooner in some states than in others. Since we had data, by state, on the earnings of men and women who graduated from college in the same year, we could estimate the independent impact of pay parity separately for each state by calculating the ratio of female-to-male earnings of nonteachers who graduated from similar colleges at the same time.

The rate of change in the degree of wage compression due to union influences also varied from one state to the next. For instance, while teachers in states like Michigan, Massachusetts, and Rhode Island were heavily unionized by the early 1960s, collective bargaining spread more slowly in other states—especially in the South. These differences were largely due to differences in state laws relating to collective bargaining for public-sector workers.

Unionization and the introduction of collective bargaining can be expected to increase average pay for all teachers but reduce the difference between average pay and the pay received by those with both high and low aptitudes, thereby discouraging entry into teaching by women with higher aptitude while attracting those with lower aptitudes. While other forces may also affect the wage spread, we have isolated statistically the portion that was caused by unionization and collective bargaining. To do so, we relied on six indicators of state laws that facilitated or forestalled unionization of teachers. From 1955 onward, states gradually enacted laws that gave teachers' organizations the rights to meet and confer with management, to conduct collective bargaining, to deduct members' dues and nonmembers' fees from paychecks, and to exclude nonmembers from teaching. Other states enacted laws that protected nonmembers' right to work or prohibited paycheck deduction of dues and fees.

Other research shows that changes in these laws caused the pace of teachers' unionization to vary considerably, even among states with very similar labor markets such as Ohio and Illinois. By restricting our analysis to changes in unionization that were associated with changes in state laws, we can be confident that we are identifying the effect on pay compression of unionization alone.

The Data

We limit our analysis to college graduates, since a college degree was required for almost all beginning teachers during the forty-year period of our study. The data come from a series of surveys conducted by the federal government for various years between 1961 and 1997. For the college graduating classes of 1975, 1977, 1980, 1984, 1986, and 1990, we relied on the surveys of Recent College Graduates (RCG), compiled by the U.S. Office of Education (later the Department of Education). For information on the classes of 1961 and 1964 to 1967, we relied on two predecessors of the RCG surveys (College Graduates of the Class of 1961 and Project Talent), and two successors to the RCG surveys (Baccalaureate and Beyond and the National Education Longitudinal Study) provide information for the classes of 1993 and 1997. The surveys contained information, for most states, on the college from which a woman graduated, her first occupation, and her earnings around one to three years after graduation. Unfortunately, the surveys did not collect direct information on a woman's aptitude. However, we were able to obtain information on the average aptitude of all students at the college she attended.

We divide the individuals from each annual cohort of college graduates into six groups according to the type of school attended: (1) highly selective colleges, where average student SAT scores were in the top 5 percentiles; (2) quite selective colleges, in the next 10 percentiles; (3) moderately selective colleges, in the next 15 percentiles; (4) above-average colleges, in the next 20 percentiles; (5) below-average colleges, in the next 25 percentiles; and (6) bottom-tier colleges, in the lowest 25 percentiles.

Organizing in this way gave us a direct measure of the extent to which teachers are being trained at more or less selective colleges, itself a question of considerable interest. The measure also provides an accurate estimate of the change in the aptitude of entering teachers, provided that their average aptitude relative to the average aptitude of all students has not changed within each of these six categories over time. That is, if the average teacher's SAT score at highly selective colleges is consistently fifty points lower (or higher) than that of the average student at such colleges, and a similar consistency holds for the other groupings, then we have a good measure of changes in the aptitudes of those entering the teaching profession.

Charting the Decline

The economic news for educators as a whole was fairly good over the approximately forty years of the study. Our data indicate that, nationwide, the real (inflation-adjusted) earnings of the average new female teacher rose by 8 percent between 1963 and 2000. But this change was not evenly distributed across aptitude groups. The earnings of teachers in the lowest aptitude group (those from the bottom-tier colleges) rose dramatically relative to the average, so that teachers who in 1963 earned 73 percent of the average salary for

Figure 10.2. Big Push

In 1963 the average salary of women teachers from highly selective colleges was much higher than the salary received by women teachers from bottom-tier colleges. By the year 2000 the two groups were earning about the same.

Relative Salaries of Women Teachers from Highly Selective and Bottom-Tier Colleges Relative to Average

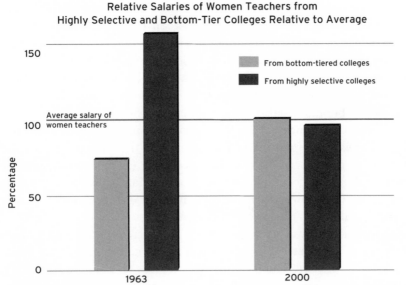

SOURCE: Author's calculations.

teachers could expect to earn exactly the average by 2000. Meanwhile, the ratio of the earnings of teachers in the highest-aptitude group (from the highly selective colleges) to earnings of average teachers fell dramatically. In states where they began with an earnings ratio of 157 percent, they ended with a ratio of 98 percent. By 2000, most states had earnings ratios near 100 percent for all aptitude groups, indicating that graduates of the most highly selective colleges earned no more as teachers than did graduates from bottom-tier schools! (See figure 10.2.)

Opportunities outside of teaching also changed differently for women by ability group, but the differences were far less pronounced. For a college graduate from the selective schools (the top 30 percent), the ratio of female earnings to male earnings in non-teaching occupations rose modestly: A woman could expect her earnings to rise as a percentage of the earnings of males with similar aptitudes from 77 percent in 1963 to 84 percent in 2000. For a woman from the bottom-tier schools, there was little change in the ratio of female earnings to male earnings. A woman could expect her earnings to drop slightly, from 80 to 77 percent, in relation to men with similar aptitude (see figure 10.3).

Figure 10.3. Little Pull

Between 1963 and 2000, the gender differences in pay outside the teaching profession changed only slightly for those from either highly selective or bottom-tiered colleges.

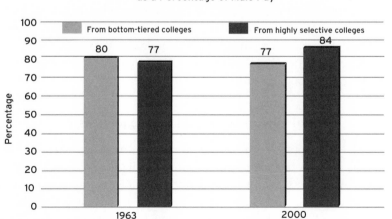

Female Pay in Nonteaching Occupations
as a Percentage of Male Pay

SOURCE: Author's calculations.

Figure 10.4. A Race to the Bottom

The share of female teachers who attended highly selective colleges fell dramatically from 1963 to 2000. At the same time, the share that came from bottom-tiered colleges more than doubled. By 2000, more than one-third of new female teachers had graduated from a bottom-tier college.

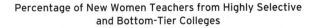

Percentage of New Women Teachers from Highly Selective and Bottom-Tier Colleges

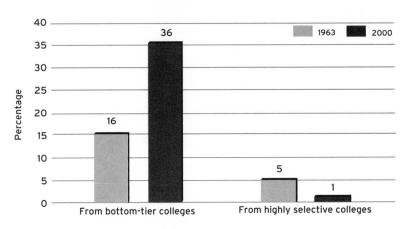

SOURCE: Author's calculations.

Our data also indicate that the share of new female teachers from highly selective colleges fell from 5 percent to 1 percent between 1963 and 2000. This five-fold drop is a strong indication in our data of the decline in teacher aptitude. Over the same period, the share of new female teachers who came from the bottom-tier colleges rose from 16 to 36 percent (see figure 10.4).

Equal Effects, Unequal Consequences

Factors with equal potential effects can nonetheless have dramatically different consequences if one factor hardly changes while the other shifts significantly. In physics, both pressure and temperature affect volume, but if only temperature changes, that is the force that explains why a kettle whistles when water comes to a boil. As we shall see, much the same can be said about changes in teacher quality in recent decades.

Equal changes in each of the four components listed above had roughly equal effects on the probability that a woman would enter the teaching profession. For example, increases in average teachers' salaries increased the likelihood that a woman would become a teacher. Changes in other occupations had a similar effect. When the base occupational wages (for men) within a particular aptitude group increased, then women were attracted out of teaching to other occupations. Also, when women came closer to achieving parity of pay in non-teaching occupations, then teaching became less attractive. A change in any of these factors had roughly the same impact on the decision of women to enter teaching as did a change in the amount of wage compression.

But while an equal change in all factors would have had a roughly similar impact on the chances that women of a particular aptitude would choose to teach, the actual size of the changes over the forty-year period were anything but equal for women from different aptitude groups. While parity of pay for men and women and the base pay for males in other occupations changed similarly for all women regardless of aptitude, the change in union-induced compression of the pay spread for teachers was especially large.

As a result teaching became much more attractive to those with lower aptitudes—and much less attractive to the most talented. Pay compression increased the share of the lowest-aptitude female college graduates who became teachers by about 9 percentage points. Meanwhile, the share of the highest-aptitude graduates who became teachers shifted downward by about 12 percentage points.

By contrast, the gains in gender equality in other occupations, while significant, were similar for female college graduates of all aptitudes. Thus they had only small differential effects on the occupational choices of talented women college graduates; the fraction of women entering the teaching profession from highly selective colleges fell by only 3.2 percentage points. For all the selective colleges (the top 30 percent), the effect was just 2.5 percentage points. For all those who attended less selective colleges, increasing pay parity had negligible effects.

Conclusions

The results reported above allow us to estimate how many teachers would have come from each type of college had pay compression not intensified and, separately, had pay parity in other occupations not improved. We find that pay compression explains about 80 percent of the decline of teachers from highly selective colleges and about 25 percent of the increase in the share of teachers from the least selective colleges. Meanwhile, changes in pay parity in non-teaching occupations explains only 9 percent of the decline in the share of teachers coming from highly selective colleges—and only 6 percent of the increase in teachers from the bottom tier of colleges. The sheer increase in the proportion of all college graduates coming from these bottom-tier colleges accounts for much of the remaining increment in the percentage of low-aptitude teachers.

These results are striking: union-driven pay compression alone accounts for more than three-quarters of the decline in teacher quality. The finding is best understood by recognizing that pay parity increased only moderately and at a similar rate for college-educated women of all abilities. Not only did the gender gap begin to disappear in such highly paid professions as law and medicine, but it also slipped noticeably in less-exalted occupations such as book-keeping and middle-level administration.

Put another way, we cannot expect high-performing college graduates to continue to enter teaching if that is the one profession in which pay is decoupled from performance. Indeed, other professions have been raising the reward for performance over the past few decades. We suspect that this trend exacerbated the degree to which pay compression pushed high-aptitude people out of teaching. A push from one direction has more effect on someone who is being simultaneously pulled from the other direction.

Our findings, though disturbing, are potentially hopeful. The decline in the quality of those entering teaching is not an irrevocable trend driven by larger forces in the society over which policymakers can exercise little control. On the contrary, education policymakers have the tools within their own hands to address the problem at hand. To attract high-aptitude women back into teaching, school districts need to reward teachers in the same way that college graduates are paid in other professions—that is, according to their performance. In all probability, such a strategy would attract male teachers of higher aptitude as well.

CAROLINE M. HOXBY is professor of economics at Harvard University.

ANDREW LEIGH is a fellow at the Social Policy Analysis, Evaluation and Research Centre in the Economics Program, Research School of Social Sciences, Australian National University.

Do Teacher Unions
Stifle Reform?

CHAPTER ELEVEN

⌁

A Union by Any Other Name

Terry M. Moe

The teacher unions have more influence on the public schools than any other group in American society. They shape the schools from the bottom up, through collective-bargaining activities so broad in scope that virtually every aspect of the schools is somehow affected. They also shape the schools from the top down, through political activities that give them unrivaled influence over the laws and regulations imposed on public education by government.

As the unions put their distinctive stamp on the nation's schools, the objectives they pursue are reflections of their own interests, which are often incompatible with what is best for children, schools, and society. This presents an obvious problem—and a serious one—for a nation that wants to improve the quality of its education system.

In recent years, certain scholars and even a few union leaders have argued the need for "reform unionism" and claimed that, with enough enlightened thinking, the unions can voluntarily dedicate themselves to education reforms that promote the greater good. This is a fanciful notion, based on a fatal misconception: that the unions can be counted on not to pursue their own interests. No such thing is going to happen.

My purpose here is to provide a simple overview of the pivotal roles that teacher unions actually play in public education—and to suggest why, if Americans want to improve their schools, something needs to be done about the unions and their extraordinary power.

The Rise of Teacher Unions

Until the early 1960s, only a tiny percentage of teachers were unionized. The American Federation of Teachers (AFT) was the only teacher union to speak of, and it organized no more than 5 percent of the nation's teachers clustered in a few urban areas. The leading force in public education was the National Education Association (NEA). It attracted about half of the nation's teachers, but it functioned as a professional association and was controlled by school administrators.

The watershed event came in 1961, when the AFT won a representation election in New York City. This victory set off an aggressive AFT campaign to organize teachers in other cities, forcing the NEA to compete as a union or risk losing its constituency. The early years of NEA-AFT competition brought thousands of districts under union control, with the NEA winning the lion's share and maintaining its position of leadership—but now as a union rather than a professional association.

By the early 1980s, dramatic increases in union membership began to level off at a new equilibrium. As of 2001, this equilibrium still prevails and is quite stable, with the vast majority of teachers (outside the South) covered by collective bargaining. The NEA, which claimed a membership of 766,000 in 1961, now claims to have some 2.5 million members, about 2 million of whom are K–12 teachers. It has affiliates in all fifty states and is politically active throughout the country. The AFT has expanded by its own count from 70,821 members in 1961 to roughly one million members today, although only about half are teachers. As in the past, the AFT's strength is in big cities.

Any effort to understand why the teacher unions succeeded as they did must begin by recognizing that their emergence was not an isolated development in the American labor movement. It happened during a time of spectacular growth among public-employee unions generally.

Several factors were responsible for this phenomenon, but a critical one is simply that the laws changed. Before the 1960s, states did not authorize public employees to engage in collective bargaining. In 1959, Wisconsin became the first state to enact a collective-bargaining law for public-sector workers, and over the next two decades most states followed suit. These laws created rights, duties, and procedures that made it easier for unions to organize and bargain. By the early 1980s, the percentage of unionized workers in government had skyrocketed from trivial levels two decades earlier to a robust 37 percent—where, as with teachers, it stabilized at a new equilibrium.

At the very time unions were succeeding dramatically in the public sector, they were stumbling badly in the private sector, in what was nothing short of a catastrophe for the labor movement (see figure 11.1). Why did teacher unions and other public-sector unions do so well when private-sector unions—which had long benefited from union-promoting legal frameworks—fared so poorly?

There seem to be various causes at work. In the private sector, most employers know they will lose business to competitors if their costs increase, and this prompts them to resist unionization. Similarly, unions cannot make costly demands without losing jobs to nonunion firms, and this too limits their ability to organize and bargain. As a general matter, competition breeds trouble for unions; and over the past few decades, the private sector has become much more competitive.

The government environment is very different. Public agencies usually have no competition and are not threatened by loss of business if their costs go up, while unions know they are not putting jobs at risk by pressuring for all they can get. Government decisions on labor matters, moreover, are heavily influenced by politics rather than simple efficiency. In jurisdictions where unions are powerful, therefore, many public officials have incentives to submit to union demands even if they know the result will be higher costs and inefficiencies.

Given the lack of competition, and given the dominance of politics over efficiency, unions simply find it much easier to prosper in the public sector. It is no accident that the American labor movement has been kept afloat by the success of public-sector unions—and that the largest, most powerful union in the country is not the Teamsters or the United Auto Workers, but the National Education Association.

Collective Bargaining

When it comes to the fundamentals of organization, the teacher unions are like all other unions: collective bargaining is their core function and the base of their economic and political power. It is through collective bargaining that they attract and hold members, get most of their resources, and gain the capacity for political action.

The teacher unions bargain with school boards, which play the role of management. As the above discussion implies, however, school boards cannot be expected to behave like the managers of private firms in resisting union demands. School boards face little competition and needn't worry that they will lose business by agreeing to union demands that raise costs, promote inefficiencies, or lower school performance. The kids and the tax money will

Figure 11.1. Ships in the Night

As unions lost members in the private sector, they used their political clout to expand rapidly in the less competitive public sector.

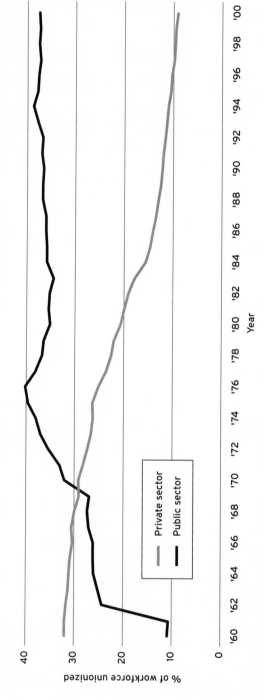

SOURCE: Union Sourcebook 1947–1983 (U.S. Bureau of Labor Statistics); Statistical Abstract of the United States, 2001 (U.S. Census Bureau).

still be there. In addition, school boards are composed of elected officials, whose incentives are explicitly political and less tied to efficiency and costs than those of private managers. Moreover, the unions, by participating in local elections, are in a position to determine who the management will be, and to give it incentives to bargain sympathetically—a stunning advantage that, for private-sector unions, would be a dream come true.

Union influence usually takes the form of rules that specify (in excruciating detail) what must or must not be done. In a typical union contract, there are so many rules about so many subjects that it may take more than a hundred pages to spell them all out. In many urban districts, where the unions are strongest, contracts may run to two or three hundred pages or longer.

There are rules, of course, about pay and fringe benefits. But there are also rules about hiring, firing, layoffs, and promotion. Rules about how teachers are evaluated. Rules about the assignment of teachers to classrooms and their (non)assignment to yard duty, lunch duty, and after-school activities. Rules about how much time teachers may be asked to work and how much time they must get to prepare for class. Rules about class schedules. Rules about class size. Rules about the numbers and uses of teacher aides. Rules about teacher involvement in school policy decisions. Rules about how grievances are to be handled. Rules about numbers of faculty meetings. Rules about how often teachers can be required to meet with parents. Rules about who has to join the union. Rules about whether dues will be deducted automatically from paychecks. Rules about union use of school facilities. And more.

Union demands on these and other scores are not random or frivolous. Fundamental interests motivate their behavior and determine the kinds of rules they find desirable. These interests arise from the primordial fact that, in order to prosper as organizations, unions need to attract members and money. Most of what they do can be understood in terms of these simple goals—which entail, among other things, securing benefits and protections for members, increasing the demand for teachers, supporting higher taxes, regularizing the flow of resources into union coffers, minimizing competition, and seeking political power.

Note that these interests and the behaviors they entail need have nothing to do with what is best for children, schools, or the public interest; indeed, they may clearly conflict with them. For this reason, collective bargaining often leads to contracts that make little sense as blueprints for effective organization.

By way of illustration, here are some common themes that give substance to the typical contract:

- Unions are dedicated to protecting the jobs of all members. The rules they insist upon make it virtually impossible for schools to get rid of even the worst teachers, not to mention those who are merely mediocre.
- Unions don't want decisions about pay, promotions, assignments, or transfers to be based on performance. As they see it, performance evaluations create uncertainty for their members, force members to compete with one another, and put discretion in the hands of superiors. The unions want personnel decisions to be based on seniority and formal education, which offer advancement to all teachers regardless of their competence.
- Unions seek to expand teachers' rights by severely restricting the discretion available to administrators. For principals and district officials, discretion means the ability to lead and manage. For unions, however, it means that administrators make decisions about where, when, and how teachers do their work and how incentives are structured—which is unacceptable. Discretion is to be driven out, replaced by rules that define realms of teacher autonomy.
- Unions tend to oppose anything that induces competition or differentiation among teachers. This applies to performance-based assessments, but also to many other policies. They are opposed, for example, to differential pay in response to market conditions (which might mean paying math and science teachers a premium to attract and hold them). Unions want teachers to have the same interests, because this promotes solidarity. The notion that some teachers are better than others, or worth more than others, is stridently resisted.
- Unions tend to oppose anything that induces competition among schools. Most fundamentally, they want all schools in a district to be covered by the same contract, because the schools not covered (and free of the costs and rigidities it imposes) would have an advantage. This would be especially true if the non-covered schools were allowed to be different in other ways too, and if parents were free to choose, for then the non-covered schools might attract kids, jobs, and resources away from the union schools. The union ideal is that all schools be regulated the same and that all be guaranteed their "fair share" of students and money.
- Unions tend to oppose any contracting-out of educational functions that involves a shift of jobs and resources from public to private. This is true even if privatization may provide better services at lower cost. The goal is to keep public employment and spending as high as possible.

- Unions want contract provisions that require all teachers to become members and that force nonmembers to pay "agency fees." They also want dues and fees automatically deducted from teachers' paychecks, as this guarantees unions a regular flow of money and shifts administrative costs onto the districts.

The unions put the best public face on their collective-bargaining demands, arguing that what is good for teachers is good for kids and that they are just fighting for quality public schools. It is obvious, however, that many aspects of union influence (not all) have negative consequences for kids and schools. How can it be socially beneficial that schools can't get rid of bad teachers? Or that teachers can't be tested for competence? Or that teachers can't be evaluated based on how much their students learn? Or that principals are so heavily constrained they can't exercise leadership of their own schools?

It is also clear that union-generated rules add tremendously to the bureaucratization of schools. The unions are responsible for making the system much more formal, complex, and impersonal than it would otherwise be. These characteristics tend to undermine school performance. Schools tend to do best when they function in an informal, cooperative, flexible, and nurturing way—which is precisely the opposite of bureaucracy.

Little research specifically links teacher unions to school performance, so it is impossible to make an ironclad, fully documented case about the direction of union effects. The few existing studies have produced mixed results, some showing negative effects and some showing positive effects. But many of these findings are probably spurious, arising because the data are very poor and hard to get and the methodological difficulties are formidable.

The most recent addition to this literature, an article by Lala Carr Steelman, Brian Powell, and Robert M. Carini in the winter 2000 issue of the *Harvard Educational Review*, claims that unions have positive effects on performance, and its findings are being touted by union enthusiasts. This analysis, too, needs to be regarded with care. Its measures of school performance, for example, are SAT and ACT scores, which clearly do not measure the actual performance of the schools (as the unions are usually the first to point out). And because these and other variables are aggregated to the state level for analysis, there are dangers in drawing inferences about causal processes (like union influence) at the school level. An analysis that minimizes these sorts of problems, and is the most sophisticated of the tests of union impact, was carried out a few years ago by Harvard economist Caroline M. Hoxby and published in the August 1996 issue of the *Quarterly Journal of Economics.* Hoxby found that unions have negative effects on school performance.

The most confident conclusion that can be drawn from this literature is that unions increase the costs of education, apparently by an average of 8 to 15 percent—and without (as far as can be determined) a corresponding increase, or any increase at all, in school quality. This tends to support the argument that, for a given level of spending, unions make the production of quality education more difficult.

Local Politics

Collective bargaining is the bread-and-butter activity of teacher unions. The key to their preeminence in American education, however, is their ability to combine collective bargaining and politics into an integrated strategy for promoting union objectives.

Teacher unions are active in politics at all levels: local, state, and national. In local politics the teacher unions are in the astounding position of being able to determine who sits on local school boards, and thus with whom they will be bargaining. Needless to say, the unions have strong incentives to mobilize for political purposes, to participate actively in electoral campaigns, and to identify and recruit sympathetic candidates. These incentives are all the stronger because districts make decisions on a wide range of policy, taxing, and funding issues of great relevance to union interests.

The details of local politics can vary across districts, due to their individual histories, demographics, and problems. But certain characteristics are common to most of them—and give teacher unions great advantages in the struggle for influence.

- School board elections usually occur in off years or times and thus tend to attract very low turnout, often in the range of 10 to 20 percent. By getting their own members and supporters to the polls, unions are well positioned to prevail.
- These elections are typically nonpartisan: candidates are not identified by party affiliation. Voters are thus denied the key information that running under a party banner conveys, and this enhances the ability of unions to control how candidates are perceived and who is elected.
- Local politics is not very pluralistic. Teacher unions tend to be the only organized force in school politics. They almost always overshadow busi-

ness and civic groups, and they always overshadow parents, who are not organized (outside the PTA, which has long been under union control in politics) and who vote in low numbers.

- Teacher unions are flush with political resources. They have money for campaign contributions, and they control an army of political workers (teachers) who are educated, informed, have a direct stake in the issues, and are organized for political action.
- Most candidates run for school board on a shoestring. This being so, candidates endorsed by the unions and boosted by their money, manpower, and organization are very likely to win.

For these and other reasons, unions are formidable powers in local politics. The upshot is that, when school boards make decisions about policy or money or about the myriad rules governing school operations, they tend to give heavy weight to the interests of unions—and may often depart, as a result, from what is best for children and effective education.

State and National Politics

Important as local politics is, the teacher unions have good reason to think more broadly about the exercise of political power. Increasingly, the big decisions on education are being made by state and (to a lesser extent) national governments, and many of these decisions have a direct bearing on union interests. Active involvement in state and national politics is more than an attractive option for the unions. It is a necessity.

The great value of higher-level politics is that state governments, especially, are in a position to adopt virtually any requirements, programs, and funding arrangements they want for the public schools. Whatever policies they adopt, moreover, are typically applied to all the districts and schools in their jurisdictions. When unions use their political power at these higher levels, then, they can achieve many objectives they might be unable to achieve through local collective bargaining, from more money to smaller classes to stricter credentialing requirements. One political victory can accomplish what hundreds of decentralized negotiations cannot.

Over the past few decades, the NEA and the AFT have acted aggressively on these incentives, and they have emerged as extraordinarily powerful players in state and national politics. A recent study at the state level asked experts to rank interest groups according to political influence, and the teacher unions came out number one, outdistancing business organizations, trial lawyers, doctors, insurance companies, environmentalists, and even the state AFL-CIO affiliates.

One reason for the unions' success is that they spend tremendous amounts of money on political campaigns and lobbying. They regularly rank among the top-spending interest groups at both the state and national levels, and in many states they are number one. Probably the key to their political fire-power, however, is that they have literally millions of members, and these members are a looming presence in every electoral district in the country. Candidates are keenly aware that the unions invest heavily in mobilizing their local activists and have considerable clout in seeing friends elected and enemies defeated.

Almost all of this firepower is employed to the benefit of Democrats, whose constituencies already incline them to favor policies the teacher unions want—more spending, higher taxes, higher public employment, more regula-tions, more job protections, more restrictions on competition, more collec-tive bargaining—and who, with union backing and pressure, can usually be counted on for support.

Within Congress and the state legislatures, the teacher unions are aggres-sive, omnipresent participants. This is often true even in right-to-work states. They monitor all relevant legislation, propose bills, carry out background research on issues, attend committee hearings, keep scorecards on legislators, and bring their formidable power to bear in getting legislators to vote their way. On education, teacher unions are the 500-pound gorillas of legislative politics.

On occasion, they also use the initiative process to put their own bills on the ballot for a direct popular vote. Here, they can use their financial resources to bankroll signature-gathering and media blitzes, and they can unleash an army of volunteers during the campaign. No other organizations are so well suited to initiative politics, and the unions have gone this route when legislatures have failed to give them what they wanted. A good exam-ple: California's Proposition 98, which was successfully promoted by the Cal-ifornia Teachers Association in 1989, and since then has required the state to spend at least 40 percent of its annual budget on the public schools.

The teacher unions also exercise their power in administrative arenas. The national and state departments of education, in particular, oversee countless education programs, distribute billions of dollars, and have substantial discre-tion in deciding what the details of education policy will be and how the money will be spent. Within these departments, officials regard the unions as key "stakeholders" who have legitimate, ongoing roles to play in shaping public decisions. The opportunities for union influence are everywhere and virtually unobservable to outsiders unfamiliar with the byzantine world of government bureaucracy.

Often the unions pursue their policy objectives by combining legislative and administrative power. An important example can be found in their recent drive for teacher "professionalism." This is a goal with obvious political appeal. Who could be against professionalism? The reality, however, is that they are active on this issue because their fundamental interests are at stake. By pushing for stricter licensing, credentialing, and certification requirements and for regulatory boards controlled or influenced by the unions themselves, they are attempting to control entry into their field and thus to limit supply and put upward pressure on salaries. This is a classic political strategy that other occupations, from doctors and lawyers to cosmetologists and plumbers, have long used with great success. The teacher unions just want to do the same.

The Politics of Blocking

Much of what the teacher unions do in politics is not about winning the policies they want. It is about blocking the policies they don't want—a strategy that the American political system, built around multiple checks and balances, is designed to facilitate. Because blocking is relatively easy, the unions are usually powerful enough to stop reforms they consider a threat to their interests, and thus to protect a status quo that benefits them. In a time of widespread pressure for improvement in public education, this is the way the teacher unions put their power to most effective use. They use it to prevent change.

Consider the movement for school choice, which represents the most farreaching movement for change in American education. From the unions' standpoint, it is irrelevant whether choice is a promising reform. The overriding fact is that choice-based reforms naturally generate changes that are threatening to the unions' interests—and the unions, quite predictably, oppose them. Much of their political activity over the past decade has been dedicated to the simple goal of blocking school choice.

The unions see vouchers as a survival issue. Vouchers would allow money and children to flow from public to private: threatening a drop in public employment and in union membership; dispersing teachers to private schools, where it is much harder for unions to organize; promoting competition among schools, which puts union schools at a disadvantage; and creating a less regulated system in which the unions have less power. Small wonder, then, that the unions have done everything they can to defeat vouchers—even when vouchers are proposed solely for the neediest of children.

The teacher unions are also battling against charter schools—which, while public, need not be unionized, and which draw students and money away from the regular public schools where union members teach. Unions sometimes claim to "support" charter proposals, but these are strategic moves designed to head off something much worse: vouchers. Moreover, they are typically accompanied by demands for strict ceilings on the number of charters, requirements that charters be unionized, and extensive district controls. Charters are on the rise nationwide, but for now most are constrained by laws that have been heavily influenced by the unions.

The teacher unions are also fighting privatization. In the 1990s, for-profit companies sought contracts with districts to run entire schools, typically those regarded as failing. The unions recognize that they have less control over private contractors than over the districts, and that the success of private contractors could well promote the flow of jobs, money, and control from public to private schools. They have done what they can, accordingly, to prevent school boards from entering into such agreements and to sabotage those that get past them.

The bottom line is that the teacher unions' greatest power is not the ability to get what they want, but rather the ability to stifle reforms that threaten their interests. School choice is not the only reform they oppose—for union interests are deeply rooted in the status quo, and most changes of any consequence create problems for them. The result is that, as our nation has struggled to improve its public schools, the teacher unions have emerged as the fiercest, most powerful defenders of the status quo, and the single greatest obstacle to the reform of American education.

Introducing Competition

For reform to succeed, something concrete must be done to remove the education system from the unions' grip. This won't be easy, because the unions can (and regularly do) use their power to "persuade" reformers to turn their sights elsewhere. Most Democrats, in particular, would be committing political suicide by trying to alter the unions' current role in public education, and they will resist any efforts to do so. In a political system of checks and balances, this alone will be enough to block most reform proposals most of the time.

If the future holds a solution to the problem of union power, it will probably develop as a by-product of the school-choice movement. The best bet is that, despite union opposition, school choice in various forms will gradually spread. As it does, the unions will be faced with an increasingly competitive environment. Children and resources will begin to flow to nonunion schools, and unions will find themselves with fewer members, less money, and a growing number of schools and teachers that are outside the traditional system and difficult to organize. Competition spells trouble for unions. It undermines their organizational strength—and with it, their political power.

Whether choice and competition will ultimately win out remains to be seen. In the meantime, the teacher unions will reign as the preeminent power in American education, and they will continue to give us public schools in their own image.

TERRY M. MOE is William Bennett Munro Professor in Political Science and senior fellow at the Hoover Institution, Stanford University.

CHAPTER TWELVE

Reform Unionism Is Here

Charles Taylor Kerchner

The pragmatic question of whether teacher unions can lead education reform is linked with an ideological question, whether they should. Is it their role to reshape public education, or should they limit themselves to pressing for their members' economic and job security? Many of those who believe that unions can't lead reform also believe that they shouldn't. On the contrary, I believe teacher unions should have both the right and the responsibility to engage in education reform. This belief is rooted in my beliefs about teaching and schooling. I believe that teaching is hard and skilled work: a mixture of craft, art, and profession. It follows that teachers should be organized as mind workers and not around the assumption that they are industrial workers subject to micromanagement. Creating an occupation built on the assumption of teachers as mind workers is the most important education policy frontier facing us. It may also be the most contentious.

There is substantial opposition within unions themselves and within the ranks of teachers to the idea of teaching as a self-policing profession. Most teachers are not accustomed to judging their colleagues' performance or their fitness to remain as teachers. However, the highest barrier to the engagement of teachers in education reform comes from conservatives who believe that teacher unions shouldn't be involved in substantive decisions about the direction of school reform. They see union involvement as an unwarranted intrusion of labor's influence into the rightful domains of school managers, school boards, or legislatures. They urge further restrictions on the scope of collective bargaining and generally seek to organize education reform around rather than with teacher unions.

Reforming the schools by restricting or ignoring teacher unions is counterproductive. The teachers' contract often channels more than half of a school district's operating budget and sets the pattern for much more than that. Unless they engage the labor contract's rules and financial flows, reform efforts are stunted. Not bringing reform issues to the bargaining table or other sites of labor relations means that reforms are never discussed, much less agreed to. Unions essentially escape responsibility for reform. They serve a role in the hearts of conservatives as political whipping boys, but political satisfaction is purchased at a high price. Engagement is better than blame.

Organizing around Quality

By the 1960s and 1970s, when large numbers of teachers entered into collective bargaining, the word unionism largely meant industrial unionism, a form of unionism designed to work within large hierarchies. Older forms of worker organization—guilds, artisan associations, and craft unions—had largely disappeared. In public education, industrial unionism was labor's answer to an education system constructed on the principles of scientific management, a system in which the content and pacing of work was designed not by teachers but by school administrators. Schools were bureaucratized long before they were unionized. It is somewhat ironic that teacher unions remain one of the strongest supporters of the very system whose managerial excesses and rigid rules they sought to tame with collective bargaining.

Still, schools never were factories. There is more than a little truth to the teacher's adage, "I'm in charge when the classroom door is closed." In the industrial sense, schools were always incomplete bureaucracies. Although the assertion would horrify most teachers, schools are dramatically under-supervised by industrial standards. Nonetheless, the logic of industrial organization created a clear division between work creation and task execution. Strictly interpreted, industrial organization would hold teachers responsible for the faithful reproduction of lesson plans and classroom routines developed elsewhere. Invention, creativity, and spontaneity would not be required or expected.

A small but growing number of teacher union locals have attempted to go beyond the industrial unionism model by fashioning new ways of organizing teaching around high-quality practice and high-performing schools (see figure 12.1). Scattered efforts—sometimes called "random acts of innovation"—have

Figure 12.1. Reform Unionism

In select, mainly urban school systems unions have negotiated reforms that alter antiquated systems of teacher pay, evaluation, and training.

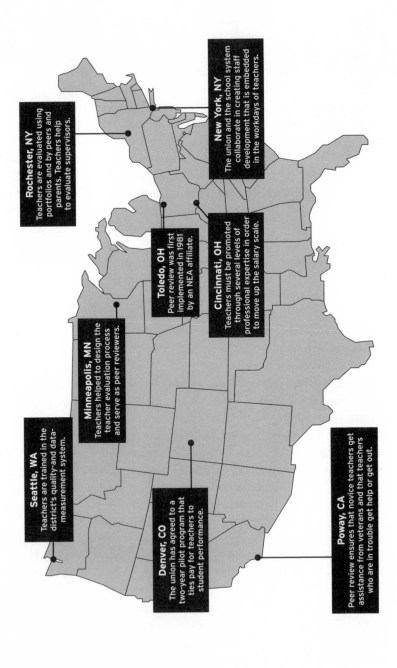

Rochester, NY
Teachers are evaluated using portfolios and by peers and parents. Teachers help to evaluate supervisors.

New York, NY
The union and the school system collaborate in creating staff development that is embedded in the workdays of teachers.

Minneapolis, MN
Teachers helped to design the teacher evaluation process and serve as peer reviewers.

Toledo, OH
Peer review was first implemented in 1981 by an NEA affiliate.

Cincinnati, OH
Teachers must be promoted through several levels of professional expertise in order to move up the salary scale.

Seattle, WA
Teachers are trained in the district's quality-and data-measurement system.

Denver, CO
The union has agreed to a two-year pilot program that ties pay for teachers to student performance.

Poway, CA
Peer review ensures that novice teachers get assistance from veterans and that teachers who are in trouble get help or get out.

begun to coalesce into a systemic connection between the everyday practices of labor relations and a quality school-reform agenda. In districts such as Minneapolis, teachers have begun assuming greater responsibility for how quality is assessed and how quality standards are enforced, and they have gained greater authority over their work lives. These expanded work roles are compatible with many organizational forms. Like those in Minneapolis, most teachers work for complex hierarchies that could become more participatory and streamlined while retaining their basic shape. Even unions in industrial settings, such as Saturn Motors, have accomplished such a transition. Charters and other more autonomous schools could function as producers' cooperatives or professional practice corporations. If schools were under private management, the union contract might call for an equity stake in the corporation, as does the agreement in Miami–Dade County for teachers working in Edison Schools.

Four labor-relations interventions form what may be called the Diamond of Quality—peer review, teacher induction, professional development, and performance rewards—all held together with a system of standards and indicators that focuses both labor relations and school operations on student achievement. All of these reforms are consistent with developing the art, craft, and profession of teaching. Some—such as peer review and new compensation systems—are controversial within labor and management, but all fall within the range of negotiability.

A Bedrock of Data

Because the central idea is to use labor relations to focus on student achievement rather than on adult privileges, the core of the quality diamond is a system of standards and indicators. If teachers don't create and analyze data on student achievement, tying a system of evaluating or compensating them to the outcomes of their students becomes capricious and counterproductive. Teachers may gain or lose money, but they are literally senseless about how actions they took or didn't take are connected to performance results.

Even though there are substantial misgivings among teachers themselves, both national teacher unions have supported a national system of educational standards. The American Federation of Teachers (AFT) has made standards the key to its quality-schools strategy. Its Task Force on Redesigning Low Performing Schools has created an intervention strategy that includes indicators of poor performance and materials, procedures, and established school-wide improvement strategies that can be used to respond.

Constructing a good system of data and indicators and training teachers and site administrators to use one is a substantial undertaking. The Seattle Public Schools and the Seattle Teachers Association have an agreement to train three teachers in each school in the district's quality and data measurement system. This is seen as a long-term project. A series of agreements between the Minneapolis Teachers Federation and the school district has created an interlocking system of data use and development. In New York City, the United Federation of Teachers has a joint project with the school district to integrate standards-based teaching in the district.

Teacher unions are potential allies in today's most far-reaching reform effort, the effort to establish and implement standards. Historically, education has not lacked for standards; it has suffered from their lack of implementation. Implementing standards means teaching differently. Teaching differently means retraining the existing work force and inducting new teachers into new ways of teaching. Creating budgets and work schedules for professional development is typically a subject of bargaining. Unions also forcefully prod state and local officials to synchronize the tests, the standards, and the curriculum so that the test can reflect what the students actually learn in school.

Peer Review

Performance review by colleagues is a hallmark of a profession, both for entrance into an occupation and for the ongoing assessment of a professional's performance. In higher education it is the norm. Union-sanctioned peer review for elementary and secondary school teachers has a record long enough for reasonable claims to be made for its success. Started in Toledo, Ohio, in 1982, it has spread to about fifty other sites, and both national unions endorse it. Although no comprehensive study exists, anecdotal evidence suggests that peer review provides a more thorough system of inducting and evaluating novices than is currently used in most school districts. Peer review also seems to be more effective than administrative evaluation in the remediation or removal of veteran teachers with serious performance problems.

A complete peer-review system, such as that in Poway, California, works at three levels. First, novice teachers get the introduction to teaching they need and deserve. In contrast, most U.S. teachers still survive sink-or-swim induction. A culture of isolationism among veteran teachers often prevents assistance to new teachers. Peer review links experienced teachers to novices and provides greater formative assistance. Ultimately supervising teachers learn to "call the question" (as they say in Rochester, New York), making a judgment about a novice's performance. Second, peer review works for teachers in trouble. They get help, they get better, or they get out. Third, it operates as an alternative to the pro forma classroom evaluations carried out by most principals. For example, in Poway, the peer-review process evaluates teachers against criteria based on the guidelines of the National Board for Professional Teaching Standards.

When peer review is established, teachers will work hard to defend it. Teachers have gone to the brink of strike to save their peer-review programs in Toledo (in 1995) and in Cincinnati (in 1999 and 2000).

Unionists disagree about whether peer review is a proper union role. Union leader Adam Urbanski is fond of saying, "Peer review is controversial in all the places that don't have it." He is largely correct. Schools and unions that have adopted the system are largely happy with it even though administrative organizations frequently oppose the idea. In Rochester, the administrators' union unsuccessfully sued the teacher union and the district over the peer assistance and review program, claiming that allowing teachers to evaluate one another violated the rights of administrators.

Peer review remains legally clouded in some states. Ohio has amended its statutes to allow peer review. California encourages it with financial incentives. Nevertheless, in some cases outside of public education, bargaining rights have been denied to employees who are considered supervisors because they are involved in assigning, disciplining, or dismissing other workers. In a much-cited U.S. Supreme Court case, faculty members at Yeshiva University were denied bargaining rights because their faculty senate and its committees made substantive university decisions. A recent National Labor Relations Board decision applied the same logic to health care workers. Public policy—in particular state labor statutes—signals what is expected of labor and management. The current signals mandate a union interest in the economics of teaching, but they do not say that educational quality is the union's responsibility. They should.

Induction

Peer review should be part of a general induction process that trains and retains new teachers. Several union locals, including those in Columbus and Cincinnati, Ohio; in Miami–Dade County, Florida; and in Minneapolis, Minnesota, have strong working relationships with local universities that provide a pathway into teaching that is grounded in teaching internships. In Columbus, the same supervising teachers who help and evaluate novices in the workplace help to train them at Ohio State University. In Cincinnati, the Cincinnati Federation of Teachers, the University of Cincinnati, and the school district overhauled teacher training based on their analysis of what is required to be an effective teacher in an urban setting. The Cincinnati plan includes a program in which prospective teachers study for two undergraduate majors, one in a discipline, another in teaching. They take an internship in their fifth year and work alongside senior teachers at a professional development school. During the fifth year they are paid half-time as interns, easing the economic burden of preparing to teach.

Unions have been roundly criticized for their opposition to opening up the teacher labor market so that those with substantive knowledge but without certification can teach. Some of the criticism is justified, but some is not. For the most part, big-city school districts do not use relaxed hiring rules in order to hire retired rocket scientists to teach math or gifted authors to teach high school composition. Districts such as New York City and Los Angeles generally use "emergency" certification to hire thousands of teachers each year who have neither a strong academic background nor good teacher training. At the same time, these districts maintain personnel procedures that discourage qualified applicants. Teacher-education directors from top-ranked schools such as Columbia and UCLA report that red tape often discourages their graduates from applying to urban school districts; the procedural delays often result in suburban schools' tendering employment offers earlier.

Professional Development

Staff development that is embedded in a teacher's workday is the logical extension of a good induction program. In New York City, the United Federation of Teachers and the school system collaborate in creating staff development that is woven into the workdays of teachers. More than 220 teacher specialists staff professional development centers in schools. Through the centers, these teachers deliver classroom coaching and mentoring and assist directly with school-adopted interventions, such as the whole-school-reform program Success for All.

Embedded staff development takes many forms: collegial planning, team teaching, study groups, or teacher centers, as in New York. Such arrangements offer fertile ground for connections with external partners. Teacher academies exist, with union collaboration, in Louisville and Cincinnati. School and university partnerships exist in scores of places. Teacher networks, such as the National Writing Project or the Coalition of Essential Schools, offer ways to bring a web of knowledge to bear on school problems.

All of these programs connect teachers' professional development with the examination and analysis of what students do.

Performance Rewards

Since its introduction in Denver and Des Moines in 1921, the single salary schedule has become virtually universal in public education. Teachers are paid the same depending only on their years of service and level of academic preparation. This was thought to be both a model of fairness and a reasonable incentive system. The salary schedule rewarded teachers for investing their time and personal funds in further education and it ended the long-standing practice of paying men more than women and white teachers more than minorities. It also took pay raises out of the hands of school administrators, which at the time was seen as a way to substitute objective criteria for favoritism and political influence in compensation. The single salary schedule was in place almost everywhere long before teachers bargained collectively. The usefulness and ease of administration of this system explain its long tenure. Only recently has there been serious discussion of alternatives. The most discussed alternative is actually a relatively slight modification of the existing system: paying for knowledge and skills.

The standard salary schedule pays teachers for additional education, but many of the acceptable courses are only loosely connected to teaching responsibilities, subject matter expertise, or knowledge of contemporary pedagogy. Allan Odden and Carolyn Kelley argue that teacher pay should be linked to formal education, as it now is, and to the achievement of knowledge and skills demanded by new curriculum standards and the new roles required of teachers in reorganized schools.

They also promote the use of contingency pay, an extension of what is commonly called "extra pay for extra work." But instead of being focused on extracurricular activities, as are most current contingent pay schemes, Odden and Kelley's plan emphasizes enhancing student achievement. Teachers who complete professional development tasks, for example, would be eligible for bonuses, as would teachers who collaborated on a project linked to creating school programs to raise achievement or who worked on valuable individual projects.

Assistance in preparing for evaluation by the National Board for Professional Teaching Standards and stipends for obtaining "board certification" are forms of contingency pay. Both unions have supported legislation to encourage teachers to become certified, and in many localities unions have bargained salary incentives for board certification. Collective bargaining allows schools to link monetary incentives to board certification. For example, the Los Angeles Unified School District and United Teachers Los Angeles bargained a 15 percent annual salary supplement for any board-certified teacher. In New York City, board certification qualifies a teacher for a salary differential of approximately $3,700.

Board certification is important in its own right, but the influence of the board's methodology—evaluating teachers based on demonstrated practice rather than credit hours alone—is already influencing other domains. Districts and unions are considering using the types of evaluation tools and standards developed by the National Board in internal evaluations of teachers.

Although a recent union election cast doubt on the durability of the arrangement, Cincinnati has become the first public school district in the country to scrap the traditional salary schedule in favor of a system that pays teachers according to their classroom performance. An agreement with the Cincinnati Federation of Teachers, first discussed in 1997, was narrowly ratified by teachers in 2000. The hallmark of the system is five career stages, not unlike the movement through professorial ranks. Advancing in rank and earning salary increments requires specified professional education and evaluations by both a principal and a supervising teacher. As is the case in colleges and universities, teachers who do not advance from the lowest ranks in a specified period are to be dismissed. Meanwhile, the Denver Public Schools and the Denver Teachers Association have captured attention for agreeing to a two-year pilot of a program that ties pay for all teachers in participating schools to student performance and to further teacher education.

Expecting More

Let's face it. Teacher unions can be a terrible nuisance. They are noisy and contentious. Their leaders espouse values that frequently differ from those of school managers and board members. Management's adage that the shortest contract is the best one is a comfortable path. Why, after all, spend time dealing with people with whom one disagrees? Why give them the privilege of having a speaking part in the drama of school reform?

The answer is simple: teacher unions control essential resources for school reform. Unions mediate much of the fiscal contract and most of the psychological contract between teachers and school districts. Teacher unions effectively define the occupation of public school teaching. If we are content with teachers who follow industrial-era scripts—who work specified hours, follow a prescribed curriculum, and follow detailed behavioral rules—we can get by with industrial-era labor relations in which the union's exclusive concerns are wages and work rules.

However, if we have higher aspirations for teachers, we must also have higher expectations of teacher unions. If we want to nurture high standards, if we want teachers to take responsibility for the quality of instruction and for student outcomes, we need public policies and school organizations that demand that teacher unions behave differently. Just as it is in our national interest to engage nations and heads of governments our leaders find disagreeable and sometimes pernicious, it is in the interest of governors, legislators, and school officials to engage teacher unions in education reform.

Engaging teacher unions does not mean forgoing criticism, debate, or confrontation. It does not mean the end to contentious bargaining. It does, however, mean expecting more of labor relations, anticipating as a matter of public policy that union leadership will lead teachers on reform issues. It means raising questions about the connections between union activities and education reform again and again until they are answered. Those who think that unions should speak for teaching as well as for teachers, for the institution of public education as well as for explicit self-interest, have both the right and the ability to ask tough questions. Those who don't think unions should lead education reforms have just let them off the hook.

CHARLES TAYLOR KERCHNER is Hollis P. Allen Professor of Education at Claremont Graduate University.

School Choice

PART A

Charter Schools

Charter Schools: Mom and Pops or Corporate Design

Bryan C. Hassel

Everyone has read the ubiquitous feature story about a charter school—Jane and John Q. Public and their friends, sitting around somebody's kitchen table, dream up a different kind of school for their kids. Putting in hours of sweat equity, charging start-up costs to their credit cards, maybe even mortgaging their homes to bring their dream to reality. Making the economics work by taking parent involvement to a whole new level—parents driving buses, cleaning school bathrooms, mastering the intricacies of state financial reporting requirements.

Charter schools with origins like these can be compelling and unique, models of the outside-the-box approaches these schools are supposed to pilot. And most of the dramatic success stories from the charter world come from schools founded by teachers or community members. For example:

- KIPP Academy, Houston. At KIPP, a middle school founded by two former Teach for America members, one recent class entered with passing rates of 35 and 33 percent on state math and reading tests. The following year, the class's rates rose to 93 and 92 percent.
- The Accelerated School, Los Angeles. Opened by two teachers in 1994 and named *Time* magazine's "Elementary School of the Year" in 2001, the school reports that its scores on the Stanford Achievement test have jumped 97 percent since 1997.
- North Star Academy, Newark, New Jersey. Based on preliminary results from the spring 2000 state test, 88 percent of the school's first 8th grade

class scored proficient or above in language arts (compared with 47 percent citywide), and 66 percent scored proficient or above in math (versus 21 percent citywide).

Numbers like these are eye-catching. But can these stand-alone, typically small charter schools serve as the basis for a sustainable, large-scale movement for change in education? Or are they likely to remain the exception rather than the rule? After all, starting an innovative, successful charter school is extraordinarily difficult, and few entrepreneurs seem cut out for the job.

Small Businesses

There are certainly reasons to think of successful stand-alone charter schools as an interesting but ultimately marginal phenomenon. Starting a public school from scratch is, in a word, difficult. It has become a cliché that charter schools, in addition to being educational institutions, have to succeed as small businesses—balancing their budgets; negotiating leases, financing packages, and contracts; and making payroll. Individuals and small teams—often teachers, parents, or community activists who have never run schools—are apt to possess some but not all of these skills and backgrounds.

Opening a new school also requires capital. Most charter schools receive federally funded start-up grants of $10,000 to $150,000 for one to three years. Beyond that, they cannot expect any public funds to flow until, if they're lucky, the July before they open. However, expenses can't wait. Principals need to be hired a few months before school starts. Ideally, teachers start at least a few weeks before students arrive. Then there are books and bookshelves, desks and desktop computers, and all the other supplies that need to be purchased. And all of that doesn't include the big kahuna of start-up costs: the charter school facility.

The first decade of charter schools has unearthed entrepreneurs who are willing and, in some cases, able to take on these herculean tasks. They've proven themselves able to secure the requisite start-up capital—by becoming enterprising fundraisers, by "partnering" with others who have deeper pockets, by finding creative ways to keep start-up costs down, or by going without amenities that are standard-issue in the typical district school. Even with all these challenges, approximately 2,700 charter schools will be open during the 2002–2003 school year, educating some 700,000 students.

This supply of entrepreneurs can work if we're talking about a reform that captures just 1 percent of the nation's public school market share. But what if we're interested in creating a set of schools that educate 10 percent, 20 percent, or an even greater share of American students? Are there enough social entrepreneurs out there to do that?

Let's consider this question. Nationally, the growth of charter schools was dramatic in the years following the passage of the initial charter laws (see figure 13.1). In 2001 and 2002, however, the number of new charter schools opening in the fall actually declined compared with the previous year.

Statutory caps on charter schools have caused some of this leveling, but not all of it. Even in jurisdictions with few restrictions on new starts, the numbers tend to decline over time. It appears that within a given geographical area lives a limited supply of entrepreneurs willing to undertake starting a charter school, a supply that peters out over time. Not to zero, but to what amounts to a drop in the bucket of public schooling in a city or state.

Enter the EMOs

"Education management organizations," or EMOs, are sometimes touted as the solution to these challenges. According to the Center for Education Reform, 19 of these companies ran 350 charter schools in 2001–2002, about 14 percent of the nation's charter schools (see figure 13.2). Since EMO-run schools are typically larger than the average charter school, EMOs actually educate an even higher percentage of charter school students—perhaps 25 to 30 percent.

Most EMOs today are for-profit companies, such as Edison Schools and Nobel Learning Communities, but not all. Aspire Public Schools, for example, is a nonprofit seeking to operate a large chain of public schools, at least initially in California. The nonprofit New Schools Venture Fund has established a "Charter Accelerator" initiative to invest in more nonprofit EMOs.

EMOs offer many answers to the leadership supply question:

- Expertise and systems. Starting and operating a school requires expertise across a range of fields—curriculum and instructional design, facilities management, community relations. EMOs can hire experts in these areas or develop expertise over time and then share knowledge and capacity with their constituent schools. They can turn expertise into systems so that every school doesn't have to reinvent the wheel.
- Economies of scale. As they operate more and more schools, EMOs can use their growing buying power to obtain favorable terms for goods and services. By negotiating bulk purchase contracts with suppliers, they can reduce per-student costs.

Figure 13.1. Growth Slowing

The early years of the charter school movement saw doubling and even tripling in the number of charter schools. In recent years, however, the rate of growth began to slow.

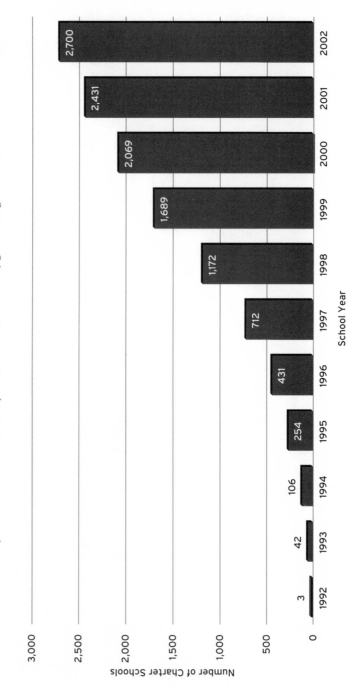

SOURCE: Center for Education Reform.

Figure 13.2. Corporate Takeover?

During the 2001–2002 school year, 19 education management organizations (EMOs) ran a combined 14 percent of the nation's charter schools. About a quarter of the charter school students are educated in EMO-run schools, due to the larger size of EMO schools compared with "mom and pop" charters.

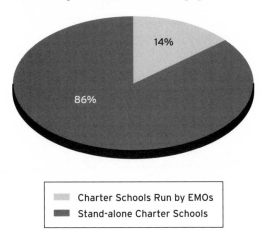

14%

86%

▓ Charter Schools Run by EMOs
■ Stand-alone Charter Schools

SOURCE: Center for Education Reform.

- Capital (for research and development and possibly facilities). At least for EMOs, the prospects of long-term profitability make it possible to raise capital from venture investors or, in a smaller number of cases, like Edison Schools, the public markets. For nonprofits, philanthropic funds serve a similar purpose. This capital allows the companies to make substantial investments in R&D—such as Edison's multiyear curriculum design project, which took place largely before the company operated a single school. Some EMOs have also deployed capital to help meet the challenge of financing facilities.
- Incentive and capacity to cultivate leaders. As important as a company's expertise and systems are to its schools, the quality of the school-level leadership is still critical for the success of EMO-run schools. EMOs have strong incentives to seek out high-potential leaders and develop their capabilities over time. And because they operate multiple schools, they are in a position to develop a "farm system" and create opportunities for career advancement that would not be possible in "mom-and-pop" charters.

- Incentive and capacity to sustain schools over time. If a stand-alone charter school experiences troubles, the founders or current leaders may try strenuously to get the school back on course. But if they fail, no institution is likely to do the hard work of saving the school. The school district may be glad to see the school go; the charter authorizer may not have the capacity or the philosophical inclination to intervene. But if an EMO school begins to sink, the EMO has strong incentives to rescue it. And they may have the resources to do so, by sending in new leadership or expertise.

The Dilemma of Scale

Nonetheless, it would be a mistake to rely on EMOs alone to sustain the charter school sector over time, for three reasons.

First, though EMOs bring substantial monetary and human resources to the table, they are not immune from financial and management challenges of their own. One of the major national EMOs, National Heritage Academies, recently reported an annual profit. But most of the scale players in the market have been for-profits only in the legal documents. Investments in capacity and marketing have swamped revenues for the typical EMO.

Second, for-profit EMOs exacerbate the built-in political challenges of creating charter schools. Under any circumstances, charter schools ignite political controversy (see chapter 14 in this volume). But when they are operated by for-profit entities, they become even more of a lightning rod. Grassroots organizations like ACORN, which have supported charter schools—even started their own—have led vigorous campaigns against Edison Schools' involvement in troubled public systems like those of Philadelphia, New York, and San Francisco.

These experiences raise questions about the political viability of a charter school movement that becomes largely composed of schools run by for-profit EMOs. Charter school policies have attracted unlikely coalitions that include free-marketeers and business leaders, but also community-based organizations, civil-rights groups, and other nontraditional allies. It seems that the support of nonconservative charter advocates depends, in part, on the fact that up to now the movement has been composed mostly of grassroots, community-based schools—not franchises of profit-seeking companies.

Finally, and perhaps most important, EMOs may not be the most likely source of innovation—and thus of the kind of dramatic gains in performance that we need to see in schools. For several reasons, the drive for scale militates against out-of-the-box approaches. To begin with, attracting sufficient enrollment is vital for EMOs; the need to fill seats is bound to drive companies to appeal to the "median" consumer, who might balk at strange new grade configurations or pedagogical approaches.

The companies' internal dynamics also push toward the conventional. EMOs face the substantial challenge of scaling up an educational and organizational model across multiple sites, perhaps across a wide geography. It makes sense in that context to select the familiar, the easily conveyed. The same goes for personnel. If a company needs thirty principals, the average hire is more apt to resemble the typical principal than the renegade that a stand-alone charter school might seek.

Herein lies a great dilemma facing the charter movement. To become a serious force for change in education, charter schools as a group need to achieve greater scale. The most obvious path to scale is the proliferation of chains of schools run by education management organizations. For financial and political reasons, though, looking exclusively to EMOs for scale is a poor strategy. In addition, the breakthrough innovations that are part of the great promise of charter schools may be more likely to emerge from schools that are, at least initially, single-site start-ups. But such schools are limited in number and small in size—hardly the basis for a large-scale movement.

Resolving this dilemma requires thinking about "scale" in two new ways. First, what would it take to enable more successful, stand-alone schools to "scale up"—by replicating themselves or through other means? Second, what would it take to create an environment in which much larger numbers of successful, stand-alone charter schools can form and thrive?

Scaling Proven Models

Education is notorious for single-school success stories that serve as fodder for 60 Minutes and feature films, but are never "replicated" elsewhere. Within traditional school systems, it's not hard to see why. The incentives to adopt good ideas from other schools are weak, and the constraints on change—from policy and culture—are strong.

The charter school strategy has the potential to overcome this conventional failure by providing a space within which it's easier to scale up what works via the creation of new schools. But most effective charter schools remain single-site successes. Charter leaders have their hands full even several years into start-up. Their "model" may actually be heavily reliant on the personal leadership of one or more founders and/or local ties and circumstances, which are difficult or impossible to "bottle."

Still, a small number of successful charter schools are beginning to explore scaling in one way or another:

KIPP Academies. Based on the success of the two initial KIPP academies in Houston and the Bronx, KIPP decided to scale up with support from the Pisces Foundation and other philanthropists. KIPP's approach to scale relies on developing leaders to open and operate new public schools—both charter and district-based. The highly selective Fisher Fellows program inducts twenty to twenty-five aspiring school founders per year and provides them with a summer training program that includes classroom instruction at Berkeley's Haas School of Business—half focused on business matters, and half on academic and school issues. Fellows then do a four-month residency in an existing KIPP Network school. By spring, fellows go to work founding a school—with intensive assistance from KIPP national. Support continues over three years, ending with an "inspection" to assess how well the school lives up to KIPP's "five pillars"—the general principles that define a KIPP school.

By 2010, KIPP aims to have started a total of 200 schools nationally. If successful, the resulting network will be an interesting model. It won't be an EMO—each school will be an independent entity, subscribing to the five pillars, but each unique. But it will capture some of the advantages of scale, primarily in the start-up phase. At this point, KIPP does not seem focused on reaping other potential values of scale, such as the power of joint purchasing or the centralization of certain routine functions.

Minnesota New Country School/EdVisions. Minnesota New Country School in Henderson, Minnesota, is unique in two respects. First, its learning program is very unusual. Almost all of its high school instruction takes place through personalized project-based inquiry, facilitated by teachers and relying heavily on the computers sitting on nearly every child's desk. More traditional forms of instruction are used as well, but only as needed to ensure the mastery of basic skills. Second, the school is run by a cooperative of teachers, who make all the key decisions about the school—from the learning program to the budget to hiring and firing. With funding from the Bill and Melinda Gates Foundation, the EdVisions cooperative is now seeking to spread this dual model to fifteen new secondary schools over five years. Gates funding will go both to the new sites and to EdVisions central, which will provide intensive start-up assistance. Six sites are currently involved at different stages.

High Tech High. Founded by tech industry leaders and educators in San Diego, High Tech High is undertaking various efforts to scale up its design, which offers a rigorous, personalized program focusing on math, science, and technology, and providing extensive connections to the "adult" world through internships and other means. Like KIPP and EdVisions, part of High Tech High's scale-up work involves helping others found similar schools in nine sites around the country. This initiative is also funded by the Gates Foundation. But High Tech's approach includes other elements as well. It has developed a Learning Resource Center, a detailed online source of information about the school's approach that allows anyone in the world to access and use the school's resources. It is engaged in various initiatives to prepare teachers to use its approaches in their own schools. And it is participating in a local effort to design 14 new high schools to be built in San Diego over the next decade.

Nevertheless, expanding beyond a single campus or city presents added challenges—challenges that so far have prevented most successful charter schools from seriously pursuing scale. What's needed is a new infrastructure that makes scale-up more feasible—a diverse range of service providers capable of helping schools with a whole array of needs. If such a system existed, it would be easier for successful schools to scale up, just as it would be easier for brand-new stand-alone schools to start.

Service Providers

Presently, starting a new school from scratch is just too difficult and painful, even for people who are capable of pulling it off. Much of the work goes into activities such as transportation, food service, accounting, regulatory compliance, zoning battles, mortgages, and the like, activities that are not where education needs innovative, fresh thinking. It seems likely that there is a large reservoir of entrepreneurial educators and non-educators who would be willing to engage in school start-up—if it were not such a nightmare.

Part of the answer certainly lies in the policy arena—giving charter schools equitable access to funding (including capital funds), cutting unnecessary regulations, ensuring that institutions other than local school boards can issue charters in every jurisdiction.

But just as important are internal or "supply side" solutions. Stand-alone charter schools need access to the same high-quality, pooled expertise that the best school systems and EMOs provide to their schools. They need a set of institutions that can shoulder the burdens of school start-up and management, allowing entrepreneurs to focus on building an excellent educational program. However, to retain their independence, stand-alone schools need to come to these service providers as voluntary, paying customers—not as units controlled by a larger system.

The creative challenge, then, is to imagine a "system" of providers that can deliver this kind of service. Within such a system three attributes, besides quality, seem most important: scope, intensity, and diversity.

Scope

Since operating a school is a complex undertaking, the service infrastructure needs to cover a wide range of issues on which charter school operators may need help. In many service areas, an industry of providers already exists—because school districts and private schools already demand the service. Prime examples include textbook and software publishers, information-management systems, developers of curricula and "comprehensive school reform models," and transportation providers. In other areas, like accounting, payroll, legal services, and facilities development and financing, a host of general-purpose providers already serve nonprofits and small businesses. Many of these companies see great potential in the charter school market and have already begun offering their products and services to charter school customers.

However, even where a sector of service providers already exists, its offerings may not be well tailored to the charter context. Charter schools tend to be small, to have limited budgets, and to face uncertain futures due to the vicissitudes of the market and the threat of nonrenewal or revocation of their charters. As a result, conventional providers may find charter schools unattractive in the end. Facilities financing stands out as one illustration, but the same holds true for many curriculum and "whole school reform" providers. While learning programs like Core Knowledge and Expeditionary Learning/Outward Bound have seen real opportunities in the charter sector, others have shied away.

New institutions will need to arise—both to meet needs that are unique to charter schools and to design service packages in older service areas that make sense for charter schools.

Intensity

Every state with charter schools has at least one "technical assistance center" for charter schools, and many have more. These organizations tend to provide assistance to charter schools on all the issues they may face. Charter schools call them with every question imaginable. They publish handbooks, newsletters, and websites that seek to address charter schools' concerns, from soup to nuts. One, the California Charter School Development Center, runs "boot camps" for new charter school leaders, running them through a litany of topics.

However, helpful as they are, technical-assistance organizations often are not able to provide intensive services to many schools. With their limited resources and broad mandate to serve all schools, it's not possible for most of them to roll up their sleeves day in and day out or to provide full services, like accounting or special education, to charter schools.

Several answers to the need for intense start-up help are emerging in the marketplace. One is the charter school "incubator," exemplified by the Education Resource Center (ERC) in Dayton, Ohio. ERC gets more involved in schools' start-up efforts than most providers of technical assistance, serving as temporary adjunct staff. It is also more selective. Like a venture-capital firm, it sizes up a client's prospects diligently before providing help. Incubators have succeeded in the small-business world, but charter incubators are too new to show results. Another avenue is a growing number of fee-for-service start-up providers, such as the Minnesota-based nonprofit SchoolStart. Charter entrepreneurs contract with these organizations to provide all-purpose help in the start-up phase—help in preparing the charter application, writing the budget, finding a facility, selecting an appropriate learning program, and hiring teachers. The Education Performance Network (EPN), the professional-services affiliate of New American Schools, is taking a different tack by creating an "education management support organization." EPN offers clients a menu of services including data management, accountability and evaluation, program design, and charter start-up and implementation. A key aim of EPN is to help build charter schools' ability to manage themselves over time.

A third trend is the emergence of leadership development programs for would-be charter entrepreneurs. Examples include the Fisher Fellowship program, New Leaders for New Schools, and the Massachusetts Charter School Resource Center's Leadership Institute. These organizations seek to provide in-depth training to potential school leaders, including both classroom and on-the-job components. Some follow up the learning with hands-on start-up assistance for graduates.

Finally, several national organizations have begun to help their local affiliates start charter schools. The YMCA is one. Another is the National Council of La Raza, a leading Hispanic advocacy and development organization. La Raza has put together the most intensive package of services—including hands-on consulting for community-based groups starting charter schools, joint professional development opportunities, and the creation of national partnerships that can be useful to all of the network's schools—which La Raza hopes will number fifty by 2005.

Diversity

Third, schools needs access to a variety of providers so they can shop around for the best quality, fit, and prices. In contrast to district-based service systems, in which the central office or its chosen contractors provide all services to schools, the essence of the charter school service system must be diversity and choice.

On this front, early trends are promising. Across the different domains of service, many different types of providers are emerging. Besides the for-profit and nonprofit providers already mentioned, charter schools in some places have formed cooperatives and associations to take advantage of economies of scale. Special education has been an especially fertile area for charter cooperatives, with models emerging in the District of Columbia, Texas, Minnesota, and Indianapolis. For example, the D.C. Public Charter School Cooperative, with twenty-one members, aims to provide information to members about the complexities of special education, hire and make available specialized staff that no school would want to employ alone, and develop a Medicaid billing system to increase reimbursements for special-education services.

Developing the range of service providers necessary to expand the charter movement will require investment on the part of firms, philanthropists, and governments at the local, state, and national level. If this comes to pass, we can imagine a charter school sector characterized by both scale and a diversity of entrepreneurial schools, a future in which grassroots charter schools remain the heart of the movement, but in a sustainable fashion.

BRYAN C. HASSEL is codirector of Public Impact.

CHAPTER FOURTEEN

Charter School Politics

Bruno V. Manno

Since 1991, thirty-nine states and the District of Columbia have enacted laws allowing for the creation of charter schools—independent public schools of choice that are freed from many regulations but accountable for their results. There are now 2,700 schools that serve some 600,000 students in these areas (see figures 14.1 and 14.2), with cities like Washington, D.C., and Dayton, Ohio, now enrolling upwards of 17 percent of all their children in these new institutions.

While such numbers are impressive—a decade ago there were no charter schools—we also see worrisome indications that the charter movement is in trouble. In July 2002, *Newsweek* reported that a raft of recent charter "reports find that too often, charters haven't lived up to their end of the bargain." A Brookings Institution study released in September 2002 concluded that student performance in charter schools was significantly lower than that of district schools on state tests in reading and math.

At the same time, signs of a vital and thriving charter school movement abound. Nationally, demand for these schools remains high, with more than 75 percent of charters having waiting lists that together could fill at least 900 more schools. The parents, students, and educators involved with charter schools report high levels of satisfaction. A California State University, Los Angeles, study of California charters, released in March 2002, found that their test-score gains outpaced those of students in regular public schools. In Massachusetts, the test scores of charter schools on the spring 2002 state test showed, according to the *Boston Herald*, "a greater number of improved scores

Figure 14.1. Gaining Market Share

*Charter schools now enroll some 600,000 students nationwide,
triple the number of students in 1998.*

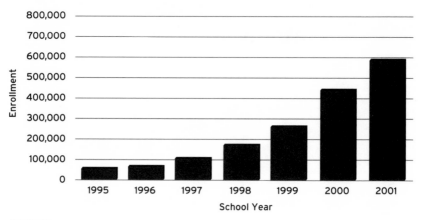

* Estimate

SOURCE: Center for Education Reform.

. . . with more and more of the [charters] scoring higher than their home districts." Even the Brookings study may say less than it seems. The investigators themselves acknowledge that their findings may be due to the fact that charters are attracting "students who were already low achieving," a suspicion supported by other studies that find charter students to be relatively disadvantaged.

Not only are many charter schools enjoying success, but they are also held accountable in a way regular public schools are not. When a charter school experiences severe troubles, it usually faces severe consequences (see figure 14.3). To wit, more than 200 failed or failing schools have been closed on fiscal, educational, and organizational grounds.

Can Success Survive?

In the education world, however, success often breeds second-guessing if not downright resentment. The more traction a successful reform gains, the more sour grapes it harvests. Despite strong, bipartisan political support, charter schools have not been immune from this attitude. America's deeply conservative public education system is striking back at this disruptive innovation,

Figure 14.2. Competitive States

Of the 39 states (plus the District of Columbia) with charter school laws, five stand out: Arizona, California, Florida, Michigan, and Texas. More than a third of the states have fewer than 20 charter schools.

State (year law passed)	Total operating in 2002–2003
Arizona (1994)	468
California (1992)	452
Florida (1996)	232
Texas (1995)	228
Michigan (1993)	186
Wisconsin (1993)	115
Ohio (1997)	97
Colorado (1993)	95
North Carolina (1996)	93
Minnesota (1991)	92
Pennsylvania (1997)	91
New Jersey (1996)	56
Massachusetts (1993)	47
District of Columbia (1996)	39
New York (1998)	38
Georgia (1993)	36
Kansas (1994)	30
Illinois (1996)	29
New Mexico (1993)	28
Louisiana (1995)	26
Missouri (1998)	26
Oregon (1999)	26
Hawaii (1994)	25
Connecticut (1996)	16
Alaska (1995)	15
Delaware (1995)	14
Idaho (1998)	14
South Carolina (1996)	14
Nevada (1997)	13
Utah (1998)	12
Indiana (2001)	10
Oklahoma (1999)	10
Rhode Island (1995)	9
Arkansas (1995)	8
Virginia (1998)	8
Mississippi (1997)	1
Wyoming (1995)	1
New Hampshire (1995)	0
Iowa (2002)	0
Tennessee (2002)	0
NATIONWIDE	2,700

SOURCE: Center for Education Reform.

Figure 14.3. Truly Accountable

As of January 2001, 86 charter schools had been forced to shut their doors for financial, academic, and other reasons.

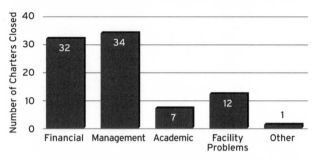

Reason for Closure

Note: Figures do not include charters that consolidated with district or private schools (26 as of January 2001) or charter schools that never opened (50 schools).

SOURCE: Center for Education Reform.

which shifts power from producers to consumers; demonstrates that more can be done with less at the school level; and moves control of resources from central bureaucracies to autonomous schools. Such tectonic shifts bring new uncertainties and imply that many hoary public education practices are no longer the only imaginable way to do things.

The initial efforts to stop the spread of charter schools took three main forms: preventing the enactment of charter laws; limiting the number of new charters; and ensuring that existing charter schools were as meagerly funded and as heavily regulated as possible.

These strategies succeeded to some extent. For example, Washington State, among other states, still has no charter school law—mostly because of intense opposition from the teacher unions and other interests vested in the status quo. Among those states with charter laws on the books, more than a third have fewer than twenty charter schools in operation. In addition, the early growth of the charter movement may be reaching a plateau—in part due to the hostile tactics of charter opponents.

One by one, however, states continue to come on board. In 2001, Indiana passed a strong law that allows charters to be granted not only by school districts but also by public universities and by the mayor of Indianapolis. To date, school districts have allowed two schools to convert to charter status; Ball State University has chartered seven new schools; and Indianapolis mayor Bart Peterson has approved four new charters. Eleven of the thirteen approved schools opened their doors in September 2002.

Three-Front War

Opponents are now regrouping, as the vigorous growth of the charter movement and its impact on traditional district schools has alarmed its adversaries. The resulting attacks come from three directions: state policymakers, local school systems, and organized public education interest groups.

State policymakers have an entire arsenal of charter-harassing weapons at their disposal. These include depriving charters of full per-pupil funding; denying them access to (or financing for) facilities; placing new restrictions on existing schools or moratoriums on future growth; and weakening charter laws. Two states provide vivid illustrations.

Indiana's entry into the charter movement was nearly arrested in early 2002 when Suellen Reid, the Republican state superintendent of public instruction, balked at giving Indiana's new charters any money during their first semester, basing her opinion on legal advice from members of her staff. Nor would these schools be reimbursed for expenses incurred during that semester. Only a contrary ruling from the state's attorney general (at the strong urging of Indianapolis's Democratic mayor, Bart Peterson) led to a reversal of that decision. The reversal, however, prompted an outcry from some legislators and from the superintendents of the eleven school districts located within Indianapolis. They protested "the adverse financial effects for public schools resulting from the formation of charter schools in our county" and called for a moratorium on the creation of new charters until the "financial inequities" were resolved. Mayor Peterson refused to yield, however, and proceeded to consider a second round of thirteen charter applications for the 2003–2004 school year.

California passed its charter law in 1992 (the second state to do so) and now has 362 operating charter schools. But the enemies are circling. The 2001–2002 legislative session passed five anti–charter school bills, four of which were signed into law by Governor Gray Davis (who felt compelled, in one of his signing messages, to claim that he still "supported charter schools"). The most controversial bill gave the state board of education extensive powers to regulate independent study or "nonclassroom"-based instruction that uses computers as the main instructional tool. The bill's intent was to force "virtual" charter schools to spend a high proportion of their budgets on certified staff rather than on technology, stifling their capacity to innovate. These "cyber" charters must now document their instructional minutes, and their per-pupil funding may be reduced if they offer less than the minimum number of student course minutes per year—a district-style regulation of the process of education without regard for outcomes.

Other proposals to cut funding for California charters emerged from the state department of finance. These would have slashed funds for students over age 18 (including former dropouts whom the charters were seeking to "recover") and ended summer-school funding for many charter students. While these proposals were defeated by an organized charter school community led by the California Network of Education Charters, charter operators expect them back in a future legislative session.

Local Opposition

The local districts where charters choose to locate, and from which they draw students, have felt the impact of charters most heavily. When a district loses students to a charter, most (sometimes all) of the per-pupil funding travels with those students. This places charters in direct competition with districts—and the districts, instead of competing, often try to influence the rules of the game.

In Houston, where 46 of Texas's 219 charter schools are located, the district estimated recently that it will lose about 13,000 students to charters during this school year (up from 12,000 the previous year) at a cost of $53.5 million in state revenues. The city's school board is thinking of asking the state to consider, before it grants any more charters, the financial impact a new charter school will have on district revenues.

Charters may cause trouble for school districts, but they often wind up saving money for the state. For instance, the Dayton, Ohio, school board claims that charters are bleeding the district of some $20 million a year. Of course, they no longer have the students to educate, either. And it costs less to educate a student in a charter than in a district school. Scholars Bryan Hassel and Deborah Page showed that during the 1999–2000 school year, charters in Ohio received about $2,300 less per pupil than local school districts. The seven largest districts in Ohio would each have received $20 to $160 million less in state funds had they operated under the charter school funding formula.

Local school districts can harass charters in many ways. They can devise application procedures with absurd timetables or use meager funding formulas to slash the dollar allocations to charters. City development agencies, zon-

ing boards, or fire inspectors can raise a host of regulatory
on the most difficult issue that charter schools face: findi
 In 2000, California voters approved Proposition 39, e
charter schools to facilities that are "reasonably equivale:
by district schools. The Sequoia Union High School L........ ... .
City, California (one of the wealthiest in the state), filed suit in May 2002 in
San Mateo County Superior Court to stop Aurora Charter High School from
receiving its fair share—in the form of either rent money or buildings—of the
$88 million bond measure that Sequoia passed in 2001. Sequoia believed that
it had no legal obligations to Aurora High because, while the school is
located in Sequoia, it was approved by Redwood City, an elementary school
district. Aurora argued that a substantial majority of its students live within
the Sequoia district. Aurora countersued the Sequoia district in July 2002. In
late August, Judge Quentin Kopp (who served in the California state senate
when the Charter Act was passed) ruled that Sequoia must provide facilities
for Aurora Charter High School. As of this writing, the district was considering an appeal of this decision.

 In Washington, D.C., both the city and the school district are making it
nearly impossible for charters to find classroom space, even though the mayor
and the school district are broadly sympathetic to charter issues. D.C. law
requires city officials to give charter schools the first option to buy surplus
buildings—unless the city can make substantially more money by selling
them to others. Naturally, this leads the fiscally strapped city to seek private
buyers for those buildings in the least disrepair and to offer charters more
dilapidated buildings that will cost millions to be made safe for children. One
charter founder reported that the building his school was offered had "$3 mil-
lion worth of asbestos issues and [would have] cost us $10 million [more] to
renovate." Meanwhile, the D.C. school system offers charters only one-year
leases on vacant schools in the (unlikely) event that the district needs to
reclaim the school for its own purposes.

Interest Group Attacks

A phalanx of interests, from teacher unions to school boards and superintendents, principals' associations, teacher colleges, disabled-rights groups,
and even private schools, often find reasons to view charter schools as a
threat. Let's consider two of these: the teacher unions and private schools.

 The unions' initial response to charter laws was defiance. In time, they realized that this looked bad—the charter idea was popular in too many quarters.

they moved from outright hostility to a highly conditional embrace, with the National Education Association beginning its own charter school project in 1996 (and subsequently abandoning it). In the words of an Education Week reporter, "Both national unions have endorsed the charter idea within fairly narrow limits, requiring district control over the schools and collective bargaining for the teachers within them." (What would distinguish such a charter school from traditional public schools remains unclear.) The American Federation of Teachers' July 2002 report, Do Charter Schools Measure Up? which calls for a moratorium on the expansion of charters, signals a renewed hostility toward charter schools.

Today, the unions' stance toward charters is convoluted, sometimes trying to co-opt the movement, other times trying to stop it cold.

A once-secret report prepared by the Pennsylvania State Education Association (PSEA) lays out a strategy that would organize all charter employees under the NEA affiliate's collective bargaining agreement, thereby depriving charter operators of a key element of their autonomy. As the authors explained, "The main source of the PSEA's influence is that almost all Pennsylvania teachers are unionized. If we want to maintain influence, our ability to do anything, we must make sure that education remains a unionized industry." Here the union is hedging its bets, trying to weaken the charter movement while also ensuring that any teachers who do slide into charter schools will remain union members.

In Ohio the unions have mounted a new effort to sink charter schools. Tom Mooney, president of the Ohio Federation of Teachers, is leading two ever-widening lawsuits seeking to have the state's charter law ruled unconstitutional. Tactics include involving all of Ohio's charter schools in the lawsuit and requiring them to deliver school records on a variety of issues, tying up time, energy, and resources in matters far removed from classroom instruction. This courtroom effort is also apt to chill charter enrollments, teachers, and public perception of the charter movement.

Private schools also sometimes see charter schools as a threat to their finances and influence. For instance, some charter schools are attracting large numbers of students from Catholic schools. The Archdiocese of Newark has lost 139 students to charter schools; the Archdiocese of Detroit, 300 students. Of the 776 students enrolled in St. Louis charter schools, 21 percent came from private schools—13 percent from Catholic schools and 8 percent from nonreligious private schools. While private-school leaders have not grumbled openly about charters, Sister Glenn Anne McPhee of the U.S. Catholic Conference has noted that they are watching the situation closely to see what effect the charter movement is apt to have on Catholic schools over time.

Enemies Within

Some self-inflicted wounds of the charter movement have strengthened the hands of its critics and opponents. These include greedy charter operators keener to make a quick buck at public expense than to educate children; inept operators whose schools are fiscally disastrous and academically inadequate; sponsors that exercise little care in reviewing charter proposals or monitoring the schools' progress; and supporters who press sponsors to leave the schools alone—even to renew their charters—notwithstanding their organizational, financial, and instructional failures.

Some of these schools have engaged in egregious misbehavior. In Houston, Reverend Harold Wayne Wilcox opened the Prepared Table Charter School in 1998. It rapidly grew to 1,500 students on three campuses, making it one of Texas's largest charters. After state auditors investigated the school's operations, however, the Texas Education Authority concluded that Prepared Table had overstated its attendance at a cost to the state of $1.3 million; that it had commingled school funds with those of Reverend Wilcox's church; and that it was governed by virtually the same board members as the church. It also found that members of Wilcox's family were working for the school and that Wilcox, who also served as head of the school, was given a $235,000 buyout package one week before the state convened a hearing to determine what to do with the school. The school was closed and its charter revoked in August 2002.

Forty-six California charters had their funding reduced when the state scrutinized their financial records during the 2001–2002 school year. They could not document how they had spent substantial sums of money and were unable to show what instructional services they were purchasing from private contractors. In some instances, the private vendors were members of the charter boards, posing conflict-of-interest questions.

In Arizona, a record number of that state's charter schools—31 of 288 reviewed—were fined in 2002 because of "late audits, ignored testing requirements, and financial fraud." This represented more schools than the total number disciplined since charters began in Arizona in 1994.

The basic charter "bargain" grants independence to school operators in return for superior academic results. But with that independence come opportunities for misbehavior—and these are apt to arise well before the results are measured. This places a heavy burden on authorizers to do careful due diligence before awarding charters and to perform ongoing reviews—without clamping down in classic bureaucratic fashion. Some sponsors are not up to this subtle, solemn responsibility.

Consider Techworld Charter School in the District of Columbia. The school was chartered by the elected D.C. Board of Education in 1997 and opened the following year. It was finally closed in June 2002 after three years of accounting irregularities, governance tiffs, and over-reporting of enrollments. It was placed on probation several times during those three years, but was never adequately monitored by the board, which in 2000 was replaced by a new hybrid board of elected and appointed members. The new school board set out to close down the school but encountered a belligerent principal. Just before its closing, he instructed the school's financial manager to award him a $20,000 bonus, along with $5,000 each to eight other employees, including his wife. The school's board of directors began to consider legal action against the principal, whose wife then changed the password to the computer files containing students' grades, hoping to force the board members not to prosecute her husband. The school's directors eventually retrieved the grades through a costly reconstruction of the computer records and turned the matter over to federal prosecutors.

The new D.C. school board moved during the 2001–2002 school year to close three other schools chartered by the previous board. They had an array of problems: overcrowded classrooms with little ventilation, high absentee rates, few textbooks and other instructional materials, abysmal academic results, and failure to file financial reports and to offer the advertised courses. This "cleanup" action could be traced to the failure of the old board to exercise adequate due diligence in approving the original charter application and monitoring the schools. This behavior contrasts sharply with the approach of the alternative, non-district chartering authority in D.C., the D.C. Public Charter School Board, which has chartered nearly 20 schools, none of which has been closed.

Counter Attack

The charter movement can no longer coast on a theory and a hope. It has a track record, if not a solid one. This has given new opportunities to those who never liked the charter movement in the first place. But there are ways to strengthen the charter movement to counter the attack. The National Association of Charter School Authorizers, created in 2001, is the kind of institution necessary to support the charter school movement as it matures. Members regularly receive information on topics of high interest to charter authorizers, such as evaluating charter applications and school performance, negotiating accountability agreements, renewal/revocation decision making, policy updates, and state-by-state information on authorizers.

Also needed is a national organization dedicated to pressing the charter movement to clean up its act and deliver the results promised by charter boosters. It would also recruit new charter supporters at the state and local policy level, especially since many governors, legislators, and local activists who gave birth to the charter effort have since moved on to other endeavors. Their successors are disposed to view charters as someone else's idea; are more aware of charters' problems than their successes; and are being skillfully manipulated by interests that have finally recognized that charters aren't going away.

BRUNO V. MANNO is senior program associate at the Annie E. Casey Foundation.

CHAPTER FIFTEEN

A School Built for Horace:
Tales from a Start-up Charter School

Nancy Faust Sizer and Theodore R. Sizer

The Francis W. Parker Charter Essential School opened in the fall of 1995, housed in an almost windowless building where the U.S. Army intelligence experts and cryptographers based at Fort Devens, Massachusetts, once were trained. The closing of the base provided the school with much of its furniture and equipment and one telling artifact: a massive map of East Germany that covered the wall of a basement classroom.

Parker's motivating idea is its common, carefully focused and interconnected academic curriculum, which is shaped by "essential" questions in two major areas: Mathematics/Science/Technology, including Health, and Arts and Humanities, including Spanish. Each of our 340 students, ages 12 to whatever it takes to meet the graduation standard, has a Personal Learning Plan, effectively a contract among student, school, and family. Students are promoted through three divisions, irrespective of their ages, by public presentation of portfolios and, for older students, exhibitions. Our limited budget (per-pupil expenditure is up to 15 percent less than nearby district high schools) allows for a spare but spirited jazz band and interscholastic athletic, debate, chess, and mock trial teams. The best measure of Parker's success? A long waiting list for the 2000–2001 academic year.

The school was born of three parents' desire to have an alternative to their town's school. They, in turn, were inspired by the ideas put forth in a book, *Horace's Compromise*, written by one of their neighbors, Ted Sizer. "Horace" is Horace Smith, a fictional representation of a typical high school teacher who is caught in a job he cannot do at the standard he knows his students deserve. He serves too many of them to know each one well, to analyze their strengths and weaknesses, to meet with them in conferences, to be trusted enough to offer the constructive criticism that is necessary for their growth. Horace's school, its routines mechanical, its purpose undefined, is an unconnected smorgasbord of programs, courses, activities, and more. In the end, it is the students who are expected to make sense of it all. And so Horace compromises to get along. Without substantial changes in the way his school is organized—indeed, in the way its best values are expressed—he will be stuck doing second-class work in a genial, well-intentioned, but basically directionless place.

Horace's Compromise also inspired the creation of the Coalition of Essential Schools in 1984, first based at Brown University and now an independent nonprofit organization situated in Oakland, California. The Coalition's mission is to help create and support the growth of schools that salve Horace's frustrations, by providing an education that is more integrated and focused than the usual. The experience of Essential Schools in New York City, especially the celebrated Central Park East Secondary School, created by Deborah Meier and her colleagues, persuaded us that it was possible to create a high school that dared to develop the most essential intellectual habits in young people—in a way that was demonstrably practical and public (meaning open to all students) and had long-term positive effects on students.

The charter school provision of the Massachusetts Education Reform Act of 1993 gave these parents, the two of us, and several other colleagues our opportunity. With the Coalition's principles of school practice in mind, we hastily began developing our school plan. Some decisions were easy: to provide a program from 7th grade through graduation; to move students through the program on an individual basis; to ask our teachers to be well educated, but to act more as generalists than specialists; to keep teachers' student loads down, and to offer advisories instead of more formal and distant "guidance counseling"; to offer only one foreign language, but to expect all to learn it; to put our money into more adults, some of them young adults, rather than into high rents or new furniture.

Other decisions were harder. How theoretical did we want our curriculum to be? How practical? In a promotion system based on demonstrated competence, what would be our benchmarks? How would they be made clear to teachers and to students and their parents without becoming rigid and meaningless? How would we help our teachers to adapt to classrooms in which projects would often replace the usual chalk-and-talk? How could we be good neighbors to the schools in our area from which we might enroll students?

How could we fashion a diverse student body, yet still draw students from towns that provide a higher per-pupil allocation?

What follows is the story of the ups and downs of going from the germ of an idea to a secondary school that serves students ages 12 and up—in short, the ways in which we avoided Horace's compromises or coped with those compromises we couldn't avoid.

Sweat Equity

The ideas behind our school and the motives for starting it were the relatively easy part. The start-up of any organization plunges its leaders into a welter of unanticipated or underestimated problems. From its very beginning, Parker confronted a number of challenges—everything from financial difficulties to engaging our teachers in a unique and demanding curriculum.

Like almost every charter school, the Parker School has had its share of financial concerns, especially during the start-up phase. For the most part, charter schools, once open, receive funds for ongoing operations, but the months before opening day are funded largely by the founders' sweat. The development of an institution's ideas takes time; not just anyone's time, but the time of experienced and busy people. And so it was that parents and students were repairing, carrying, and washing furniture late at night, while teachers were doing every kind of job, from planning classes to washing windows to driving to the store to buy erasers. In each of our first meetings, whether we were hashing out our guiding principles or writing the charter application or recruiting our first potential students or deciding when—and how—to hire our first employees, we must have worked for love because we certainly were not working for money. When we trustees stopped by, we were likely to be put to work. Save for some federal money (which came late), the detailed planning of the Parker School and the training of its staff had to be done pro bono.

Massachusetts' charter schools—places that were to break the mold and chart new directions, no less—apparently were to be designed in persuasive detail by spontaneous combustion, with hardly any support from the state. That some of us designing Parker had substantial experience made our task easier—though never easy—but we were the exception. Only the big for-profit companies have the financial horsepower to create fresh material. Schools that have sprung from the grassroots public interest of a community have had to make do with very little to nothing. It is, therefore, no surprise that too many charter schools are either weak or, in their unthinking copying of existing practice, still hampered by the compromises that bedeviled Horace. Powerful new, complex institutions require up-front research and development. That means money. Charters are getting little of it, and rarely at a scale that could make a substantial difference. Serious start-up schools need ready physical facilities, adequate R&D funds for the initial planning, and at least half of the faculty hired and involved in planning and training for at least nine months before the school opens.

Left Hand, Right Hand

Like most applicants for a charter, we were attracted by the idea that we could shape our own mission, present it to the state's chartering authorities, and then be held to our own, but externally validated, standards. Thus Parker wrote an application for a charter that detailed our educational goals, our strategy for meeting those goals, and a means of carefully assessing, internally and externally, whether we had reached those goals. Parker chose to keep doggedly to the "essentials"—designing a curriculum that covered a small number of topics in extreme depth, rather than lightly touching on a broad range of material.

Parker's planners worked "backwards." We visualized the kinds of graduates we would be proud to send into the world. We started with the habits, skills, and content we wanted our students to learn, and then we planned the curriculum and teaching styles to reach those aims. We found that being reasonably clear about what a student should know and be able to do as a matter of habit led to an ever narrower and deeper program.

For example, if the school expected every graduate to display clear and even marginally graceful expository prose, then there had to a great deal of writing, not just in Humanities but in the other domains as well. That writing had to be assessed—which meant teacher time, often preceded by teacher training. We had to ask ourselves: What will be our standard for Division III expository writing? How will we determine whether students have met it, and what will it take to get most, if not every last one, of our kids to that level? And what standard should apply to children who are identified as having "special needs"?

Such "backwards planning" is commonsensical yet rare in public education. Instead there are lists of topics to cover and skills to achieve, and these are rolled out in central headquarters with little regard to pedagogical and scholarly realities. The giant textbooks so familiar in American high schools are testament enough to that; in most, there is something included for every political pressure group. The result is "scholarship" by hop, skip, and jump, one of Horace's most painful compromises.

At times, these conflicting approaches made life at Parker rather difficult. For instance, the state Board of Education approved all the aspects of our charter proposal. But in a different policy context it asserted that the state's charter schools had to follow the unusually comprehensive state curriculum frameworks (thus, in our view at least, guaranteeing a curriculum that will be geared toward superficial mastery by most students). Our students also had to pass standardized tests derived from those frameworks. In many ways, these conflicting signals reflected little more than the left policy hand not knowing what the right policy hand was doing, but it placed and still places Parker in a compromised position. Nevertheless, and counterintuitively, our students score competitively on state tests.

The strains of the state's dual agenda are especially evident during testing season. Since we group our students (on the basis of their exhibited performance) into three Divisions, each with an approximately two-year curriculum designed by our teachers, the state's pattern of testing 8th and 10th graders (a designation we don't make, on philosophical grounds) is especially hard on our students. Our emphasis in Arts and Humanities shifts from world topics one year to American topics the next, which means that those who take the tests may well have studied the material only in the previous year. Furthermore, when "10th graders" are pulled out of class to take extensive tests, new curricula must be devised for the "9th graders" who are left behind. Too much energy must go toward mitigating the disruption, even more than in other schools. Everyone is stretched, with little actual learning to show for it.

In the spring of 2000, we had yet another dilemma. For several weeks, the entire curriculum in Division II Arts and Humanities was devoted to preparing for a trip to Washington, D.C., during which every student participated in a visit to the office of a member of Congress to advocate for a bill that was before Congress. The students learned about the substantive reasons for and the politics behind the legislation they were researching, the ways in which bills become laws, the opportunities citizens have to take part in the process, and the most persuasive ways of presenting their cases. It was a superb civics lesson, and the vast majority of the students showed, in a variety of observable ways, that they had learned powerfully from it. However, while their enthusiasm about their experiences augurs well for the fate of the republic, what they learned is not likely to be an item on this year's test. Effective charter school policy requires consistency from the state, both in protecting what the approved charter asserted and in assessing a charter school's success in ways that are consistent with its charter.

Building a Staff

The challenge of any "new" school, charter or otherwise, and especially a school that wishes to adopt new ways of teaching, is to build a competent, experienced staff with the expertise and energy to work in a start-up. Teacher education has largely been a matter of the "great old dogs" teaching eager new dogs the best of their tricks. The problem is that some of the old tricks are not very effective in schools that rest their programs, as does Parker, on one or another branch of serious contemporary research. Teaching toward intellectual academic habits such as, in Howard Gardner's phrase, "thinking like a scientist" is more than mere "coverage" of "material" to be displayed only at the immediate completion of a "course." Truly demanding intellectual training is not cookbook, easily routinized stuff. It is challenging work, particularly if high school students are used to getting by within the old, familiar system. The clash of minds, the give-and-take that leads a young person to a responsible and usable grasp of a consequential idea is sophisticated business.

In such a school, teachers must have time away from children each day to focus on their teaching, on their students' work, and on learning from their colleagues. Every teacher at Parker has one to two hours daily away from class. Within a tight budget, this is accomplished by offering only a narrow core program. Parker's designers regarded this as a worthy trade-off.

Another personnel trade-off we tried to make didn't work as well. In order to achieve low teaching loads, we tried to conserve money by keeping overhead low. Parker started with a "leadership team" consisting of only two "lead" teachers, a business manager, and a part-time "coordinator." This helped to achieve low student loads—sixty-five or fewer per teacher, including advisories of twelve students per teacher—but, by January of our first year, the trustees and the faculty knew this leadership arrangement would not work. The workload was more than an overworked quartet could handle.

And so, still believing that less is more when it comes to "administration" (which we too easily confused with "leadership"), we hired a proven teacher/ principal. He carried both tasks for eighteen months and then everyone, including him, cried Uncle. The work was too demanding. So much of the school was new, and creating (and then re-creating) fresh practices took time, intense concentration, coordination, and a level of imagination that rarely emerges for overworked people at 2 a.m. Young teachers needed support. Parents and prospective parents needed endless explanations of our school's design. The state expected the principal to serve not only as a typical Massachusetts school leader, but also as superintendent. Money, being in short supply from state sources, had to be raised. The list was endless.

At this point Parker's trustees turned to two retired school veterans on the board (the authors of this essay) to act together, pro bono, as the principal. This bought Parker a year to think through its leadership requirements, to restructure the budget to allow for the appointment of experienced administrators, and to complete a search for a senior leader. But the general problem remains: There is a severe shortage of adequately prepared people rising to leadership, especially educational leadership of new ventures.

Culture Matters

We tried to create a distinct culture in our school, one that taught lessons in its own right. From the beginning, we were determined to include our students as full-fledged fellow pioneers. We valued them and admired their bravery and told them so often, especially as they progressed through our performance-based program. We tried to keep external motivators like grades and punishments at a minimum, in the hope that our students would develop internal motivators. Yet we knew that most of our students and many of their parents were coming to school with a different sort of expectation.

Parker, like most schools, has rules. It also aspires, however, to have a "culture" that will make these rules necessary only at extreme moments. No issue has been more difficult to master, especially since the school believes in giving students substantial say in shaping the community's mores and life. On the surface, it is easier to "run" a "tight" school. However, any secondary school where the "rules" are merely delivered from on high without intense discussion by all parties of their meaning and application is a poor place for students to learn how to be members of a thoughtful community. Parker has made becoming such a community one of its goals, not only to make life in our building pleasant, but, equally important, to "teach" the restraints that make a community respectful and yet also free. This is easy to articulate, but exceedingly difficult to do, as it must be done one person at a time.

Creating a healthy school culture almost demands small scale. A community where people do not know one another is a place that must be policed rather than gathered. Developing the habits of getting along in constructive, principled ways is not simply a matter of building small schools, though. It must be worked at just as deliberately as a student works at his calculus. There are no short cuts to a lasting "moral education."

Commencement

As we write this, we have just returned from attending Parker's first commencement. If ever a charter school sought validation, this was it. Offered the chance to speak, a third of our graduates chose to do so. Most moving for those of us who have worked to bring this school into life and sturdy health was the message and the tone in their speeches. Their school was different, they said; different in ways that benefited them. The students have been part of an institution that, as they described it, was challenging and yet was always clearly on their side, was in fact designed around their growth. Student after student thanked the adults who had made it happen.

The state Board of Education asserted that charter schools had to follow the unusually comprehensive state curriculum frameworks, guaranteeing a curriculum that will be geared toward superficial mastery.

To have the chance to attack Horace's compromises head-on is a worthy undertaking. In Massachusetts, to be able to run a public school that is open on a lottery basis to any child wherever that child may live—rich suburb or poor city—finally gives an honest definition to the word "public." Though it will still take time, effort, and money to make this access across residential communities a practical reality, the state is headed in the right direction.

We still worry that too many policymakers and citizens will assume that "standards" by definition require "standardization"; that "reform" can be achieved by a combination of jawboning, regulation, and low-cost testing; that humiliation is a necessary part of competition; and that the universities will not wake up to their obligation to support reform vigorously. As pioneers, we all have summoned the extra energy required to climb mountains, but if long-term improvements are to be made, we need to have policies that will make life sustainable on the other side.

NANCY FAUST SIZER is a trustee at the Francis W. Parker Charter Essential School and adjunct lecturer at the Harvard Graduate School of Education.

THEODORE R. SIZER is a trustee at the Francis W. Parker Charter Essential School and visiting professor at the Harvard Graduate School of Education.

PART B

School Vouchers

CHAPTER SIXTEEN

‿‿

The Impact of Vouchers
on Student Performance
William G. Howell, Patrick J. Wolf,
Paul E. Peterson, and David E. Campbell

Just ten years ago, the only data available on the impact of school vouchers came from a poorly designed public-choice program conducted during the 1960s in Alum Rock, California. But the early and mid-1990s brought new privately and publicly funded voucher programs to cities such as Milwaukee; Dayton; Cleveland; Indianapolis; San Antonio; Washington, D.C.; and New York City. With them came a wealth of new research opportunities.

The privately funded voucher programs in New York City, Dayton, and the District of Columbia are especially conducive to study. In each city, vouchers were awarded randomly, generating treatment and control groups that are statistically indistinguishable from one another. Before conducting the lotteries, our evaluation team collected data on student test scores and family background characteristics. One and two years later, we retested the students. Since the two groups of students—the lottery's winners and losers—had similar average abilities and family backgrounds, any subsequent achievement differences observed between them can be attributed to the effects of the vouchers.

As a result, our evaluations of the New York, Dayton, and D.C. voucher programs have yielded the best available information on students' test-score outcomes and parental assessments of public and private schools. Here we use the data from all three cities to analyze the one- and two-year effects on academic performance of switching from a public to a private school. We find that vouchers have a moderately large, positive effect on the achievement of

African American students, but no discernible effect on the performance of students of other ethnicities.

The Literature

Earlier comparisons of public and private schools generally have found that low-income and African American students who attend private schools outperform their public-school peers. For instance, University of Wisconsin economist Derek Neal's analysis of the National Longitudinal Survey of Youth found that, even after adjusting for family background characteristics, students from Catholic schools were 16 percentage points more likely to go to college than were public-school students. The gap between Catholic-school students and public-school students was largest among urban minority children. Other studies have reached similar findings. University of Wisconsin political scientist John Witte's review of the literature on school effects led him to conclude that studies of private schools "indicate a substantial private-school advantage in terms of completing high school and enrolling in college, both very important events in predicting future income and well-being."

All of these studies, however, have one important limitation. They can account for only observed family background characteristics, such as the mother's educational level, a student's ethnicity, or family income. There is no assurance that these studies have successfully controlled for an intangible factor: the willingness of parents to pay tuition to send their children to private school and all that this implies about the value they place on education. As a result, it remains unclear whether these studies have unearthed actual differences between public and private schools or simply differences in the kinds of students and families attending them.

The best way to compensate for this limitation is to assign students randomly to experimental and control groups whose only substantive difference is whether they are offered a voucher. Past evaluations of voucher programs have not been able to take full advantage of a random-assignment research design. Consequently, the findings from New York, Dayton, and D.C. provide a unique opportunity to examine the effects of school vouchers.

The Programs

In several key respects, the three voucher programs followed similar designs. All were privately funded; all were targeted at students from low-income families, most of whom lived in the inner city; all provided only partial vouchers, expecting the families to supplement them; and all of the students in the evaluations previously had been attending public schools. Brief descriptions of the three programs follow.

New York City

The School Choice Scholarships Foundation (SCSF) in New York City offered 1,300 scholarships worth up to $1,400 annually toward tuition at a private school for at least three years. To qualify for a scholarship, children had to be entering grades 1 through 4, live in New York City, attend a public school at the time of application, and come from families with incomes low enough to qualify for the U.S. government's free or reduced-price school-lunch program. More than 20,000 students applied between February and late April 1997. By the end of the scholarship program's second year, 64 percent of the lottery-winning students were attending a private school.

Dayton, Ohio

In the spring of 1998, Parents Advancing Choice in Education (PACE) offered low-income students in grades K–12 the opportunity to win a scholarship to attend private school. For the 1998–1999 school year, PACE offered scholarships to 515 students who were in public schools and to 250 who were already enrolled in private schools in the Dayton metropolitan area. During the program's first year, the PACE scholarships covered 50 percent of tuition at a private school, up to $1,200. Support was guaranteed for at least four years, with a possibility of continuing through high school, provided funds remained available. Of those students offered scholarships, 49 percent enrolled in a private school during the second year of the program.

Washington, D.C.

Established in 1993, the Washington Scholarship Fund (WSF) is the oldest of the three programs. By the fall of 1997, the WSF was serving approximately 460 children at 72 private schools. On receiving a large infusion of new funds from two philanthropists, the WSF announced a major expansion in October 1997.

To qualify, applicants had to reside in Washington, D.C., and be entering grades K–8 in the fall of 1998. Families with incomes at or below the poverty line received vouchers that equaled 60 percent of tuition or $1,700, whichever was less. Families with incomes above the poverty line received smaller scholarships. Families with incomes higher than two-and-a-half times the poverty line were ineligible. The WSF claims that it will maintain tuition support for at least three years and, if funds remain available, until students complete high school. In April 1998, the WSF awarded more than 1,000 scholarships by lottery, with the majority going to students previously attending a public school. Of those students offered scholarships, 35 percent were still using them to attend a private school in the second year of the program.

Evaluation Procedures

The evaluation procedures used in all three studies conformed to those used in randomized field trials. Our evaluation team collected baseline test scores and family background information before the lottery, administered the lottery, and collected follow-up information one and two years later.

Students took the Iowa Test of Basic Skills (ITBS) in reading and mathematics. Students who were entering grades 1–4 in New York City and grades 2–8 in Dayton (and other parts of Montgomery County, Ohio) and Washington, D.C., were included in the evaluations. Parents responded to survey questions about their satisfaction with their children's schools, their involvement in their children's education, and their demographic characteristics. Students in grades 4 and higher completed similar surveys. In all three cities, the follow-up procedures replicated the pre-lottery procedures: students again took the ITBS in reading and math; parents and older students filled out surveys about their backgrounds and educational experiences.

More than 5,000 students participated in pre-lottery testing in New York City. Of the families that did not win the lottery, approximately 1,000 were selected at random to compose a control group of approximately 960 families. All of these students were attending public schools at the time. In Dayton, 1,440 students were tested before the lottery; 803 of them were attending public schools at the time. In Washington, D.C., 2,023 students were tested before the lottery; 1,582 of them were attending a public school. In Dayton and in D.C., separate lotteries were held for students who were enrolled in public and private schools at the time of application. The fact that only public school children were eligible to apply for a scholarship in New York obviated the need to hold separate public and private lotteries there. In all three cities, only those students who were in public schools at the time of the lottery are included in this study.

In New York City, 42 percent of the students participating in the second year of the evaluation were African Americans; in Dayton, 74 percent; and in D.C., 94 percent. Hispanic students accounted for 51 percent of the New York City group and 2 percent and 4 percent of the Dayton and D.C. groups, respectively. Whites accounted for 5 percent of New York City's evaluation group, versus 24 percent in Dayton and 1 percent in D.C. The remaining students came from a variety of other ethnic backgrounds.

In New York City, 80 percent of the students included in the evaluation attended the first-year testing sessions; 66 percent attended the second-year sessions. In D.C. the response rate after one year was 63 percent; after two years, 50 percent. In Dayton, 57 percent of families attended follow-up sessions after one year, 49 percent after two years.

We are reasonably confident that these modest response rates do not undermine the integrity of our findings. First, with the exception of the second year in New York, response rates were similar for both the treatment and the control groups after one and two years in all three cities. Second, comparisons of baseline test scores and background characteristics revealed only minor differences between the composition of the test and control groups in all three cities. Finally, to account for the minor differences between respondents and nonrespondents that we did observe, the test scores of children who, based on their demographic characteristics, were more likely to attend follow-up sessions were weighted less heavily, while the test scores of children who were less likely to attend follow-up sessions, but nevertheless did, were weighted more heavily. Given the slight differences between respondents and nonrespondents, however, the weights had little effect on the results.

The randomized lottery ensured that lottery winners as a group were not significantly different from the control group (those who did not win a scholarship). In all three cities, the demographic characteristics and pre-lottery test scores of scholarship winners and losers (the treatment and control groups, respectively) resembled one another. Only in Dayton were there minor differences in the pre-lottery test scores: those offered a voucher scored 6.5 percentile points lower in math and 3.1 points lower in reading than those not offered a scholarship, a statistically significant difference.

To measure the effect on children's test scores of switching to a private school, we estimate a statistical model that takes into account whether a child attended a public or a private school, as well as baseline reading and math test scores. Baseline test scores were included to adjust for the minor baseline differences between the treatment and control groups on the achievement tests and to increase the precision of the estimated impact.

The lottery generated two groups: those who were offered a voucher and those who were not. We're not interested, however, in the effect of being offered a voucher. Rather, we're interested in the effect of using a voucher to attend a private school. A significant number of the students who were offered vouchers did not use them; similarly, a smaller proportion of those students not offered a voucher attended a private school anyway. Therefore, a simple comparison between public and private school students is inappropriate because certain students may be more likely to take advantage of a voucher. Their parents may place greater value on education and be more willing to supplement the voucher, or they may live in a neighborhood with a broader selection of private schools. If these children differ from students who won a voucher but failed to use it in ways that are related to student achievement, it could bias our findings. To solve this problem, we used as an instrumental variable whether or not a student was offered a voucher to predict the probability that she attended a private school; with these predicted values, we can provide an unbiased estimate of the actual impact of switching from a public school to a private school. This two-stage regression technique was first used in medical research and is now commonplace in econometric studies.

Results

Our findings varied by ethnic group. In all three cities, there were no significant differences between the test-score performance of non-African American students who switched from a public to a private school and the performance of students in the control group—after either one or two years. For African American students, however, the receipt of a voucher made a substantial difference. In the three cities combined, African American students who switched from public to private schools scored, after one year, 3.3 percentile points higher on the combined math and reading tests (expressed as National Percentile Ranking [NPR] points, which run from 0 to 100 with a national median of 50). After two years, African American students who used a voucher to enroll in a private school scored 6.3 percentile points higher than African American students who remained in public schools (the control group) (see figure 16.1).

We emphasize the overall test scores, which represent the average of the math and reading components. When using one-hour testing sessions to gauge student performance, combined reading and math scores serve as a better indicator of student achievement than either test separately. Theoretically, the more test items used to evaluate performance, the more likely performance will be measured accurately.

Nevertheless, the differences after two years were approximately the same for both the reading and the math tests. On average in the three cities, African American students who switched from public to private schools scored 6.3 percentile points higher than their peers in the control group on the reading portion of the test and 6.2 points higher on the math portion.

Figure 16.1. The Voucher Gap

*After two years, African American students who
used vouchers to switch from public to private schools scored
6.3 percentile points higher in math and reading than those
who remained in public schools. This represents a difference
of 0.33 standard deviations—or roughly one-third of the
black-white test-score gap nationwide.*

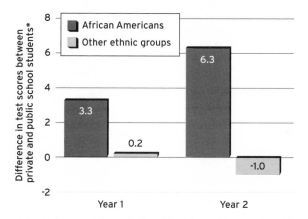

* *Weighted average difference in three cities. Measured in percentile rankings.*

The largest test-score differences between African American students in private schools and African American students in public schools were observed in the D.C. program. Black students who attended D.C. private schools for two years scored 9.0 percentile points higher on the two tests combined than did students in the control group. The smallest differences after two years were observed in New York City, where the combined test scores of African American students attending private schools were 4.3 percentile points higher than those of the control group. In Dayton the difference was 6.5 percentile points for African American students.

The trend over time also varied from city to city. In New York City, at the end of the first year, African American students in private and public schools displayed substantial differences in test scores, but these diminished slightly in the second year. After two years the difference in scores is 4.3 percentile points, which is slightly but not significantly (in statistical terms) less than the 5.8 percentile point difference observed after one year. It is reasonable to conclude that African American students' initial gains in the New York City school voucher program were preserved but did not increase between year one and year two.

In Dayton, there appears to be a steady upward trend in the combined test-score performance of African Americans. African American students who switched from public to private schools performed 3.3 percentile points higher on the combined test in year one and 6.5 percentile points higher in year two.

In some ways, the most striking results in terms of trends over time concern African Americans in D.C. After one year, no significant differences were observed for African American students as a group, but older and younger students experienced significant differences. While younger students may have benefited slightly from the voucher program after one year, the older students who switched to private schools scored significantly lower than their public school peers after one year. By the end of the second year, however, these students seemed to have overcome the initial challenges of changing schools. Both younger and older African American students who switched from public to private schools posted positive and significant gains. On the combined reading and math tests, younger students in private schools scored 9.3 percentile points higher than those who remained in public schools. Older African American students in private schools scored 10.3 percentile points higher.

The lottery ensured that scholarship winners as a group were not significantly different from those who did not win a scholarship. In all three cities, the demographic characteristics and pre-lottery test scores of scholarship winners and losers resembled one another.

Controlling for Demographics

Most research on the impact of private schools attempts to control for differences in family income and other background characteristics among students attending public and private schools. When a lottery is used to assign research subjects to experimental and control conditions, however, such statistical adjustments are generally unnecessary simply because the two groups being compared are virtually identical.

After two years, African American students who used a voucher to enroll in a private school scored 6.3 percentile points higher than African American students who remained in public schools.

Nonetheless, after the release of our study, some analysts objected to the apparent absence of controls for family background characteristics. Bruce

Fuller and his colleagues at the University of California, Berkeley, for instance, argued, "The experimental group may have been biased as some of the most disadvantaged voucher winners did not switch to a private school, and therefore were excluded from the group (possibly boosting mean achievement levels artificially)." An interest group, People for the American Way, lodged a similar complaint: "The . . . study's key finding improperly compares two dramatically different groups and may well reflect private-school screening-out of the most at-risk students."

In the three cities roughly half the students initially took the voucher that was offered to them (the takers), and about half did not (the decliners). Takers had higher family incomes in New York and D.C., but lower incomes in Dayton. The New York and D.C. findings are not surprising, given that the voucher awards did not cover all the costs of a private education. These additional costs were the reason most frequently given by families for not using the voucher. Presumably acceptance rates would rise if the monetary value of the vouchers were increased.

However, we did not drop the decliners from the analysis, as some of our critics have charged. All voucher applicants were invited to follow-up testing sessions, and each of the families who participated, including those who declined a scholarship, is included in the analysis. To estimate the impact of switching from a public to a private school, we did not simply compare those students who used a voucher to enroll in a private school with all those who did not. Such a comparison would have introduced bias and squandered all the advantages of a random-assignment evaluation. Instead, we used a familiar technique, often used in medical and econometric research, that preserves the essence of a random-assignment evaluation. The outcome of the lottery, a random event, was used to create what statisticians refer to as an instrumental variable, which obtains unbiased estimates of the effects of attending private school on students' test scores. According to the statistical theory that underpins this technique, results from lotteries are powerful instrumental variables, because the lottery, being a random event, is not directly related to students' test-score performance. In other words, the use of this statistical technique fully corrects for any differences that arise from the fact that not all of the families who were offered a voucher made use of one.

To see whether the instrumental variable worked in practice as it should in theory, we conducted a second analysis in which we controlled not only for the students' pre-lottery test scores but also for their mothers' educational level, her employment status, family size, and whether the family received welfare. If the critics were correct, the introduction of these background characteristics into the analysis should have diminished the estimated effect of attending a private school, because only after these adjustments were made would the analysis have adjusted for the background differences between those who used the voucher and those who did not. But if the use of the lottery as an instrumental variable works in practice as it is expected to work in statistical theory, it would already have corrected for these differences. The results should remain essentially the same.

As statistical theory anticipates, the average difference in the combined reading and math test scores of African Americans in all three cities remained exactly the same—6.3 NPR points—after the adjustments for family background characteristics were introduced. Minor differences in the two estimates were observed within each city. The impact of switching to a private school without controlling for family background in New York City was originally estimated to be 4.4 NPR points; after accounting for family background, the impact was estimated to be 4.2 NPR points. Introducing controls in Dayton decreased the estimated impact from 6.5 to 5.9 NPR points. In Washington, D.C., the estimated impact increased from 9.0 to 9.1 NPR points. In New York and Washington, the estimated impacts, after adding controls for family background, remain statistically significant. In Dayton, the impact just missed the standard threshold for statistical significance.

Discussion

It is possible that conditions specific to each city or minor fluctuations in testing conditions might skew results one way or another. But when similar results emerge from the evaluations of school voucher programs in three very different cities, we can be fairly confident that the intervention is the main cause of the differences in achievement.

In general, we found no evidence that vouchers significantly improved the test scores of ethnic groups other than African Americans, most notably Latinos in New York and whites in Dayton. The impact of vouchers for African Americans, however, was moderately large. After one year, black students who switched to private schools scored 0.17 standard deviations higher than the students in the control group. After two years, the difference grew to 0.33 standard deviations, roughly one-third of the test-score gap between blacks and whites nationwide. These effects are approximately the same as those observed in Tennessee when class sizes were reduced from twenty-four students to sixteen students, a much more costly intervention.

Whether the gains from these small, private scholarship programs will translate to large-scale, publicly funded school-choice programs in urban areas is unknown. Only a small fraction of low-income public school students in New York, Dayton, and D.C. were offered vouchers, and these students made up a small share of the cities' private school populations. A much larger program carried out for longer periods of time could yield quite different outcomes. But we'll never know unless we try. The nation's capital, the city where the largest effects were observed, would be a good place to begin.

WILLIAM G. HOWELL is associate professor of government at Harvard University.

PATRICK J. WOLF is associate professor of public policy at the Georgetown Public Policy Institute.

PAUL E. PETERSON is Henry Lee Shattuck Professor of Government and director of the Program on Education Policy and Governance at Harvard University, and editor-in-chief of *Education Next: A Journal of Opinion and Research.*

DAVID E. CAMPBELL is assistant professor of political science at the University of Notre Dame.

CHAPTER SEVENTEEN

Do Vouchers and Charters Push Public Schools to Improve?

Caroline M. Hoxby

The most scathing critique of voucher programs and charter schools is that they may bleed traditional public schools of their best students and most active parents, leaving the children who are left behind even worse off. Moreover, as the students leave, taking their per-pupil funding with them, the public schools will find themselves stripped of the human and monetary resources necessary to answer the call of competition. "Skimming," the term of art for this hypothetical phenomenon, may lower overall achievement, as the downward spiral of the public schools swamps any gains made by the students who take advantage of school choice.

Market enthusiasts have always argued the very opposite: that competition will improve the public schools, just as the entry of Federal Express and DHL into the package-delivery market forced the U.S. Postal Service to lower its costs and offer new services, such as Express Mail. Few analysts expected the Postal Service to be able to compete with its new rivals, yet several decades later it is a worthy opponent. Supporters of school choice believe that public school administrators and teachers would respond with equal vigor to the prospect of seeing their students and funding walk out the front door. Their professional pride and livelihood in jeopardy, they would work harder, adopt more effective curricula, hire more talented staff, and turn the district office into more of a support center than a maker and enforcer of rules. They would be spurred to innovate in ways that improve student achievement and parental satisfaction. Competition would be the proverbial rising tide that lifts all boats.

For the most part, the research is in on the question of whether students in private schools, using a publicly funded voucher or paying tuition, perform better than their peers in public schools after adjusting for all the background characteristics that affect achievement. Studies comparing students in private Catholic schools with students in public school, and students who receive a voucher to attend a private school with those who don't, show substantial achievement gains as a result of attending a private school. How competition affects the students who remain in public schools, however, is a relatively unstudied question. In the vast majority of cities and states, charter schools and voucher programs are either too young or too limited for the public schools to have responded in any significant way.

Only in one city, Milwaukee, and in two states, Arizona and Michigan, have the new choice reforms created truly fluid education marketplaces for a sustained period. Students in Milwaukee have been using vouchers to attend private schools since the 1990–1991 school year, though only in 1998–1999 was the cap on the number of voucher students raised from 1 percent of the district's enrollment to 15 percent. The Milwaukee district loses a significant amount of state aid to the voucher program, enough at least to notice if not to elicit some kind of competitive response. This study examines the trend in student achievement in Milwaukee schools where large shares of the student body are eligible for vouchers.

Both Arizona and Michigan have generous charter school laws, approving their applications more easily and funding them more fully than other states. They were both early converts to the charter movement, and some of their public schools are now suffering noticeable enrollment and funding losses as a result of competition from the charter school sector. This study examines achievement trends in districts and municipalities in both states where charters have captured significant market share. Taken together, the findings presented here, from Milwaukee, Arizona, and Michigan, offer a first glimpse at how public schools are responding to these new forms of school choice. They suggest that the fears of a downward spiral aren't merely overblown. They're simply wrong.

Time-Tested Choices

It is important to recognize, before discussing the effects of charters and vouchers on public schools, that these new forms of choice simply add to the varieties of de facto choice already available in many parts of the country. It is not at all unusual for parents in a metropolitan urban area to be able to choose from among many schools and many school districts and from a variety of low-cost private school options. These kinds of choice have been around for so long and are so universally taken for granted that we tend not to think of them as choice. But take a family living in the Boston area. They can choose among seventy independent districts located within a thirty-minute drive of downtown and many more in the metropolitan area. Towns looking to attract families and raise property values face clear incentives to safeguard the quality of their schools.

Other metropolitan areas offer far less competition among local districts. A family living in Las Vegas, Miami (where one school district, Dade County, covers the entire metropolitan area), or Hawaii (where the entire state is one school district) will be served by the same school district no matter where they choose to reside; the district has a virtual monopoly over public schooling in the area. Comparing public school performance in highly competitive metropolitan areas with performance in less competitive areas is one way of discovering how competition affects public schools.

My research shows that metropolitan areas with maximum interdistrict choice elicit consistently higher test scores than do areas with zero interdistrict choice. The 8th grade reading scores of students in highly competitive areas are 3.8 national percentile points higher than those of students in areas with no competition; their 10th grade math scores are 3.1 national percentile points higher; and their 12th grade reading scores are 5.8 national percentile points higher. Moreover, highly competitive districts spend 7.6 percent less than do districts with no competition. In other words, interdistrict competition appears to raise performance while lowering costs—the result predicted by market enthusiasts.

School districts face competition not only from other school districts but also from private schools. Metropolitan areas vary in this regard as well. Areas with long-standing religious populations, such as Catholics in the Northeast and Lutherans in the Midwest, tend to have developed a large market for private schooling, with many options whose tuition is substantially subsidized by donations of land, buildings, and money given primarily during the first half of the twentieth century. Private schools in areas whose religious populations are relatively young or supportive of public schools tend to be less competitive; they simply don't have the endowments or contributions to keep their tuition low enough to make them accessible to most parents. With strategies similar to those used to analyze the effects of interdistrict choice on public schools, I compared public school performance in areas where public schools face strong competition from private schools with public school performance in areas where little competition between public and private schools exists.

If every school in the nation were to face a high level of competition both from other districts and from private schools, the productivity of America's schools, in terms of students' level of learning at a given level of spending, would be 28 percent higher than it is now.

My comparison showed that all schools perform better in areas where there is vigorous competition among public and private schools. Areas with many low-cost private school choices score 2.7 national percentile points higher in 8th grade reading; 2.5 national percentile points higher in 8th grade math; 3.4 national percentile points higher in 12th grade reading; and 3.7 national percentile points higher in 12th grade math.

In short, both traditional forms of choice—choice among school districts and between public and private schools—influence public schools in a positive manner. To place the influence of competition on school performance in perspective, if every school in the nation were to face a high level of competition both from other districts and from private schools, the productivity of America's schools, in terms of students' level of learning at a given level of spending, would be 28 percent higher than it is now. And that is with a relatively diluted form of competition; traditional forms of choice do not provide strong competition because money does not follow students in a direct way. Furthermore, traditional forms of choice are not available to many families, either because they live in an uncompetitive area or because they are too poor to move to another district or to pay private school tuition.

New Competitors

One advantage of studying traditional forms of school choice is the insight they give into how competition unfolds over the long run—over the many decades traditional forms of choice have been in place. Only the short-term effects of competition can be seen through the study of vouchers, charter schools, and their impact on the public schools against which they compete. Therefore, for this study it was crucial to isolate those instances where competition was lively and long-standing enough to potentially provoke a competitive response from the public schools. As noted earlier, only charter schools in Arizona and Michigan and the voucher program in Milwaukee met this basic criterion.

School vouchers in Milwaukee. In Milwaukee, students from families with incomes at or below 175 percent of the poverty line are eligible for vouchers to attend a private school. For every student using a voucher to leave the Milwaukee public schools, the school loses state aid equal to half the value of the voucher. During the 1999–2000 school year, the year studied here, the voucher was the lesser of $5,106 or the cost of tuition at the private school the student chose. So the district lost $2,553 of its $8,752 in per-pupil spending, or 29 percent, for every student who used a voucher. More than 90 percent of the vouchers went to students in grades 1–7 during 1999–2000 because the vouchers were sufficient to cover tuition only at private elementary schools; high schools tend to charge more. Thus the only public schools in Milwaukee that faced serious competition from the voucher program were elementary schools, so I focused on students' scores in 4th grade, the only elementary grade in which all Wisconsin students take a statewide exam.

It was not until the cap on the voucher program was raised from 1 percent of the district's enrollment to 15 percent in the 1998–1999 school year that vouchers generated real competition for the public schools. Therefore, it made sense to compare public school performance during the 1996–1997 (before significant competition) and 1999–2000 (after significant competition) school years. I divided Milwaukee schools into those that were more "treated" to competition because at least two-thirds of their students were eligible for vouchers, and those that were less treated because less than two-thirds were eligible. I expected that the more-treated schools would respond more strongly than the less treated, but the latter is not a true control group. A full 25 percent of the students in the least-treated schools were still eligible for vouchers. The response of these schools to vouchers might be attenuated, but it would still be a response. To find schools to serve as a true control group, I used the following criteria: (1) the schools were not in Milwaukee (and so entirely unaffected by vouchers); (2) the schools were urban; (3) at least 25 percent of the students were eligible for free or reduced-price lunch; and (4) African Americans composed at least 15 percent of the student body.

Only twelve schools in Wisconsin met all these criteria. Overall, these schools are still richer and have fewer minority students than the Milwaukee schools. The same is true of the less-treated schools in Milwaukee: they are richer and have fewer minorities than the most-treated schools. Research has shown that these richer schools outside Milwaukee and the less-treated schools in Milwaukee are ordinarily likely to improve more rapidly than the most-treated Milwaukee schools. Put another way, the rates of improvement in the schools facing the most competition from vouchers will probably look less impressive than they actually are. It is simply more difficult for performance to improve in these low-income schools than in the less-treated control group schools.

Given this, the results for Milwaukee's most-treated schools are remarkable. As shown in figure 17.1, 4th-grade math scores rose by about 7 percentile points per year in the most-treated schools, 5 percentile points per year in the less-treated schools, and just 4 percentile points in the control schools. Social-studies scores in the most-treated schools rose by 4.2 percentile points per year, while in control schools the scores rose by only 1.5 percentile points per year. The scores of the students in the most-treated schools, the schools facing the most potential competition from vouchers, improved by more in every subject area tested than did the scores of the students facing less or no competition from vouchers. In fact, though reading scores improved only slightly in the most-treated schools (by 0.6 percentile points per year), reading scores actually dropped in the less-treated schools (by −0.4 percentile points per year) and control schools (by −1.4 percentile points per year), perhaps due to Wisconsin's adoption of a controversial new "whole language" reading curriculum.

Recall that the most-treated schools were those with the most to overcome in terms of raising their scores, yet they bested the less-treated and untreated schools on every measure of improvement. Their mostly poor and minority students experienced an upward spiral in achievement as a result of competition, and the improvement is even more impressive than the mere comparison of the numbers suggests. Of course, it cannot yet be known how long these schools will be able to maintain their rates of improvement. It is possible that improvement will slow after a few more years of competition.

Charter schools in Michigan. Michigan's charter school program was established in 1994. It was relatively easy to isolate the schools targeted by competition in Wisconsin: no school outside Milwaukee faced competition from vouchers, and the degree of competition faced by Milwaukee schools varied with students' poverty. In Michigan, I had to choose a threshold level of charter school enrollment, above which I would classify the neighboring public schools as being subject to charter competition. Because enrollment in Michigan schools normally fluctuates by about 5 percent a year, even when there is no competition from alternative schools, I chose a threshold of 6 percent. That is, I defined a treated public school as any school in a district where charter school enrollment was at least 6 percent of regular public school enrollment.

There are advantages to studying Michigan. For one, a Michigan district that loses a student to a charter school loses a substantial amount of money—

Figure 17.1. Vouchers Spur Public School Gains in Milwaukee

Public schools in areas where many students are eligible for vouchers to attend private schools made greater gains from year to year than schools elsewhere.

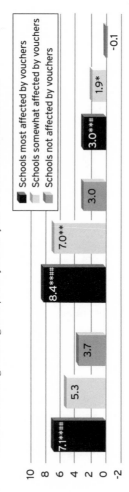

** Statistically significantly different from the trend for unaffected schools at the 0.05 level.

* Statistically significantly different from the trend for unaffected schools between the 0.05 and 0.15 levels.

Statistically significantly different from the time trend for the somewhat affected schools at less than the 0.05 level.

Statistically significantly different from the time trend for the somewhat affected schools at the 0.05 to 0.15 level.

SOURCE: Wisconsin Department of Public Instruction (various 2000); United States Department of Education, School District Data Book.

the state's minimum level of per-pupil spending, given the characteristics of the school's student population. During the 1999–2000 school year, the average spending on a charter school student was $6,600, compared with $7,440 for the average public school student. Also, charter schools in Michigan receive their charters from statewide organizations, such as universities. Unlike charter schools in many other states, they do not have to get their charter approved by the very district that would be their competitor. Big-city, small-city, and small-town schools are all well represented among the schools that face charter competition in Michigan.

As in Milwaukee, achievement improved in Michigan public schools faced with significant competition. As shown in figure 17.2, their scores climbed by 2.4 scale points more per year in 4th grade reading and 2.5 scale points more per year in 4th grade math (4th grade is, again, the only elementary grade in which Michigan administers a statewide test). These improvements are above and beyond their achievement trends before they were subject to charter competition. Moreover, they are above and beyond the improvements made during the same period in public schools that did not face charter competition. Just to give a sense of the magnitude of these improvements, one can compare Detroit (a district that did face competition) with one of its most affluent suburbs, Grosse Pointe (a district that did not face competition). If Detroit were to maintain its faster rate of improvement, it would close the achievement gap between its students and Grosse Pointe's students in just under two decades.

Charter schools in Arizona. Arizona's charter school law, passed in 1994, is widely regarded as the friendliest to charter schools. It gives charter schools considerable financial and legal autonomy and imposes few constraints on their growth. Consequently, about 5 percent of Arizona's public school enrollment attended charter schools during the 1999–2000 school year, the highest share of any state in the country. Charter schools in Arizona can be state sponsored, in which case they get a fee equal to the state's share of revenue (45 percent of the total revenue for a regular public school). They can also be district sponsored, in which case they get a fee equal to local per-pupil revenue but are less able to compete since they must seek renewal of their charters from the very districts with which they compete.

I followed the same strategy in evaluating Arizona that I used with Michigan, with one exception. A single municipality in Arizona may contain several school districts, so rather than associate regular public schools and charter schools with a district, I associate them with a municipality. As in Michigan, I used charter school enrollment of 6 percent of regular public

Figure 17.2. Competition from Charters Improves Public Schools in Michigan

School districts that lost more than 6 percent of their students to charter schools in Michigan responded to the competitive threat, by improving their scores in math and reading.

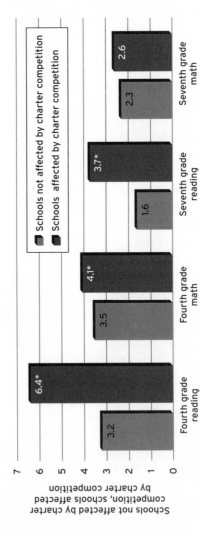

* Difference between these two figures is statistically significant at the 0.05 level.

SOURCE: Michigan Department of Education (various 2000).

Figure 17.3. Competition Improves Public Schools in Arizona

Students in districts in Arizona that lost more than 6 percent of enrollment to charter schools began increasing achievement at rates greater than in schools that weren't affected by charters.

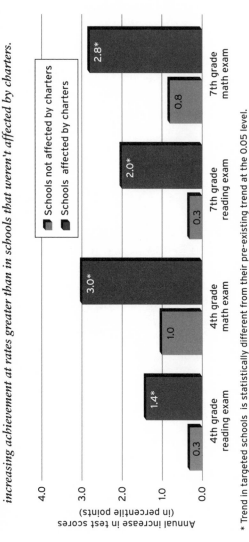

* Trend in targeted schools is statistically different from their pre-existing trend at the 0.05 level.

SOURCE: Arizona Department of Education (1988 through 1995 and various 2000).

school enrollment as the threshold for classifying a municipality as facing charter competition. Also, as in Michigan and Wisconsin, I focused on 4th grade scores because it is the elementary grade that has been tested statewide for the longest time.

The results in Arizona were similar to those in Michigan and Milwaukee. As can be seen in figure 17.3, regular public schools that faced charter school competition improved both their 4th grade reading scores and their 4th grade math scores by 1.4 national percentile points a year. These improvements are above and beyond their achievement trends before charter competition. They are also larger than the improvements made over the same period by public schools that did not face charter competition. Again, for perspective, let's compare a municipality that did face charter competition, such as Phoenix, with its affluent suburbs. If Phoenix were to maintain its faster rate of improvement, it would close the achievement gap between its students and those in its affluent suburbs in less than ten years.

Conclusion

The findings presented here consistently show public schools' responding favorably to competition. In Milwaukee, schools facing more competition from vouchers improved at rates faster than schools facing little or no competition from vouchers. Public schools in Michigan and Arizona began improving at faster rates after they lost significant shares of their enrollment to charter schools. It is risky to extrapolate from these short-term results, but the long-term results found in my studies of traditional competition among districts and between public and private schools seem to confirm that competition is in general good for the public schools.

In fact, say the critics' worst fears were realized: A school in Milwaukee went from being the best school in the city to the worst as students began leaving on vouchers; an extreme creaming effect took place. The top 10 percent of Milwaukee schools performed 32 percentile points better than the worst 10 percent of Milwaukee schools on Wisconsin's statewide math exam. Consider a student in this hypothetical school: not only the school's average score but the student's score on the statewide math exam dropped 32 points. Even in this case, so bad as to be barely plausible, if the student's rate of growth in achievement were the same as in the Milwaukee schools that were most treated by voucher competition, after five years the student would be achieving at a higher level than he was before vouchers induced some students to choose a new school.

The mostly poor and minority students in schools facing the most competition in Milwaukee experienced an upward spiral in achievement, and the improvement is even more impressive than the mere comparison of the numbers suggests.

If one critique can be leveled against these findings, it is the very opposite of skimming: that schools subjected to the most competition might have seen their lowest-performing students leave for charter or private schools. In that case, any achievement gains among the public schools would be at least partly an illusion, simply the result of having lost their worst students to schools of choice. This seems somewhat plausible: the worst students might have highly displeased parents who are eager for new options. But the worst students might also have apathetic parents who could care less. There is no way of knowing. Regardless, those who have studied the test scores and family backgrounds of students switching from public schools to the new choice schools have found repeatedly that the students are about average, not much different from those left behind. Still, if opponents of school choice wish to stipulate that schools of choice actually attract the worst students, leaving the public schools to teach the so-called cream of the crop, so be it. You'll get no argument here.

CAROLINE M. HOXBY is professor of economics at Harvard University.

CHAPTER EIGHTEEN

_⌒_

School Choice and Social Cohesion
David E. Campbell

As the civic participation of young people continues to plummet, it becomes ever more important that we learn how schools can teach students to be active citizens. Indeed, "producing better citizens" was the original justification for creating America's public schools. In the 1800s, Horace Mann and others successfully argued that the public schools could assimilate immigrants into the norms of American civic life. Today essentially the same objective remains. In a 1996 Phi Delta Kappa/Gallup Poll, 86 percent of Americans reported that they feel "preparing students to be responsible citizens" is a "very important" purpose of the nation's schools; just 76 percent considered it very important that schools "help people become economically self-sufficient."

Today a broad consensus exists on three objectives characteristic of an education that develops good citizens. The first objective is to equip the nation's future voters with the capacity to be engaged in the political process. This is especially salient against a backdrop of declining rates of political activity, most notably among young people. The second objective is to have citizens not only participating in democratic institutions, but also doing so knowledgeably. Students should understand the nation's history and political system. The third objective stems from political philosopher Amy Gutmann's idea that the defining characteristic of a democratic education is that it imparts the "ability to deliberate" in a context of "mutual respect among persons." The general public would seem to agree. According to a 1999 Phi Delta Kappa/Gallup Poll, 93 percent of Americans believe that the schools should teach "acceptance of people of different races and ethnic backgrounds." Seventy-one percent stated that the schools should also teach "acceptance of people who hold unpopular or controversial political or social views." In other words, an education that prepares students for democracy teaches them to respect the opinions of others and promotes social and political tolerance.

Different types of schools pursue various strategies for meeting these objectives, some with more success than others. Here I ask the simple question: How well do different types of schools promote civic education? For instance, do private schools foster social divisiveness, as their critics often claim? Does attending a religious private school rather than a secular one have different civic consequences?

Building Social Capital

There is only a small but nonetheless growing body of research on the civic effects of public versus private schools. Researchers have shown that Catholic schools are more racially integrated than public schools and that voucher programs do not have an adverse effect on integration. Another study found that Hispanic adults who were educated in private schools are more likely to participate in politics than those who attended public schools. Evidence from the National Education Longitudinal Study further demonstrates that students in private schools are more likely to participate in community service than are their peers in public schools. Similarly, private school administrators more often rate their schools as "outstanding in promoting citizenship" than do their public school colleagues. Research from the voucher programs in Dayton, Ohio, and Washington, D.C., found that parents of private school students were more civically engaged than parents of public school students.

In 1966, before school vouchers were on the nation's political agenda, Andrew Greeley and Peter Rossi used extensive survey data collected from American Catholics to argue that Catholic schools do not depress civic engagement or promote intolerance. The 1998 National Assessment of Educational Progress (NAEP) Civics Report Card for the Nation reports that students in private schools (both Catholic and non-Catholic) have higher average scores on the NAEP civics test than do their peers in public schools. However, this is without adjusting the data for background characteristics that may affect students' level of civic knowledge, such as their parents' educational level. James Coleman and Thomas Hoffer did control for family background and found that students in private schools, both Catholic and non-Catholic, scored higher on the High School and Beyond civics test than did public school students, although the results were not statistically significant. Taken together, these results give no reason to suspect that private schools do a worse job of providing a civic education than assigned public schools and some reason to think they do a better job. Yet reasonable doubt remains.

More broadly, Harvard University professor Robert Putnam's research on civic participation provides reason to think that private schools should be better able to deliver civic education than are public schools. Since the publication of Putnam's *Making Democracy Work* (1993) and the follow-up, *Bowling Alone* (2000), it has become increasingly common for political scientists to discuss political participation as driven by social capital. As Putnam defines it, "social capital refers to features of social organization such as networks, norms, and social trust that facilitate coordination and cooperation for mutual benefit." Before Putnam employed the concept to explain differences in governmental performance between northern and southern Italy, Coleman and his colleagues developed it to theorize why students in Catholic schools excel academically relative to their public school peers. Perhaps the same characteristics that cause Catholic schools to excel academically enable them to produce better citizens.

Comparing public and private school students is difficult, given that most Americans attend a public school in the elementary and secondary grades. In 1995, 91 percent of American secondary-school students were enrolled in public schools. It is even more difficult to make comparisons within the private sector, which comprises Catholic schools, religious schools sponsored by other faiths, and secular schools. Even within the public sector, there are schools to which students are assigned based on geography and schools they choose to attend (magnet and charter schools, for example). Here I use five types of schools: assigned public, magnet public, Catholic, secular private, and other religious. This last category combines schools from a broad range of faiths, including Christian fundamentalists, Quakers, and Muslims.

I used survey data from the 1996 National Household Education Survey, a large nationally representative survey of both parents and their children. This analysis draws on questions asked of students (and their parents) in grades 9 through 12, for a total sample size of 4,213. Even with a sample this large, the number of students attending other religious and secular private schools is still quite small (80 and 102 cases, respectively).

Throughout the analysis, except where noted, I adjusted the data to account for a variety of factors that might influence students' civic education and knowledge other than the kind of school they attend. At the individual level, I controlled for the usual demographic factors: students' age, gender, race, ethnicity, whether they spoke English, and whether they lived in the South. I also controlled for their academic performance, expectations of going to college, their expressed ability to take political action, their interest in the news, and the number of hours they spent at a job. Since adolescents' family lives exert a strong influence on their values, I controlled for a variety of family-based factors. These included parents' educational levels, family income, church attendance, whether students grew up in a two-parent household, parents' volunteer work, parents' political participation, parents' civic skills, and parents' political tolerance. I also considered factors such as the racial composition of a school, school size, whether the school arranges volunteer service, whether students' opinions matter, whether courses with political content are offered (so-called civics classes), and whether the school has a student government. Owing to the richness of the control variables, there can be reasonable confidence that these results capture the effect of the school a student attends.

Civic Engagement

Voter turnout is the most commonly used measure of civic engagement, but it is inadequate here because very few secondary school students are old enough to vote. Instead, three other measures can be used. One, voluntary community service, is a measure of what students are doing in the present. The second, acquiring "civic skills" in the classroom, is a measure of what students have learned to prepare them to be civically engaged in the future. The third is a measure of whether students feel confident that they could actually use their civic skills outside of the classroom.

Community Service

Past studies have found civic activity while young to be a "pathway to participation" in adulthood. Students were asked whether they engaged in "any community service activity or volunteer work at your school or in your community." Without any adjustments to the data, the results show that, statistically, there is no difference between assigned public schools and magnet public schools or secular private schools. However, students in both Catholic and other religious schools are more likely to engage in community service than are students in assigned public schools. Forty-seven percent of assigned public school students perform community service, compared with 64 percent of students in other religious schools and 71 percent of students in

Catholic schools. This is not surprising, given the religious character of these schools. Other research has shown that religious people are more inclined to volunteerism.

A reasonable objection to these results is that they are potentially misleading because many religious schools require their students to perform "voluntary" service. Seventy percent of students in Catholic schools report that their schools require community service in the 9th through 12th grades. This compares with 16 percent of students in assigned public schools, 22 percent in magnet public schools, 28 percent in other religious schools, and 38 percent in secular private schools. It is unclear what these differences mean for students' long-term commitment to community service. On the one hand, students who are compelled to perform service may only grow resentful. On the other hand, requiring service in the community would presumably introduce to volunteer work students who would not otherwise have had that experience. They may find that they enjoy it and wish to continue even after they have fulfilled their school's requirement. Regardless, after excluding from the analysis those students whose schools required them to perform community service, the results were very similar—with the notable exception of religious/non-Catholic schools. While more of their students participate in community service than do students in assigned public schools, the difference ceases to be statistically significant.

These results, however, still do not account for differences in the backgrounds and characteristics of students who attend these types of schools that might in turn affect whether they engage in community service. After again excluding students whose schools require community service, I took into account the various factors listed above. The results still show that students in Catholic schools are more likely to perform community service than those in assigned public schools (see figure 18.1). Forty-eight percent of public school students participate in community service, compared with 59 percent of Catholic school students. That is, Catholic schools contribute about as much to the likelihood of students' providing community service as does having a parent or guardian in the home who participates in community service (which also increases the share of students participating in volunteer activity by about 11 percentage points). Catholic schools contribute almost twice as much to a student volunteering as does raising a parent's educational level from a high school diploma to a college degree. There is no statistically significant difference between students in assigned public schools and those in secular private, magnet public, or religious/non-Catholic schools.

Figure 18.1. Service for the Soul

Schools with a religious mission appear to promote civic engagement, as more of their students participate in voluntary service than do public school students.*

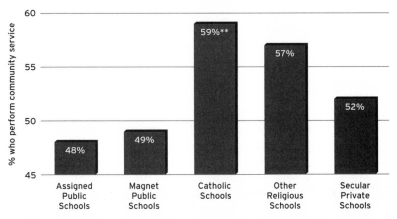

* Excluding schools that require their students to perform community service and controlling for a variety of student-level, family-level, and school-level factors that are known to influence whether students volunteer.

** Difference between this type of school and an assigned public school is statistically significant at the .05 level.

SOURCE: National Household Education Survey, 1996. For details see www.educationnext.org.

This suggests an answer to one of the essential questions in the debate over voucher programs—that is, will sending students to private schools harm their civic education? The answer appears to be no; in fact students in Catholic schools are more likely to engage in voluntary service than are students in assigned public schools, and there were no significant differences between students in assigned public schools and those in the three other types of schools. These findings are consistent with the research of Anthony Bryk, Valerie Lee, and Peter Holland, who explored the relationship between Catholic schools and their communities. They report that in all of the Catholic schools they included in their study, community service work was available as an elective course. Furthermore, an ethic of service was frequently found among both the staff and students they interviewed. They write:

> These service programs signify Catholic schools' commitment to a just social community. One board member of a field-site school remarked, "A school should not call itself Catholic if it doesn't have a volunteer service program."

The director of the program at St. Edward's [one of their case-study schools] commented: "I'm a believer in service. It's important for students to realize that the things they do make a difference. We can heal people and make their lives better. We can raise the awareness of others. Physical contact is vital for Christianity. Some of our students are sheltered from poverty and from people of different races. This program is important because it makes them more aware."

Civic Skills

People differ in their capacity to perform the mundane tasks that constitute virtually all political activity—skills like giving speeches, holding meetings, and writing letters. Those who lack these skills are extremely unlikely to participate in politics. While the authors focused on how adults learn civic skills on the job or through participation in voluntary organizations, it is in school that people are most likely to learn them when young.

An index of civic skills was created to test for systematic differences across the five types of schools. The household survey asked students, During this school year, have you done any of the following things in any class at (your current) school:

- Written a letter to someone you did not know?
- Given a speech or an oral report?
- Taken part in a debate or discussion in which you had to persuade others about your point of view?

Once again, the result for students who attend a Catholic school is statistically significant at the .05 level. Given the litany of control variables included in this analysis, this variable has quite a statistical hurdle to clear to reach statistical significance. Compared with a student who attends an assigned public school, a Catholic school student learns an average of .13 more civic skills. Not a dramatic difference, but completely consistent with the other findings reported here, it bolsters the evidence that Catholic schools deliver a high-quality civic education.

Civic Confidence

Learning civic skills is one thing; being able to use them is another. The household survey also asked respondents whether they feel that they could use two of the civic skills learned inside the classroom elsewhere. The questions ask:

- Suppose you wanted to write a letter to someone in the government about something that concerned you. Do you feel that you could write a letter that clearly gives your opinion?
- Imagine you went to a community meeting and people were making comments and statements. Do you think that you could make a comment or a statement at a public meeting?

Students in secular private, Catholic, and other religious schools are more likely than students in assigned public schools to have confidence in their ability to exercise civic skills if called upon to do so. Of these three, the religious/non-Catholic school students display the greatest degree of civic confidence. Civic confidence is the only component of civic education included in this analysis for which each type of private school displays a positive and statistically significant effect. The bottom line is that public schools can take a lesson from private schools about how to prepare students for civic life, not only in providing skills, but also in providing the confidence to use those skills.

Political Knowledge

The second objective of a civic education is to teach future voters specific, factual information about American politics. Indeed, of the three objectives I have listed, this one is most clearly the province of the schools. While there may be disagreement over whether schools should require community service, presumably everyone agrees that schools should require the acquisition of knowledge. Without understanding the particulars of American politics, people are unable to engage fully in the political process. In fact, political scientist John Zaller argues persuasively that factual knowledge about politics is the best measure of political engagement.

The National Household Education Survey includes a series of factual questions about American politics. Each respondent was asked five of the following ten questions. To avoid contamination effects, whichever five questions a student answered, her parent answered the other five:

- What job or political office is now [in 1996] held by Al Gore?
- Whose responsibility is it to determine if a law is constitutional . . . the President, the Congress, or the Supreme Court?
- Which party now has the most members in the House of Representatives in Washington?

- How much of a majority is needed for the U.S. Senate and House to override a presidential veto?
- Which of the two major parties is more conservative at the national level?
- What job or political office is now held by Newt Gingrich?
- Whose responsibility is it to nominate judges to the federal courts . . . the President, the Congress, or the Supreme Court?
- Which party now has the most members in the U.S. Senate?
- What are the first ten amendments of the U.S. Constitution called?
- Which of the two major parties is in favor of the larger defense budget?

Before making any adjustments, the average scores of students in assigned public schools are lower than those in Catholic, religious/non-Catholic, and secular private schools. Students in assigned public schools got an average of 2.4 questions out of five correct, while students in Catholic, religious/non-Catholic, and secular private schools scored an average of 3.2, 3.4, and 3.2 respectively.

Once the statistical adjustments are made for all the factors that can influence students' political knowledge except the type of school they attend, only students in Catholic schools still perform better than do students in assigned public schools. Therefore, we can conclude that only students in Catholic schools display more political knowledge when accounting for a slew of potentially confounding demographic factors, many of which are themselves statistically and substantively significant. Older students score better on the index, as do males, whites, and non-Hispanics. Having higher grades, expecting to attend college, expressing greater political interest, and spending more time watching or reading the news are all positively related to political knowledge. At the family level, both parents' educational levels and political knowledge are positive factors predicting students' greater political knowledge.

Political Tolerance

While all three objectives are equally important components of a civic education, it is the third—respect for opinions different from your own, or political tolerance—that may be most relevant to the debate over the civic consequences of attending private schools. This is often expressed as a concern that private (particularly religious) schools exacerbate social tensions. In the words of the late union leader Al Shanker, widespread voucher programs that send students to private schools "would foster divisions in our society; they would be like setting a time bomb." Amy Gutmann stresses the need for students in religious schools to be taught democratic norms under direction from the state, presumably fearing that these schools cannot be trusted to provide instruction in a "common democratic character" on their own. Certainly, the concern for teaching a respect for universal civil liberties is well placed, as democracy is defined as much by respect for minority rights as by simple majority rule.

The question of adolescents' attitudes and how they are related to enrollment in different types of schools has been virtually unexplored. The research literature suggests two alternative hypotheses, drawn from different perspectives on what fosters political tolerance. The first hypothesis is derived from distinguishing between schools as public versus private institutions. By this reasoning, private schools may be thought to foster an exclusivity among their students that translates into a disregard for minority opinions. In particular, religious schools may foster civic divisiveness, a fear reinforced by survey data that show religiosity to be negatively related to political tolerance. The second hypothesis follows from studies showing the positive academic effects of attending a private school. One widely noted study reports that education increases tolerance by enhancing students' general cognitive proficiency. It would follow that tolerance is greatest in those schools where students display the strongest cognitive performance, generally private schools.

The household survey contains two questions gauging political tolerance:

- If a person wanted to make a speech in your community against churches and religion, should he or she be allowed to speak?
- Suppose a book that most people disapproved of was written, for example, saying that it was all right to take illegal drugs. Should a book like that be kept out of a public library?

The question about churches and religion particularly challenges the political tolerance of students in religious schools, since it confronts them with an opinion they will almost certainly reject. Students in Catholic and secular private schools have higher tolerance scores than students in assigned public schools, averaging 1.6 and 1.8 tolerant responses respectively, compared with 1.4 tolerant responses among assigned public school students. Students in other religious schools have an average score (1.2 tolerant responses) lower than that of public school students. Students in magnet public schools have slightly higher scores than assigned public school students, although the difference does not approach statistical significance.

Figure 18.2. Freedom of Speech

Students in Catholic and secular private schools tend to be more tolerant of other perspectives than are public school students and students in other religious schools. *

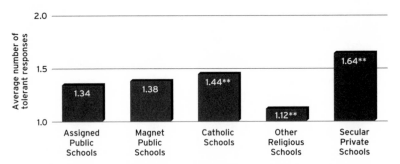

Students were asked two questions probing their openness to other perspectives: (1) If a person wanted to make a speech in your community against churches and religion, should he or she be allowed to speak? (2) Suppose a book that most people disapproved of was written, for example, saying that it was all right to take illegal drugs. Should a book like that be kept out of the public library? Answering Yes to the first question and No to the second were considered tolerant responses.

* Controlling for a variety of student-level, family-level, and school-level factors known to influence students' level of tolerance.

** Difference between this type of school and an assigned public school is statistically significant at the .05 level.

SOURCE: National Household Education Survey, 1996. For details see www.educationnext.org.

After again making the statistical adjustments listed above, students in secular private schools scored substantially higher on the political tolerance index than students in assigned public schools, while students in religious/non-Catholic schools scored substantially lower (see figure 18.2). Catholic school students still score higher than assigned public students, though the difference is only a third as large as that between secular private schools and assigned public schools. It is possible that there is some credence to the concern expressed by critics of private education that it has the potential to foster political intolerance. While students in Catholic schools (the most common form of private education) and secular private schools are more politically tolerant than students in assigned public schools, the 2 percent of America's students in other religious schools—an amalgam of schools sponsored by many different faiths—score lower on the political tolerance index.

One should not necessarily conclude that other religious schools breed intolerance. It may be that students' attitudes are shaped more by family background than by the schools they attend. For all its virtues, the National Household Education Survey has poor measures of parents' religious involvement. Because family tolerance is poorly measured and the sample size, for this group of students, is small, we should be cautious in drawing firm conclusions.

Evaluation of responses to survey questions about civil liberties must also take into account the content of the question. Because one of the questions on the tolerance index deals specifically with the rights of a speaker who is opposed to religion, students in religious schools might be expected to be especially wary of granting full freedom of expression. This is not to diminish the importance of respect for religious differences as an important component of political tolerance, but only to suggest that other questions might provide more of a "hard case" for students in secular schools. And lest it be thought that there is something inherent in religious education that breeds intolerance, remember that Catholic school students show higher levels of tolerance than students in assigned public schools.

Make Democracy Work

The results reported here are consistent with four similar studies—the 1973 High School Seniors Cohort Study, the National Educational Longitudinal Study, the Latino National Political Survey, and data collected from participants in school-choice programs in Washington, D.C., and Dayton, Ohio. Few findings in social science can be replicated in five independent sources of data (six, if you count the Washington and Dayton surveys separately). In short, it seems that strong evidence has accumulated that private—particularly Catholic—schools are a private means to the very public end of facilitating civic engagement.

This conclusion is admittedly provocative, if only because of the connotations the words "public" and "private" carry in contemporary discourse. In the United States, the word "public" is supposed to refer to the source of a school's funding and not to the population served by a school. Nevertheless, critics of private education often implicitly extend the limited definition of "public" to mean the population served by the school. Critics speak of high-priced preparatory schools as though they are the only, or at least the most common, type of private education in the United States. Often all private schools are grouped together and caricatured as exclusive and insular. While it is true that privately funded schools have the prerogative to apply virtually any criteria they want for admissions, in practice Catholic schools, at least, are very inclusive.

Catholic high schools are not highly selective in their admissions. The typical school reports accepting 88 percent of the students who apply, and only about a third of the schools maintain a waiting list. Anthony Bryk and his colleagues also report that "religious affiliation is not a routine consideration" in admissions to Catholic schools. Even though Catholic schools charge tuition, 87 percent offer financial aid. By contrast, public schools almost exclusively enroll students who live in the geographic area surrounding the school. How "public" is a school in an exclusive suburb with high housing costs, especially when compared with a Catholic school that offers financial aid to assist with its tuition (which, in turn, is usually only around $2,500 a year)?

Critics also tend to define public schools as the only institutions providing an education that promotes publicly spirited citizens. By this definition, the evidence presented here suggests that Catholic and private secular schools are really more "public" than schools funded by the state. The claim that private organizations can contribute to the quality of a community's public life is hardly original. Echoing Alexis de Tocqueville's *Democracy in America*, Putnam found that measures of civic associational life, everything from choral societies to soccer clubs, are the primary explanation for effective governance across Italy's regions. Voluntary associations like these produce social capital, and social capital "makes democracy work." In fact, our public schools seem to have much to learn from private, especially Catholic, schools about what makes democratic education work.

DAVID E. CAMPBELL is assistant professor of political science at the University of Notre Dame.

CHAPTER NINETEEN

How Vouchers Came to D.C.

Spencer S. Hsu

"We walk away from these kids in every regard. We never fix these schools," said a disgusted Rep. Richard K. Armey (R-Texas). The date was May 23, 2001, and the Republican-controlled House of Representatives had rejected a proposal to fund a pilot school voucher program that would have provided a token voucher of $1,500 to students in five schools nationwide. "Where is the heart?" Armey, then the House majority leader, asked his own members.

Less than three years later, President George W. Bush delivered a far different message to voucher supporters—a declaration of victory. In January 2004, Bush signed legislation providing grants worth as much as $7,500 each to children from dozens of public schools in the District of Columbia for their use at private or religious schools in a five-year experiment. The recipients of the first federal "opportunity scholarships," as advocates named them, were announced in June.

After the vote, in a speech at the Heritage Foundation, a Washington-based conservative think tank, Secretary of Education Roderick R. Paige predicted that Washington's example would trigger campaigns in state legislatures across the country. "We have turned a corner," the secretary said. "This is just the beginning. We can't just sit and wait five years to see what happens here."

The D.C. program is a landmark, representing the first federally funded school voucher program. Moreover, by design the D.C. vouchers are more generous than those approved in Milwaukee, Cleveland, Florida, and Colorado, although they are generally limited to fewer children (see table 19.1).

Table 19.1. Publicly Funded Voucher Programs in the United States

	D.C. Opportunity Scholarship Program	Colorado Opportunity Contract Pilot Program*	Florida A+ Plan Opportunity Scholarship Program	Cleveland Scholarship and Tutoring Program	Milwaukee Parental Choice Program
Year Vouchers Inaugurated	2004	2004	1999	1996	1990
Voucher Amount	Up to $7,500, based on financial need	Lesser of private schools' per-pupil cost or 37.5% of district per-pupil operating revenue for kindergartners 75% for elementary and junior high students 85% for high school students approximately $4,500	State's share of eligible student's educational expenses, about $4,000 during 2003 school year	Up to $2,700 for K-8 and $2,430 for grades 9 and 10 during 2004–2005 school year Capped at 90% of tuition and based on financial need	For 2003–2004 school year, the lesser of $5,882 or private school's per-pupil costs
Eligible Students	Students eligible for federal lunch program	Students must be eligible for federal lunch program and come from a district designated by the states as "poor performing" or that voluntarily participates	Students in schools that received an F on the state report card twice within a four-year period	Students in the Cleveland school district	Students with household incomes at or below 175% of the poverty line
Potential Number of Students	Funding available for as many as 1,700 students Program is authorized for 5 years	Participation capped at 1% of a district's enrollment in program's first year, rising annually to a maximum of 6% In the first year, 11 districts were set to participate and a maximum of 3,400 vouchers were to be available. By the program's 4th year, 21,000 students could be using vouchers	Not capped During the 2003–2004 school year, 1,611 students used an opportunity scholarship. Of those students, 640 attended a private school	Budgetary cap 5,281 students received tuition scholarships during the 2003–2004 school year	Capped at 15% (about 15,000) of Milwaukee public school students 13,258 participants during the 2003–2004 school year

*Program invalidated by Colorado Supreme Court pending legislative revisions.
NOTE: All programs allow vouchers to be used at religious schools. Florida also has the McKay Scholarship for Disabled Students, which are available to students with special needs whose parents are dissatisfied with their academic progress. During the 2003 school year, 13,739 Florida students used a McKay Scholarship to attend a private school.

How school voucher advocates engineered the breakthrough is the story of a complex alignment of interests among conservative education activists, the Republicans who control Washington, and the local leaders of a majority African American city. The legislation's passage, the culmination of a nine-year fight in Congress, attested to the school choice movement's persistence, deep pockets, and ability to capitalize on Washington residents' frustration with their struggling public schools.

To opponents, the creation of a federal program that pays for children to attend private schools can only foster the spread of vouchers. But Tanya Clay, legislative director of People for the American Way, a liberal advocacy group, said it is not clear if state legislatures will follow suit or if other black urban politicians will join them. The Washington fight was unique in many regards, not least in that the legislators who approved the voucher program are unaccountable to the voters whose lives it will affect, since the District of Columbia has no vote in Congress.

The latter is a chief bone of contention among some critics. In the words of Eleanor Holmes Norton (D), Washington's elected, nonvoting delegate to the House of Representatives, "[Republicans] used our denial of representation in the Senate, where vouchers would have been disposed of as a matter of senatorial courtesy, to force vouchers on the city."

A Ripe Target

The D.C. School Choice Incentive Act of 2003 provides $65 million (plus $5 million for administrative costs) over five years to send as many as 1,700 low-income D.C. students to private and parochial schools starting in the fall of 2004. The grants are limited to those households earning up to 185 percent of the poverty level, about $34,873 for a family of four in 2004. Scholarships are aimed at students from low-performing D.C. public schools.

The victory came at a price. To win the support of local officials, the Bush administration and Congress had to pledge $2 in additional aid to the District's regular and charter public school systems for every $1 in new tuition grants for private schooling. The concessions confounded some voucher purists, who say the deal undermined the competitive incentive for public schools to improve.

Voucher advocates who supported the deal calculated that, whatever the concessions, the movement would benefit in the long term from a pilot program. The outcome provided advocates with not only a high-profile laboratory for the idea, but also fresh evidence that a political strategy aimed at fusing support from African American urban leaders to a coalition of Republican groups can work under certain circumstances. As one example, participants cited the cultivation of D.C. mayor Anthony A. Williams, whose backing proved decisive. "We had never had a locally elected black official, a Democrat from a city like D.C., asking for something like this before," said Nina Shokraii Rees, director of the U.S. Department of Education's Office of Innovation and Improvement, which is implementing the program. "That's the single strongest factor that got people's attention."

Rees, a veteran of the school choice movement, said Washington was a ripe target. Movement strategists consider five factors when selecting battlegrounds, she said, and the District met each condition: a legislative and an executive branch controlled by supporters, local political champions for education or urban renewal, local business support, a weakened teacher union, and grassroots backing.

Advocates enjoyed important institutional advantages in swaying D.C.'s local government. Even though residents of the nation's capital elect their own local leaders to oversee most city and state functions, the District has no vote in Congress, and final oversight remains the province of the president and Congress. Consequently, Republicans have made regular attempts to enact a voucher program for the District—despite fierce opposition from local politicians—ever since they took control of Congress in 1994. Congress narrowly approved one such bill in 1998, knowing that President Clinton would veto it. George W. Bush's election in 2000 removed that obstacle, and the transition to unified Republican control of the federal government led some District officials to calculate that voucher legislation for the city would eventually come to pass.

One other factor unique to local Washington politics would shape events: the most powerful force opposing vouchers in D.C. politics, the local teachers union, had fallen into disarray. Responding to teachers' complaints of unusually high deductions for union dues from their paychecks in the summer of 2002, the American Federation of Teachers launched a financial audit and found at least $4.6 million missing from the treasury of its local affiliate, the Washington Teachers Union. Over the next two years, a federal investigation revealed that top union leaders had siphoned away dues to fund their lavish lifestyles. The episode neutralized the union's clout just as its political influence would be tested most.

The Mayor Signs On

It was in this unsettled environment in 2002 that Williams—together with a small group of other black Washington Democrats previously opposed to school vouchers—began back-channel talks with supporters close to White House and congressional leaders. In Williams, the school choice movement discovered an unexpected ally, motivated by a combination of personal biography, pragmatism, and political survival.

The adopted son of two postal workers, Williams, 52, graduated from Loyola, a Catholic, mostly white high school in Los Angeles, before serving in the Air Force and earning undergraduate, law, and public policy degrees from Yale and Harvard. Running for mayor in 1998, Williams called the parents who scraped together the money to send him to private school the greatest influence in his life. Nonetheless, as a candidate and officeholder, Williams called vouchers a divisive distraction benefiting the few at the expense of the many in public schools. "While the District's public school system . . . must be reformed, school vouchers are not the answer," he said at the time. "Rather than using taxpayer dollars to provide vouchers to a few, we must focus our resources and efforts on concrete reforms that make our public schools better for all of the District's schoolchildren."

By 2002, a reelection year, the mayor had found the problems of the D.C. public school system intractable and a growing political weight. Williams routinely promised quality schools as the linchpin of a vision to lure middle-class residents back to the city. His failure to deliver on this promise had worried his base of business supporters and made him appear feckless to skeptics.

For its part, the school system has churned through a new superintendent every two years on average since 1994. Over that period, the performance of D.C.'s students has remained distressingly low compared with students in other large urban school districts. The system reports needing $2 billion more to maintain crumbling schools, whose dilapidation delayed the start of the school year twice in the 1990s. Meanwhile, per-pupil spending reached $13,355 in 2002–2003, compared with a national average of less than $10,000 a year, according to U.S. Department of Education statistics, although, unlike other school systems, the District figures include the equivalent of both state-level and local education spending.

The list of familiar big-city woes continues. Violence remains a menace, with school-related shootings claiming three teenagers in a three-month span in 2003. A new D.C. school board study concluded that the system was beset by a lack of accountability, an "incoherent" curriculum, haphazard instruction, and "abysmal results." Disparities between the test scores of black and white students are among the nation's widest, in a student body that is 84 percent African American. Finally, the system's long-term flaws are evident in the city's functional illiteracy rate of 40 percent among adults. If the D.C. public school system were in any other city, some observers have concluded, it would long ago have been taken over by a state legislature. Congress, however, is ill equipped and disinclined to undertake that local function.

So when a council of chief executives of the area's largest corporations identified school reform as their top priority, Williams listened. In 2002 he gave a private pledge to business leaders organized by Terence C. Golden, a former Reagan administration Treasury official and chief executive of Host Marriott, to support vouchers as part of a broader initiative to help charter and regular public schools.

One key figure was Joseph E. Robert Jr., a local real-estate mogul who has spent millions promoting school vouchers and supporting local education and youth groups. Robert recalled the CEO dinner in the fall of 2002 at which Williams abandoned his anti-voucher stance. "The question came up, what big idea should we be working on in his administration the next year with regard to education," said Robert. With the mayor coming out in support of vouchers, Robert pushed ahead with a full-scale campaign. "We called it 'Capital Gains,'" he said, and embarked on a series of meetings with business and community leaders "in every office, in restaurants, and homes . . . to get vouchers right here in Washington."

Robert supported grassroots organizations such as D.C. Parents for School Choice, a group of about fifty activists and hundreds of supporters that had become the public face of the District of Columbia voucher movement. In addition, Robert capitalized on his ties to such national figures in the voucher movement as Wal-Mart heir John Walton and his American Education Reform Council; Howard Fuller, the former Milwaukee superintendent who now heads the Black Alliance for Educational Options; and the Institute for Justice, the voucher movement's legal brain trust. Also involved were J. Patrick Rooney, chairman of the Golden Rule Insurance Company; the family of Richard M. and Betsy DeVos Jr., founders of Amway Corporation; and former Circuit City chief Richard Sharp. "These are people who have connections on the Hill, who have friends. Without them I think it is fair to say this wouldn't have gone anywhere," said Rep. Thomas M. Davis III (R-Virginia), an eventual sponsor of the D.C. voucher legislation.

In explaining his change of heart, Williams said after years of effort he had learned that "trying to do the same thing just doesn't work." He also cited public opinion research showing that voters believe government spends enough on education but does not spend it well enough. At the same time, the mayor said he got the best deal he could for the city because he secured additional dollars for public schools. He explained, "Here's the way to think about it. Let's say you have 2,000 students choose a voucher program. You hold harmless the public schools because another $13 million can go into enrichment of one sort or another. That's real money over a period of five years if we're serious in pushing it through to the public school system, dealing with issues of juvenile crime, the lack of structure, the whole panoply of social issues. Reorganizing education is a first step. I think it's an important precedent that other places in the country might follow, and it's important for us."

The Tradeoff

The Washington talks did not take place in a vacuum. In February 2003, President Bush leaked word through aides that his 2004 budget would include $75 million for school choice experiments in a handful of cities, including the District of Columbia. White House officials had been kept apprised of developments in the District through Republican intermediaries active in city affairs such as former GOP cabinet members William F. Bennett and William T. Coleman. "The secretary had heard from several people that the mayor in private conversations had expressed interest in school choice," said one official close to Secretary of Education Paige.

Within days of the Bush leak on vouchers, Paige opened direct talks with city officials, meeting with Mayor Williams and with D.C. school board president Peggy Cooper Cafritz and D.C. council member Kevin P. Chavous.

Dead set against vouchers when he ran against Williams for mayor in 1998, Chavous had come around to supporting charter schools, reflecting Democratic orthodoxy. At a February 2003 dinner with the chief executives at a downtown hotel, he announced his further conversion to vouchers. "More money alone wouldn't do it," Chavous recalled. "Public schools won't reform themselves internally. They will only respond to external pressures and a more educated electorate."

Where Cafritz in early February had declared the school board "solidly against vouchers" and proponents "people whose goals are different than the people who live here," she shifted course in a newspaper opinion article the following month. She began by conceding, "Some version of this legislation is certain to pass. . . . We must accept the federally proposed voucher or scholarship program." In exchange, she sought money for the public system, limitation of vouchers' use to private schools in the city, and discussion of a "Marshall Plan" for public schools, charter schools, and other nonprofit education facilities in the city.

With the mayor, the school board president, and a key city council member on the team, voucher supporters had cracked the solid wall of local opposition that had stalled past campaigns.

Congress Debates

Throughout the summer of 2003, voucher opponents were mobilizing. As a September showdown neared, their coalition included the major teacher unions and public education associations, People for the American Way, the Leadership Conference on Civil Rights, and several Jewish organizations, among others. Opponents hammered at the theme that vouchers would divert taxpayers' money from public schools, weaken public education, and leave tens of thousands of children behind. Teacher union officials began calling in chits with swing members; local school board members flooded Capitol Hill switchboards; and party-whipping organizations went to battle stations.

The White House turned up its pressure. For the first time in recent memory, a president sent emissaries to meet with appropriations committee members to press them to include funding for a single initiative. President Bush's senior congressional lobbyist, David W. Hobbs, called the voucher program as high a priority for the administration as passage of No Child Left Behind in 2001. He portrayed the vote as a test of Republicans' loyalty to their president and said Bush himself lobbied lawmakers.

The floor debate was familiar. While opponents said that vouchers had no track record of improving student performance, supporters countered that no alternative could be worse than Washington's public schools, which in any case were in line to receive more federal aid. Critics also said that private schools receiving taxpayer aid would be less accountable to voters and would operate free of some antidiscrimination laws.

Meanwhile, advocates invoked the "hypocrisy" of voucher critics in Congress who were rich enough to send their own children to private schools but would deny that option to the city's poorer families. Finally, they said accountability would be ensured by the U.S. secretary of education and Mayor Williams and by rigorous research studies supported by the department. The result was one of the closest votes of the year. On September 9,

2003, the full House approved a District of Columbia voucher bill by a single vote, 209–208.

Meanwhile, the Senate was waging its own pitched fight. Both sides focused on the Senate Appropriations Committee and a handful of centrist members who held the balance of power. Under Senate rules, the committee's vote would be crucial to the bill's fate. If the measure reached the floor, the Republican majority would have the upper hand in parliamentary maneuvering to force final passage. However, in July, one of the committee's Republican senators, Arlen Specter of Pennsylvania, had made clear his opposition, citing concern that the voucher program would lead to religious discrimination and scuttling hopes for a quick committee vote.

Feinstein's Conversion

From the logjam emerged Democratic senator Dianne Feinstein of California. Like Williams, Feinstein had served as a big-city mayor, in her case nine years in San Francisco. Like him she had spent her career, thirty years in elective office, opposing vouchers. But like Williams, she credited her family's decision to enroll her in a Catholic school, as one of a few Jewish students, with setting her on her life's course, from Stanford University into public life and to the U.S. Senate. In an abrupt break with California's powerful teacher unions, Feinstein reversed course and embraced the D.C. choice legislation on July 22.

"Local leaders should have the opportunity to experiment with programs that they believe are right for their area," Feinstein said. "If supporting the mayor's proposal will help us to better understand what works and what doesn't in terms of educating our youth, then I believe Williams should be allowed to undertake this experiment." She also made clear that she was supporting vouchers in a Washington test case, not for her home state. The Senate committee forwarded the District bill on to the floor with the help of Feinstein and ranking panel Democrat Robert C. Byrd of West Virginia.

Both sides launched a final blitz. D.C. Parents for School Choice ran television advertisements targeting key senators including Massachusetts Democrat Edward M. Kennedy, accusing him of fighting efforts to help black children and comparing him to segregationist Bull Connor, the police chief in Birmingham, Alabama, who used violent tactics to disperse civil-rights demonstrators in the 1960s. The ad said, "Senator Kennedy, your brothers fought for us. Why do you fight against us? Are the unions really more important than these children?"

The Black Alliance for Educational Options bought a full-page ad in a New Orleans newspaper accusing Louisiana senator Mary Landrieu of turning her back on African Americans and noting that her two children attend private school in Washington.

Voucher opponents also fought fiercely. The National Education Association called on the four Senate Democrats then on the presidential campaign trail to be ready to return to Washington to vote against the measure. State NEA affiliates arranged meetings with wavering members, such as Sen. Tom Carper (D-Delaware), from whom the union had withheld its endorsement after past disputes. Together with wavering Republicans in states where vouchers are unpopular, opposing Democrats held firm.

In the end, a de facto filibuster by opponents kept the measure from passing for four months. But if the GOP leadership could not muster the sixty votes needed to cut off debate and pass the bill, opponents could not muster the fifty-one votes to kill it outright. Using prerogatives of the majority, Majority Leader Bill Frist (R-Tenn.) and Senate Appropriations Committee chairman Ted Stevens (R-Alaska) ultimately rolled the District measure into a catchall federal spending bill and defied Democrats to risk a government shutdown. Opponents took comfort in the fact that the Senate never voted directly on the voucher provision. Nevertheless, the measure was passed on January 22 and quietly signed by Bush the next day.

The Fallout

Meanwhile, in Washington, the fallout from the program lingers. According to a November 2003 poll for two Washington radio and television stations, Williams's approval ratings among D.C. Democratic voters plummeted to 45 percent, compared with 64 percent among residents at large in 2002. Mayoral aides blamed the drop in part on the voucher fight and his bucking Democratic Party orthodoxy. The Washington Teachers Union withdrew its support, and Williams faced a nascent recall effort.

The mayor appears unfazed, although his broader education reform initiatives have been rejected by the city council. "This is not a partisan issue. It's not Republican, it's not Democratic, it's for the kids," Williams reflected about his voucher stance. "What percentage of kids in public schools in D.C. are African American? I've got to believe, it's not just suburban parents who are upset about education."

Those who question Williams's decision to support vouchers argue that the promises of greater aid to public education are nothing more than a short-term sweetener to win passage of programs that may erode support for public schools, a penny ante in a broader contest over billions of dollars in government education spending. The mayor's change of heart notwithstanding, they say the outreach to African American urban leaders is politically motivated and will fall short, just as the Republican Party has failed to win over black voters with its choice of issues and leaders for thirty years.

To school choice movement veteran Nina Rees, the decision to provide more funding for public schools as well as vouchers for private tuition was a virtue. It shifted the debate to focus on improving education for young people, said Rees, not the mechanism by which they are taught.

As for the voucher program, organizers announced in June that about 1,200 low-income children (out of 2,600 applicants, 1,700 of whom were eligible) will receive vouchers this fall. The Washington Scholarship Fund, a nonprofit supported by Robert that has raised private funds to help provide tuition scholarships for private school students, was selected by the Department of Education to administer the effort. While a lottery to select voucher recipients chose first from among students in fifteen D.C. public schools that failed for two years to meet goals under the federal No Child Left Behind Act, about one in six D.C. children who will receive tuition grants are students who already attend private school. The Fund also announced that fifty private schools have agreed to participate.

Private schools are having to adjust to the new world of federal funding. Under the law, they can apply their own admissions criteria and placement tests to voucher students. They can also raise their tuition as long as they demonstrate in writing that any annual increase of more than 10 percent is warranted. Schools must submit tuition and fee schedules, comparative data to help parents select sites for their children, and documentation showing lawful operation such as certificates of occupancy, independent financial audits, and compliance with D.C. health, safety, and fire codes.

Meanwhile, the Catholic Archdiocese of Washington, whose private school system is expected to provide the bulk of the seats for new voucher students and which was involved in passing and developing the program, is seeking additional money, noting that their tuition rates on average cover only about 50 percent of the system's costs to educate each child. Voucher administrators are ironing out such key details as what fees to cover under the program, while making sure that voucher students are charged no more than other pupils.

For most Washington schoolchildren headed back to class this fall, any change in their lives as a result of the 2003 voucher battle in Congress will remain remote. When fully phased in, the $14 million-a-year voucher program is expected to serve about 2,000 students, a small portion of the roughly 80,000 children enrolled in the city's regular and charter public schools.

SPENCER S. HSU is a staff writer at the *Washington Post*.

PART C

Other Ways of Increasing School Choice

CHAPTER TWENTY

Contracting Out:
The Story behind Philadelphia's
Edison Contract

Jay Mathews

Gwen Carol Holmes, a tall, slender Kansan, suppressed a smile whenever angry Philadelphians attacked the track record of her company, Edison Schools. Edison, the New York-based for-profit school management firm, was seen by many in the nation's seventh-largest city as a greedy, slick huckster. Edison's opponents cited the company's failures, such as the two schools Edison had to give up in Holmes's hometown of Wichita, Kansas.

If Edison failed in Wichita, the critics said, it had no chance in a metropolis like Philly. And so Holmes would have to explain again that she was the principal whose school, Colvin Elementary, had outperformed those two Edison schools in Wichita. But she had succeeded because she was using Edison's methods and because the competition from Edison enabled her to squeeze more resources out of the central office. She was so transformed by the experience that she joined the enemy.

The Wichita school board had resented the idea that it needed an outside company—from NuYawk, no less—to save its worst schools. To assuage its pride, it assigned one of its best principals—Holmes—to run a school that would use Edison methods and show everybody that the locals were just as good as any bunch of out-of-towners (contradictory as that may sound). The fact that Holmes, the symbol of local resistance, switched to preaching for a tested national approach gives hope to many educators who think private enterprises with track records have a place in the solution of the nation's worst education problems.

Figure 20.1. Rising Demand, Falling Price

As Edison Schools' student enrollment skyrocketed, its continuing failure to turn a profit sent its stock price plummeting below $1 a share. The company opened its first school in 1995 and went public in November 1999.

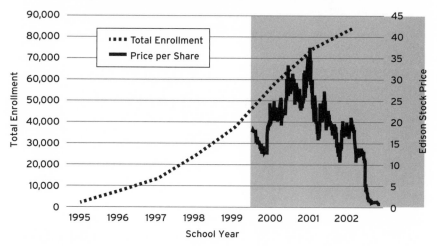

SOURCES: Edison Schools; cnn.com.

The stakes and the risks for Edison are, of course, far greater in Philadelphia than they were in Wichita. The company's $11.8 million contract to run twenty of the city's worst-performing schools is the largest challenge Edison has ever had in one metropolis. As such, it has the potential to become a referendum not just on Edison but also on privatization as a reform strategy. Moreover, Edison has been hobbled by both the terms of the Philadelphia contract and a run of financial and legal problems. The firm was not assigned the twenty schools it was to manage until April 2002, four months before the new school year, giving it little time to install its program and train school personnel. By then the company's stock price had plummeted (see figure 20.1) and it was unclear how much longer Edison could survive without turning a profit. It secured a new round of financing, but on terms highly unfavorable to the company.

The arrival of a new superintendent, former Chicago schools CEO Paul G. Vallas, has made the situation even cloudier. Vallas's insistence on strict accountability and regular testing of all schools fits the Edison model well, but one never knows what will happen when new leadership tries to make its imprint on a school district. Consider this then, whatever Edison's fate, to be a case study of an effort to bring a relatively new and data-based education product to a very old and tired city, an experiment that is taking place in one form or another in nearly every large school district in the country.

At Ridge's Invitation

More than 200,000 students attend the Philadelphia city schools, fewer than 20 percent of them non-Hispanic whites, 78 percent of them from families poor enough to qualify for federally subsidized school lunches. Just before Edison arrived in Philadelphia, the city government had tried to sue the state for more school funding. Mayor John F. Street eventually agreed to put aside the suit in return for negotiations between the city and the state, the state demanding reforms and the city in turn asking for more money to pay for them.

Street, an African American lawyer who once taught at a city elementary school, is a veteran of Philadelphia's racially tinged politics. Mayor Frank Rizzo was a lightning rod for racial tension in the 1980s. To the present day, politics in Philadelphia still tends to focus on issues of black and white more than in other cities—cities like New York and Los Angeles, where the massive inflow of Latino and Asian immigrants has created a more diverse political scene. But Street was a practical man, willing to overlook old battles if he could persuade the state to help and to defuse the feeling among many African Americans in Philadelphia that the white power structure in Harrisburg was under-funding and discriminating against their schools.

His negotiations on the funding issue were with Pennsylvania governor Tom Ridge, a popular Republican who had beaten his Democratic opponent almost two to one in 1998. Ridge grew up in Erie and had been an infantryman in Vietnam. As governor, he proposed a voucher program for public school parents whose children were stuck in bad schools. His proposal won the support of some black Philadelphia legislators, but he could not overcome the resistance of the mainly Republican suburbs. Ridge did manage to persuade Street to sign a memorandum of understanding in July 2001 that gave him permission to order an analysis of the financial and educational condition of the school district. The state resisted giving the schools more funds when many observers thought the district was grossly mismanaging its finances and operations. It wanted some kind of assurance, backed by independent research, that any new money would be spent more effectively. Enter Edison Schools.

Rising Scores . . .

Ridge and his aides were impressed with Edison's track record. Created in 1992 and starting its school management program in 1996, Edison had contracts to run more than 100 public schools. It was the brainchild of entrepreneur Christopher Whittle, whose controversial Channel One program had placed specially produced television news shows and advertising in public school homerooms.

Edison had gone further than any other private firm in demonstrating what business could do for the nation's most impoverished children. Most of its schools were charter or contract schools, run independent of school dis-

Figure 20.2. Achievement Gains

Edison Schools has reported substantial gains in student achievement, pointing to positive achievement trends in 84 percent of the schools for which long-term data were available.

Edison Schools Average Annual Achievement

Type of Test Scoring	Number of Schools	Average Annual Gain Since Schools Opened, 1995–2001	Average Gain in 2000-'01
Criterion-referenced tests[1]	47	6% (gain in % proficient)	7% (same)
		6% (gain in % not failing)	9% (same)
Norm-referenced tests[2]	27	5 percentile points	5 percentile points

[1] Criterion-referenced scoring is used in most state-required tests.

[2] Norm-referenced scoring is used on the Terra Nova, SAT9, MAT7, and ITBS tests.

NOTE: The group Parents Advocating School Responsibility has faulted Edison for including only 74 schools in the study at a time when it was operating 113 schools. Edison explains that test-score gain data (which require information both before and after attendance at an Edison school) were available for only 74 schools. (Most of the schools not included had only recently opened their doors.) An article in the *New York Times* said Edison's use of school-wide averages masked declines in specific grades. Edison replied that only 2 out of the 62 schools with positive ratings showed such declines.

SOURCE: Edison Schools.

trict supervision but using tax dollars. Edison was educating some 85,000 students scattered across twenty-three states and the District of Columbia, making it the equivalent of the 45th-largest school district in the country (see figure 20.1). Edison executives promised to save money and spread technological innovation by running those schools from a central administrative point. Many parents gravitated toward Edison as a fresh alternative to traditionally low-budget, low-tech inner-city schools. Schools like the Edison Friendship Public Charter School in Washington, D.C., had waiting lists from the moment they opened.

Just how successful Edison has been in raising student achievement remains a matter of debate (see figure 20.2). John Chubb, Edison's chief education officer, says that "student achievement is rising faster—much faster—in Edison schools than in any other similar system of schools in America." Though critics dispute these numbers, there is little doubt that Edison has taken on significant challenges.

Edison's portfolio is almost entirely made up of schools in distressed neighborhoods, areas with a demographic profile similar to that of the city of Philadelphia. About 70 percent of Edison students are poor enough to qualify for federal lunch subsidies, and more than 80 percent are black or Hispanic.

Edison officials say their schools are doing better because of innovative systems for hiring principals, checking student progress monthly, and teaching reading to older children. Edison schools use the Success For All system, which places students in small, well-paced, frequently tested groups for teaching reading. It gives home computers to students in the 3rd grade and up. It has longer school days and school years than ordinary public schools. Thomas Toch, a writer at the Washington-based National Center on Education and the Economy, praised innovations such as computer cameras for preliminary principal-hiring interviews and frequent dismissals of underperforming managers.

. . . But No Profits

If educational performance were the only yardstick, Edison would probably rank among the best urban school districts. But it has to please more than just parents and policymakers. Edison has to turn a profit, and its continuing failure to do so had pushed its stock price well below $1 a share by the end of August 2002 (see figure 20.1).

Moreover, the teacher unions, whose members work in schools Edison is trying to manage, tend to bristle at the suggestion that a private company might make a profit on their turf, further complicating the company's progress and provoking fervent protests in some cities. The demonstrations in Philadelphia began when Ridge announced in the summer of 2001 that he was awarding Edison a $2.7 million contract to study and make proposals for dealing with the financial and academic crisis in the Philadelphia schools.

The local union, the Philadelphia Federation of Teachers (PFT), repeated its long opposition to a state takeover and to any private companies running schools. There was also resistance from some students. Eric Braxton, the 26-year-old director of the Philadelphia Student Union, an organization of 4,000 politically active high school students, began to organize marches and sit-ins. "Edison had a huge debt and they were trying to alleviate their difficulties by opening more schools," he said. "We saw an inherent conflict of interest."

Lois Yampolsky led parental opposition in northeast Philadelphia. Her neighbors were mostly white, middle-class Catholics and Jews, but she embraced the anti-Edison views of some African American leaders in poorer parts of the city. "From the moment I read about Edison and its history," she said, "I was determined to keep them out of the Philadelphia schools." Edison officials said Yampolsky resisted their peace offerings. Adam Tucker, an Edison executive working on community relations, said she refused an invitation to visit an Edison school. "She said, 'I am not going to a dog and pony show,'" Tucker said.

As expected, the report Edison submitted to the state was a long list of Philadelphia's failings. Fifty percent of Philadelphia students dropped out before graduating from high school. In the past decade, the report said, the Philadelphia schools had spent more than $10 billion "with no clear accountability for the results." The school district "finds itself overwhelmed with considerable, institutionalized issues across many critical functions, including a dizzying array of curricula with little centralized district control over them . . . and a poor and uncoordinated [information technology] system that leaves the District powerless to understand and use both student and educator performance data."

The report was loudly denounced by Edison's critics. "They pointed out everything they thought was being done poorly . . . and said they were the solution," said U.S. representative Chaka Fattah, a former state legislator.

But Ridge, who praised the report, had unique leverage over the future of the Philadelphia schools. Under a law passed in 1998, the state could take over the city's education system if it experienced any of a long list of financial problems, including a severe deficit. In the summer of 2001, Philadelphia schools were $215 million in the red, the result of long years of under-funding, according to city officials, or long years of mismanagement, according to their critics. The city had made up the difference with expense cuts and one-time revenue infusions. This left the city vulnerable to a determined move in Harrisburg, where the Republicans controlled the legislature.

Ridge was called to Washington to become President George W. Bush's homeland security adviser, but a plan for a state takeover of the city schools was already under way. Debra Kahn, Philadelphia's secretary of education, said Street had three choices: (1) continue to go from crisis to crisis, (2) endure a hostile state takeover, or (3) form a partnership with the state to change the way the schools were run. Ridge was replaced by the lieutenant governor, Mark Schweiker, in October 2001. In December, Schweiker and Street agreed to the creation of the five-member School Reform Commission, which would replace the city school board. Three members would be appointed by Schweiker, two by Street.

Commissioning Edison

Schweiker, a wealthy management consultant, was, from the very beginning of his governorship, a lame duck. He announced that he would not run in 2002 for a full term, a move that Edison's opponents saw would make him less effective in fighting for Ridge's plan.

Nonetheless, the new School Reform Commission had the authority to hire independent contractors to run the school system's headquarters as well as individual schools. State officials had suggested that Edison might run the central office, but city groups—particularly the teacher union—were intensely opposed. For Edison to take over a system based on its own recommendation "was a clear conflict of interest," said Barbara Goodman, a spokesperson for the PFT. Street said he thought the state was underestimating the challenge and overestimating Edison's abilities. He set up an office at school headquarters and said he would not leave until the idea of Edison's running the building was discarded. Schweiker bowed to the pressure, withdrawing the original proposal in exchange for Street's agreement to let Edison be a consultant and run several schools.

With the political campaign against Edison in high gear, the School Reform Commission announced a compromise. Edison would get only half the number of schools it asked for, but more than any other private group. The commission identified seventy schools in need of special help, of which Edison would manage twenty. Another twenty-five were assigned to two other for-profit companies and two universities. Twenty-one schools were to be restructured under the direction of a district team—an attempt to show what locals could do, just as Holmes did in Wichita—while four other schools were to be turned into charter schools.

Turning twenty schools over to Edison was a victory for advocates of school privatization. But it was a failure in the eyes of Wall Street, where the expectation was that Edison would receive forty schools. Edison also suffered a series of blows to its financial image. The company accepted a Securities and Exchange Commission finding that it had improperly reported its receipt of money for teachers' salaries and other expenses as revenue in four out of sixty-two contracts. In June, however, Edison announced that two financial institutions, Chelsey Capital and Merrill Lynch, had agreed to loan the company $40 million. (In August Edison said the deal had been revised, with Chelsey Capital being replaced as a lender by a new company, School Services, Inc.)

Community Relations

For local educators and parents, the events leading up to Edison's arrival were traumatic. Truddie Kellam, who had both a child and a grandchild at Kenderton Elementary, said she had not liked the state takeover of the city schools. "I felt like we didn't count," she said. Kelley Elementary principal Mike Garafola had reacted viscerally to his school's being placed on the list of seventy elementary and middle schools in need of special help. "It was like being kicked in the stomach," he said. The school's 400 children, 94 percent of them poor enough to qualify for federal lunch subsidies, scored far below national averages, but they had shown some improvement and Garafola resented the school's getting no credit for that.

At a community meeting organized by Edison, Kellam asked many questions. She read the pamphlets, but they were too vague for her. She kept pushing and found herself appointed by Edison to the panel interviewing candidates for principal of the school. Like other parents, she had concerns about a private company taking over, but that was nothing compared with her frustration at the many failures of the past. "The problem is the children and their education," she said. "Money has been spent and they still are not getting it." So, she said, she was willing to give Edison a chance.

Among the Edison executives leading the community meetings were Holmes, from Wichita, and Ken Cherry, just arrived from Maryland. In Baltimore, Cherry had been a public school teacher and then an Edison academy director, partly responsible for one of the company's most celebrated recent successes. The Maryland state school board had taken over three of Baltimore's lowest-scoring elementary schools, Templeton, Gilmor, and Montebello, and given them to Edison. In April, just after the Philadelphia commission announced it was giving twenty schools to Edison, the *Baltimore Sun* reported big improvements in the Edison schools in Baltimore.

To make the same thing happen in Philadelphia, Edison officials said, they had to have the right principals. The company called an evening meeting at its temporary headquarters at the Buttonwood Hotel for the principals of the twenty schools it had been assigned. Garafola, who had been principal of Kelley Elementary since 1993, said the body language at the long table was unmistakable. "I could have written down how many would stay at Edison and how many would not," he said. Some crossed their arms. Some turned their backs. But Garafola and others liked what they heard.

Several principals said they liked the fact that Edison promised to weave character education into every class. Holmes had seen how that had worked in Wichita. "A lot of the children we are working with are coming out of a culture of poverty that is very different from the culture of the middle-class world and the working world," she said. "A lot of times teachers who come out of the middle-class world expect behaviors out of children that the children don't even know they are expected to do because they haven't been taught. So you just explain to them, hey, let me tell you . . . what you will do when you become an adult and go to the adult world." By July, Edison knew that eight of the twenty principals had agreed to stay at their schools, including Garafola.

New Leadership

In July 2002 the commission named Vallas, a finance expert widely praised for his work as chief executive officer of the Chicago schools, as CEO of the Philadelphia schools. He squashed what remained of a proposal to have Edison also serve as a consultant to district headquarters for an additional $18 million to $24 million. "We don't need a lead education consultant," said Vallas, who signed a $225,000-a-year contract. "That's what I'm here for." Nonetheless, he promised to make sure the delicate arrangements between city and state would go forward, with Edison running more schools in Philadelphia than any other independent group.

The story of Edison in Philadelphia, however it works out, is likely to demonstrate two truths about improving schools. First, factors that have little to do with children are often very important. The strength of the PFT and its resistance to change, the desire to find a political compromise that would give all combatants some sense of victory, the vestiges of old battles over money and race, and Edison's precarious financial status all had great influence over the number of schools Edison received and the initial support it had from teachers and parents.

Second, improvement in achievement is not going to be big or fast. Edison can point to overall gains and to recent increases in scores in Baltimore and Washington, D.C. Its critics can point to drops in Edison scores in some grades in a few cities. But few programs have succeeded in sustaining significant annual improvement in a significant number of schools for several years in a row. The most impressive rises in student achievement have occurred in isolated cases in a few schools—for instance, the Advanced Placement program at Garfield High School in East Los Angeles or the KIPP middle schools in Houston and the Bronx.

Holmes expects more though. "I came to work for Edison because I believe in their design and saw what a unique opportunity they had in Philadelphia," Holmes said. "If they can prove that twenty schools can be reformed en masse, then why not an entire district?" When she first went to Colvin, the school in Wichita that bested Edison with Edison's methods, "I would never have allowed my children to attend there," she said. "Now many of the staff bring their children to Colvin. When the Philly schools are good enough for my children, we will have succeeded."

JAY MATHEWS is an education columnist at the *Washington Post*.

CHAPTER TWENTY-ONE

Home Schooling: The Nation's Fastest-growing Education Sector

Christopher W. Hammons

In recent years, home schooling, once considered a method born more of religious zealotry than a concern for academics, has captured a surprising amount of positive attention. This is due in no small part to the success of home schoolers at the nationally televised Scripps Howard National Spelling Bee. This year, 13-year-old Sean Conley of Anoka, Minnesota, became the third winner of the annual spelling bee in the past five years to have been home schooled. The previous year had been a sort of coming-out party for home schoolers: Eight of the finalists had been home schooled, with the top three slots all going to home schoolers. The winner of the 2000 spelling bee, 12-year-old George Thampy of Missouri, was also first runner-up in the 2000 National Geographic Bee. An astounding 10 percent of the 2001 spelling bee contestants were home schooled, even though home schoolers make up no more than 2 percent of the student population. Sean Conley's parents seem to have favored an approach high on self-discovery, called "unschooling" in some quarters of the home schooling movement. "Basically, home schooling lets me learn whatever I want," Conley told Scripps Howard. "There are a lot of different ways to home school, and the way that I did it, my parents didn't necessarily teach me. They taught me some things, but a lot of things I just learned on my own."

Home schooling is a small but fast-growing movement that includes, but is certainly not limited to, an eclectic mix of Christian fundamentalists, aging hippies, and inner-city minorities chastened by highly dysfunctional public schools. Their motivations range from conservative concerns about the values taught in public schools to more liberal worries that public schools stress conformity over creativity. Stereotyping is no longer possible in a movement that is just as likely to include Creationists as it is avid fans of Howard Gardner's theories of multiple intelligences. In fact, the standardized-testing binge in many states may be the largest source of new converts to home schooling.

In the political arena, home schoolers, faced with repeated efforts to bring them within the regulatory reach of local, state, and federal governments, have developed potent defensive strategies—to the point that home schooling has become an almost invincible part of the U.S. education system. For instance, during the 1994 reauthorization of the federal Elementary and Secondary Education Act, California congressman George Miller offered an amendment that would have required all public school teachers to be certified in the subjects they teach. As reported by political scientist Morris Fiorina in *The New American Democracy*, advocates of home schooling such as the Home School Legal Defense Association were convinced that this might require home schoolers to obtain formal certification in order to teach their children at home. The word was quickly spread via electronic communications, and Congress was soon deluged with attacks on the amendment. Within a few days Congress received more than half a million communications from enraged home schoolers and their ideological allies. A floor amendment to kill Miller's proposal added statutory language that exempted home schooling from the legislation; it passed 424–1. For good measure, the Democratically controlled Congress then passed another amendment declaring that the legislation did not "permit, allow, encourage, or authorize any federal control over any aspect of any private, religious, or home school." In another demonstration of home schoolers' political clout, Congress, by unanimous consent, declared October 1–7, 2000, National Home Education Week.

The exact number of students schooled at home is difficult to pin down, but estimated growth is rapid (see figure 21.1). In 1990, the federal government estimated that some 300,000 students were being home schooled. Just six years later, Patricia Lines of the U.S. Department of Education put the number of home-schooled children at approximately 700,000 during the 1996–1997 school year, potentially increasing to 1 million by 1997–98. In 1997, Brian Ray of the National Home Education Research Institute estimated the home-schooling population during the 1996–1997 school year at 1.15 million and predicted it would rise to at least 1.3 million by 1999–2000. The most recent survey, released in August 2001 by the Department of Education, estimated that 850,000 children—1.7 percent of all K–12 students

Figure 21.1. A Burgeoning Movement

The number of students taught at home has increased at least threefold in less than ten years.

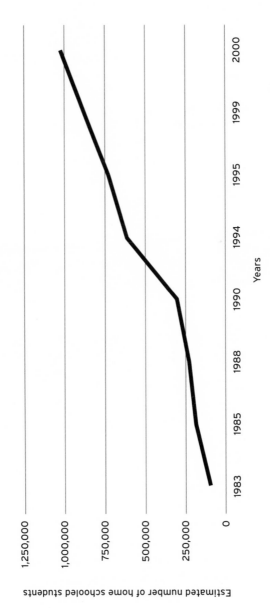

Estimated number of home schooled students

Years

SOURCE: Sam Abrams, from Department of Education reports.

nationwide—were being home schooled in the spring of 1999, noting that the total could range from 700,000 to 1 million students.

Two years later, let's use a conservative estimate of 1 million students during the 2001–2002 academic year. This still represents a large swath of students carved out of the public school system—twice the total number of children attending charter schools and about a quarter of the nation's private school population.

More and more of these home-schooled students are applying for college admission. Of students taking the ACT college entrance exam, the number of students labeling themselves "home schooled" rose 35 percent between 1997 and 1998, from 1,926 students to 2,610 students. (Note that the data are limited because the American College Testing Board only began tracking home schoolers in 1997.) Between 1998 and 1999 the numbers continued to increase rapidly, from 2,610 to 3,257 students. The largest gain occurred between 1999 and 2000, when the number of home schoolers increased from 3,257 students to 4,593—an increase of more than 41 percent.

Home schoolers perform well on these college entrance exams—slightly better than national averages, in fact. For three consecutive years, home-schooled students have scored higher on the two major college entrance exams—the ACT and SAT—than their traditionally educated peers. For the 1999–2000 school year, home schoolers' average score on the ACT was 22.8, compared with a national average of 21 points. On the SAT, home schoolers earned a score of 1100, compared with a national average of 1019. The 81-point difference is significant given that many college-bound students pay hundreds or thousands of dollars for SAT prep courses in an effort to raise their scores by 50 to 100 points.

Home schoolers scored highest on the ACT Reading and English test, outscoring traditional students by at least three points. Home schoolers also did better on the ACT Science test, but by only one point. On ACT Math, home schoolers scored lower than traditional students by a tenth of a percentage point. On the math portion of the SAT, however, home schoolers scored 532 points, compared with the national average of 514 points. Home schoolers also did better on the verbal portion of the SAT, scoring 568, compared with the national average of 505 points. Of course, these data only compare college-bound home schoolers with other college-bound students, thus giving an incomplete picture of home-schooling performance.

The finding that home schoolers score slightly higher than traditional students on standardized tests is not new. In 1998, the Home School Legal Defense Association commissioned the largest research study to date of home education in America. Conducted by Lawrence Rudner of the ERIC Clearinghouse on Assessment and Evaluation, the study analyzed data from the achievement-test scores of about 21,000 home-schooled students. All students took the same tests: the Iowa Test of Basic Skills in grades K–8 and the tests of Achievement and Proficiency in grades 9–12. Home schoolers scored higher than students in public or private schools at every grade level. On average, home schoolers appear to perform about three grade levels above their public school peers. It is important to note, however, that Rudner's study was based on a survey given by Bob Jones University to a sample of families who used the university's standardized testing program. No data exist on the percentage of home schoolers who take standardized tests; these data may be comparing the top 21,000 home schoolers with the average regular student. Nevertheless, we can safely say that Wayne Johnson, president of the California Teachers Association, was seriously misinformed in telling *Time* magazine, "Putting money into home schooling is throwing money down a rathole. You have no idea if that money is being spent properly or children are benefiting." Many children clearly are benefiting.

Home schoolers also find ways to succeed outside the classroom. Besides their disproportionate success in spelling bees, home schoolers participate in debate tournaments, public-speaking contests, and competitions that involve applied math and science. For instance, Chris Mayernik, a 12-year-old home-schooled student from Fairfax, Virginia, won the 1998 Lego Deep Sea Challenge Build-a-Thon. Contestants had to build a model of a futuristic underwater exploration vehicle out of the colorful blocks and describe how the vehicle would operate. Entries were judged on their creativity, usefulness, and scientific basis. Mayernik won for his multitiered creation, a high-tech research facility dubbed the "Titanic Search Station." Such contests are popular among home schoolers, at least in part because they provide a way to prove themselves to skeptical college admissions officers.

A Class Size of One

Rudner attributes the success of home schooling mainly to the parents, who tend to be well educated, financially secure, and greatly concerned about the education of their children. This high level of parental involvement may lead to a more rigorous academic environment at home than children would find in a traditional classroom setting. "Home schools can and do place a greater emphasis on study skills, critical thinking, working independently, and love of learning," writes Rudner. "Home schooling is typically one on one. Public schools typically have classes with 25 to 30 students and an extremely wide range of abilities and backgrounds. Home school parents are, by definition, heavily involved in their children's education; the same, unfortunately, is not true of all public or private school parents."

The individualized attention of home schooling means that students can learn at their own pace and master material before moving on. The opposite is also true: they are not held back by slower students. Parents can personalize the student's lessons, making home schooling more reminiscent of a classic tutorial system than a modern classroom setting. A minority of home schoolers even advocate "unschooling," which allows students to determine which subjects they will study based on their individual interests rather than follow a more rigid curriculum.

Interviews with parents who home school their children reveal a more traditional emphasis on reading, writing, and arithmetic, with less emphasis on social activities like gym, band, or study hall. In many cases, home-schooled students too young for high school reported studying advanced math, Greek, and Latin, and reading full-length biographies of historical figures. In short, the curricula followed by many home schoolers are certainly no less demanding than those offered in the public schools. Parents give many reasons for home schooling their kids, from worries about safety to the failure of schools to teach values, but their chief concern is still academics. Many parents simply feel that public schools do not teach their children what they need to know.

It is easy to dismiss the success of home schooling as simply further proof of the tenacious link between family background and academic achievement. Defenders of the public school system maintain that the majority of home schoolers, children reared in financially stable, two-parent families, are those most likely to succeed in any educational setting. But the differences between home schoolers and the rest of the student population are often overstated.

Parents who home school do tend to be better educated. Almost half (47 percent) of all home-schooled students have parents who hold a college degree, compared with only 33 percent of students in schools (see figure 21.2). This still means, however, that more than half of all home-schooled students learn from parents who do not hold a college degree. Unfortunately, there is no research available to determine whether the success of home-schooled children varies with parental education.

Meanwhile, there is virtually no difference between home schoolers and their peers in terms of income. In its 2001 study, the Department of Education found that an equal share—64 percent—of home-schooled students and those in schools live in households with incomes of $50,000 or less (see figure 21.3).

Figure 21.2. Educated Teachers

Almost half of all home-schooling parents hold a college degree, compared with a third of parents who send their children to school.

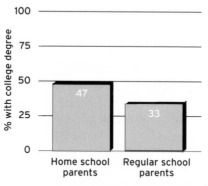

SOURCE: Department of Education, 2001.

Figure 21.3. No Wealth Effect

The share of home-schooling families with incomes below $50,000 is the same as among families who send their children to school.

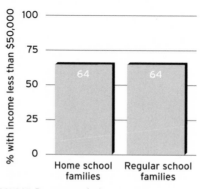

SOURCE: Department of Education, 2001.

To be sure, there is often a world of difference, academically speaking, between being raised by two college graduates, one of whom stays home to school the kids while the other goes off to a well-paying professional job, and being raised by two parents without college degrees, whose combined salaries total only $50,000. More than half, 52 percent, of all home-schooled students live in two-parent homes where only one parent works, compared with only 19 percent of those in school. Eighty percent of home schoolers live in two-parent homes, compared with 66 percent of those in school. Many home schoolers are reared in strong, stable families where the parents have made a nearly Herculean commitment to their children's education. Nevertheless, home-schooling families are by no means wealthy; they are largely middle class, with incomes slightly below the national average for all other families.

Higher Education

According to a 1997 study by the Home School Legal Defense Association, 69 percent of home schoolers go to college, compared with 71 percent of public school graduates. As a growing number of home schoolers prepare to leave home, colleges and universities will be forced to make tough decisions regarding the admission of these unique students. Home schoolers face some unusual challenges in applying for college. For instance, how much weight will admissions officers put on letters of recommendation from Mom and Dad or on transcripts produced by home-schooling parents on their home computer?

Common to most college admissions requirements is some record of what the student has achieved or learned during the home-schooling process. Many home schoolers maintain portfolios of their work and a list of their accomplishments (books read, papers written, contests entered, awards won) to submit as part of their application. As many as two-thirds of American colleges will accept transcripts drafted by parents. There are also education companies that will test students in particular subjects and provide transcripts based on their performance.

To further buttress their applications, many parents enroll their home schoolers in college summer courses and then submit their grades as proof that their students can handle college-level work. Letters of recommendation are often obtained from employers, volunteer coordinators, or outside educators. Home-schooled students are now enrolled at institutions as varied as Appalachian Bible College, Dakota County Technical College, the University of Oregon, the United States Military Academy, the University of Chicago, and Stanford University. Home schoolers are enrolled at nineteen of the top twenty national universities in the country. Thirty-six home-schooled students applied for admission to Stanford during the 2000 school year. Nine were admitted and joined the 2000 freshman class. This constitutes a 25 percent acceptance rate for home schoolers, nearly double the acceptance rate for other students.

The larger question is how home-schooled students are faring in college settings. A report released at the 1997 National Christian Home Educators Leadership Conference in Boston, Massachusetts, tracked 180 students—60 from public schools, 60 from private schools, and 60 home schoolers—over four years of college. The study compared the students in five areas determined to be important to college success—academic, cognitive, spiritual, affective-social, and psychomotor skills. In academics, home schoolers ranked first in 10 of 12 indicators. Other studies have shown home schoolers to have above-average grade-point averages.

In many ways the nature of home schooling, with its emphasis on independent study, seems to prepare students for college in a way that public schools may not. "Home schoolers bring certain skills—motivation, curiosity, the capacity to be responsible for their education—that high schools don't induce very well," a Stanford University admissions officer recently told the *Wall Street Journal*.

By far the most frequent criticism of home schooling is that it fails to prepare children to deal with the social aspects of college life—or, for that matter, the social aspects of life in general. A National Education Association (NEA) position paper claims that "home-schooling programs cannot provide the student with a comprehensive education experience." But there is plenty of evidence to the contrary. The 1997 Home School Legal Defense Association study found that 98 percent of 1,926 home-schooled students surveyed were involved in two or more extracurricular activities. More than 80 percent said they played frequently with people outside their family and went on field trips. Almost half of those surveyed indicated that they participated in group sports or music classes outside their home. Many public schools even allow home schoolers to participate in organized extracurricular events such as team sports, science labs, or social organizations. The same critics who say that home schooling is detrimental to the socialization of children, namely the NEA, would also deny them access to extracurricular activities in the public schools.

In fact, parents often mention socialization as one of the key reasons why they decided to home school their children in the first place (see figure 21.4). Citing increased school violence, lack of discipline in the classroom, overcrowding, and a poor learning environment, many parents simply feel that

Figure 21.4. Why Home School?

Parents give many reasons for home schooling their children, but none so often as the feeling that they can provide a better education at home.

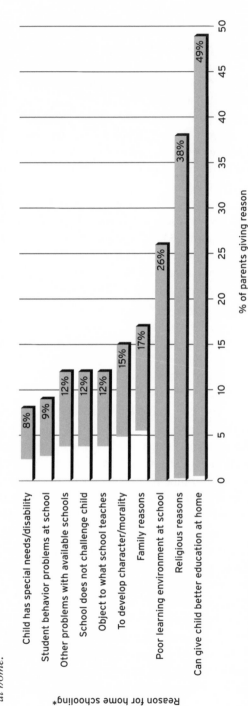

* Parents could give more than one answer.

SOURCE: Department of Education, 2001.

they can do a better job at home. Furthermore, some scholars note that classroom socialization is not always a positive experience. The crucible of adolescence, especially in an environment as mean-spirited and competitive as a middle school or high school can be, may lead to weak social skills, low self-esteem, and dependence on one's peers for self-definition.

The strongest evidence against the charge that home schoolers tend to be socially inept, however, is found in the stories of home schoolers who are enrolled in colleges and universities across the nation. Marlyn Lewis, director of admissions at Harvard University, maintains, "The home-schooled students at Harvard are indistinguishable from the other students. They are all high-caliber individuals. They are highly motivated, excel academically, and have no unusual problems adapting to campus life."

The *New York Times* has done a number of follow-up stories tracing home schoolers as they leave home and enter college life. Their interviews reveal that these students do not consider home schooling a barrier to college success, do not have abnormal anxieties, and generally meet the college challenge with few difficulties. In many cases, these students were among the best on campus, noted for their high GPAs, maturity, ability to express themselves, and intellectual curiosity. None of these students expressed any difficulty adapting to college social life.

Not for Everyone

Home schooling certainly has its limitations; it is not a panacea for modern education. It seems to thrive in stable two-parent families where one parent stays home, an increasingly endangered species of family organization. Home schools also lack the resources of public education. Most home-schooling families cannot afford the variety of materials that public schools make available to students. Such limitations are most acutely felt in the sciences, where lab equipment and supplies are outside the budget of most families. Many home schoolers simply do without. In addition, many parents feel uncomfortable teaching more-demanding subjects such as physics and chemistry. It is no surprise, then, that many children are home schooled until they reach high school and then enter the public school system.

On returning to the public school system, home schoolers do not always excel. One Houston-area high school teacher noted that home schoolers often suffer from a sort of culture shock when confronted with a modern high school. "More than anything, they have trouble adjusting to the rigid schedules and structure of a formal classroom. They are used to learning at their own pace, and they sometimes feel overwhelmed when they are hit with six subjects a day whether they like it or not. Their grades sometimes suffer because they can't keep up." One local area administrator also noted that home schoolers often suffer from "delusions of grandeur." Low test scores are assumed to be the fault of the teacher or school system, when in reality the parents' grading standards were simply more lax than those of the student's current teacher.

To complicate all these issues, the data on home schooling are very limited. By definition, parents who home school take a more active role in their children's education. It may very well be the case that these kids would succeed in most any academic environment, precisely because their parents have made education a family priority. It is thus difficult to come to definite conclusions about home schooling as an educational method.

My analysis of college admissions scores and acceptance rates suffers from the same selection effect, but perhaps to a greater degree. Here I am focusing not just on home schoolers, but on only those home schoolers bound for college. When I look at college admission tests, I am limiting the sample to those home schoolers who value higher education. The stories of superior academic achievement, higher test scores, and campus success may be less a function of home schooling than an indication of students who take their academic careers very seriously.

Nevertheless, home schoolers clearly do no worse than students educated in schools. Moreover, for many students, home schooling appears to be a flexible, engaging method that unlocks their creativity and inspires them to greater pursuits. Home schooling may not be for everyone, but for students and parents who are committed to the endeavor, it appears to be a viable alternative to public education.

CHRISTOPHER W. HAMMONS is associate professor in political science at Houston Baptist University.

CHAPTER TWENTY-TWO

⌒

School Choice in
No Child Left Behind

William G. Howell

James Caradonio can barely contain his odium for the federal government's latest efforts at education reform. The mere mention of the No Child Left Behind Act (NCLB) sparks a tirade: "Reductio ad absurdum, you know. But this is what we're dealing with in terms of this insanity. Oh, it's numbers and it looks great. We've got numbers. Simple. And it all looks great and it's just killing, killing teachers and killing principals." He should know. As the superintendent of schools in Worcester, Massachusetts, and the only superintendent to serve on the inaugural statewide NCLB Implementation Team, Caradonio possesses intimate knowledge of, and influence over, the law's local successes and failures.

The impact of NCLB, which Caradonio terms the No Teacher Left Standing Act, was supposed to be felt most strongly in urban centers with large minority and disadvantaged populations—places just like Worcester. Instead, during its first two years, NCLB appeared to have little impact at all.

As of June 2003, twelve of Worcester's fifty public schools had been labeled "in need of improvement" for two consecutive years, and five schools for three years in a row. During the 2002–2003 school year, under the new law's choice provisions, almost 4,700 students were entitled to transfer out of their failing schools and into one of the district's higher-performing schools. Roughly 1,800 students had the right to use Title I funds to obtain supplemental academic services from qualified public or private providers, another carrot the new law extends to children enrolled in underperforming schools.

As of December 2003, however, only one child in Worcester had switched schools. And just one more had taken advantage of the supplemental services provision to obtain tutoring from a provider outside of the public school system.

For the most part, local officials have taken the fact that so few parents have switched schools or demanded private supplemental services as confirmation of the district's excellence. But is there really no more than one family that wishes to change schools? If there are others, what is limiting their exercise of choice? And why aren't parents taking advantage of the supplemental services by private providers that are guaranteed to them under the law?

Obviously, the implementation of any major piece of legislation proceeds in fits and starts, making it much too early to proclaim NCLB an unmitigated success or failure. Nevertheless, for reasons inherent in the writing of the law, districts' incentives to implement it, and parents' current knowledge of its provisions, early returns suggest that NCLB is not likely to revolutionize public education in Worcester anytime soon.

Already on the Move

Worcester is the third largest school system in the state of Massachusetts, serving roughly 25,000 students in 46 public schools (36 elementary, 4 middle, 5 high, and one pre-K–12 school). The federal government provides just 10 percent of the district's $265 million annual budget, with state appropriations, local contributions, grants, and revolving funds covering the balance.

Worcester's schools house an increasingly diverse and disadvantaged population of students. During the past two decades, the percentage of nonwhite students has more than doubled, from roughly 20 percent in 1980 to slightly more than 50 percent in 2002. The district provides 7 percent of its students, representing no fewer than fifty different languages, with English as a Second Language (ESL) tutorial programs. More than 50 percent of the district's students qualify for the federal lunch program, a common measure of disadvantage. And on the Massachusetts Comprehensive Assessment System (MCAS)—the state's standardized test, first administered in the spring of 1998—Worcester public school students in different grade levels were 8 to 20 percentage points less likely to score at or above proficiency than were students statewide.

Making matters worse, Worcester's schools serve an extremely mobile population of families. Between 1999 and 2002, on average, 23 to 37 percent of elementary students changed schools within a given academic year; among middle schools, mobility rates ranged from 24 to 32 percent; and for high schools, from 24 to 28 percent. Much of this movement occurred across district lines. For instance, during the 2001–2002 school year, 12 percent of Worcester elementary students changed schools and another 21 percent left the district altogether. That such a high proportion of Worcester's families are moving in and out of the district exacerbates the problems of tracking students and delivering a coherent education program.

Schools that failed to meet their "adequate yearly progress" targets, as required by NCLB, serve some of the most mobile student populations. Among those elementary schools that were deemed in need of improvement between 1999 and 2001, mobility rates reached as high as 51 percent. When determining whether a school has made adequate progress, the state does not account for these mobility rates—a fact that almost every public official in the district is quick to point out. "You really can only determine whether you're making progress or not if you're testing the same kids, year after year," says Worcester mayor Timothy Murray. "And that's something that is not lost, I think, on parents or the School Committee."

The causes of mobility vary widely, though by most accounts it has little to do with parents seeking better schools. As Brian O'Connell, vice chair of the city's School Committee, notes, "Parents are moving from one apartment to another or husband and wife separate, mother and boyfriend separate, evictions take place, friends go off, parents move, parents are homeless, parents leave in November to go back to Puerto Rico and come back in the spring and come back to a different school."

In short, even without satisfying the choice provisions of the new law, the Worcester school district must cope with a dizzying amount of movement in and out of its schools. Schools struggle just to keep track of their students from year to year. Moreover, the district already provides a significant amount of choice. During the 2002–2003 school year, only 61 percent of students attended their neighborhood public school. The rest attended one of two charter schools or six citywide magnet schools, participated in the interdistrict choice program, or joined in the district's desegregation plan.

Friendly Discouragement

Ultimately, districts are responsible for informing parents of their rights and opportunities under NCLB. But given the challenges that Worcester faces, along with the incentives to safeguard public finances, it should come as no surprise that administrators subtly, and not so subtly, discouraged families from transferring their children out of underperforming schools.

In the spring of 2003, the district notified families at underperforming schools of their rights under NCLB. The designation "in need of improvement," the letters explained, "means that although these schools are succeeding in some areas, there is still room for growth." After highlighting limitations of the NCLB grading system, the letter underscored unattractive features of the law's choice provisions. For example, "In most instances, because of space limitations, we may not be able to transfer every child in a family to the same school." Furthermore, the letter noted, families with children at underperforming schools who switch schools forfeit their rights to supplemental services.

The letter goes on to cite many exciting developments in Worcester public schools. "We believe that your child's school is on its way towards achieving the NCLB goals. The principal and teachers at your child's school have implemented new programs and services during the school day as well as after school. These include: a proven literacy approach designed to meet the individual needs of the students; the Everyday Mathematics program for students in grades K–6; an after-school program to help students improve MCAS scores; and other special programs."

The district then set up a multistage procedure for parents to exercise their right to choose another school. The first step involves a meeting between a parent and her child's principal, wherein the parent has an opportunity to explain why she is unhappy with her child's school. The principal can then clarify the problems with NCLB and show why the family ought to stay put. Principals also explain why students are best served by receiving supplemental services within their schools. (The district offers an academically based after-school program for Title I students, which qualifies as supplemental services under NCLB. More than 800 students are currently enrolled in this program.)

Not surprisingly, very few parents requested a meeting with their principal. According to Elaine De Araujo, principal of Harlow Street Elementary School, "Nobody has wanted to change. Not one parent has come forward. If you were here, you would see why. You would see what a nurturing, wonderful place this is." Ruthann Melancon, the principal of Elm Park Elementary School, notes, "A couple of parents came to me thinking that the school was going to close. I sat down with these sets of parents and reassured them. They've been here since preschool and they have liked what they've seen." Under NCLB, both Harlow Street and Elm Park have failed to make adequate progress every year that the schools have been evaluated.

If, after consulting with the school principal, parents still want to change schools, they must schedule yet another meeting at the Parent Information

Center. Robert Vartanian, the center's director, says that he has met with just two families interested in NCLB choice, and only one of those families ended up switching their child to a different school. Each time, Vartanian has taken the opportunity to reiterate many of the points made by the school principal. Perhaps most consequentially, though, Vartanian informs parents that the district may not be able to accommodate their request to attend any specific school. Indeed, since the district is obligated only to offer parents a choice of two schools that did make adequate progress, that is all they can expect to receive. There are also no guarantees that either of these schools will be near the family's home or that transportation will be provided over the longer term of a child's education. As district official Joan Fitton explains, "The feds told us we had to offer a choice, not the parents' choice, but a choice."

Standing on the Sidelines

The Worcester district also uses its control over the flow of information to limit the influence of NCLB's supplemental services provision. While the district can advertise its tutoring and after-school services directly to parents, private providers hoping to capture a piece of this market have few opportunities to get their foot in the door. As Seppy Basili, vice president of Kaplan K12 Learning Services, notes, "The school district is the owner of the relationship between provider and the parent. And I can't get in." The five companies with contracts to provide supplemental services in Massachusetts—Brainfuse (The Trustforte Corporation), Huntington Learning Centers, Kaplan K12 Learning Services, Princeton Review, and the Summit Educational Group—do not even know which students are eligible for Title I funding and, thus, supplemental services. Therefore they must rely on the district and its representatives to present their services to parents in as favorable a light as possible.

Curiously though, private providers are not complaining yet—at least publicly—perhaps for fear of alienating district administrators, on whose cooperation and goodwill they depend. Meanwhile, for some companies that provide private tutoring, the state-mandated amount involved ($1,238 per year, per student in Worcester) is simply insufficient to warrant serious investment.

For instance, Huntington Learning Centers, which have the distinct honor of having served the only Worcester student to obtain supplemental services from outside of the public school system, typically contract with families for 100 to 150 hours of individual tutoring. The Title I money available for supplemental services, however, covers just thirty to forty hours of tutoring, which would require either an abbreviated or an entirely restructured program.

Notes Mark Shobin, the owner of three Huntington franchises in Massachusetts, "From a financial perspective, it doesn't make sense for us to try to corral these students into our program. We are happy to work with and develop programs for those students who seek us out. But I am not going to seek them out."

Transportation problems further inhibit parents' interest in sending their child to private providers. "We don't provide transportation for supplemental services," explains Joan Fitton. "And neither do the supplemental service providers provide transportation. So, there, right away, is a big glitch in the whole program. We're not required to provide transportation. And, to be honest, to send money out of the district, I'm not sure that we would even offer to do that." As long as children continue with their own school's program, parents need not worry about transporting them across town during the middle of the day. The district benefits as well, since it avoids losing Title I funds to private providers.

What Parents Know and Want

Many parents in Worcester simply do not know much about their school's performance or their rights under NCLB. In a telephone survey conducted during the summer of 2003, public school parents routinely expressed confusion over basic points of fact. Overall, 25 percent of parents surveyed in Worcester had children who attended underperforming schools. However, when asked whether their child's school was on the list of underperforming schools, just 6 percent of parents said yes, 54 percent said no, and 41 percent said that they did not know (see figure 22.1). Fully 93 percent of parents of children in underperforming public schools either did not know that their school was deemed in need of improvement or incorrectly thought that their child attended a school that had made adequate yearly progress.

As one might expect, levels of knowledge varied depending on parents' socioeconomic status and ethnicity. Whereas 54 percent of whites knew whether their child attended an underperforming school, just 28 percent of African Americans and Hispanics did. Just 26 percent of parents born outside of the United States and 17 percent of parents of children who receive English as a Second Language instruction knew whether their school was underperforming.

Are parents interested in choice? Among those with children in underperforming schools, just 13 percent said there was another public school in the district to which they were interested in sending their children (see figure 22.2). By comparison, 8 percent of parents of children in schools that had

Figure 22.1. Status Unknown

When Worcester parents with children in failing schools were asked if they knew of this fact, just 6 percent answered correctly. Just 29 percent of parents in the ten largest school districts in Massachusetts knew their child was attending a failing school.

Responses from Parents with Children in Failing Schools When Asked the Status of Their Child's School Under NCLB

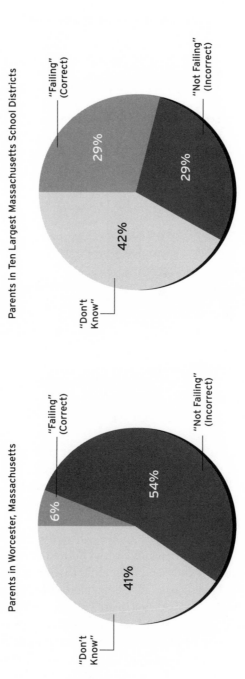

Parents in Worcester, Massachusetts

Parents in Ten Largest Massachusetts School Districts

Note: Percentages total more than 100 percent due to rounding. Survey was of a stratified random sample of 1,000 public school parents conducted in the summer of 2003. Worcester sub-sample was 250 parents. "In need of improvement" is official term for what has generally become known as failing schools.

SOURCE: Author.

Figure 22.2. Going Private or Bust

*Just 13 percent of Worcester parents with children in failing schools said
there was another public school in the district to which they were interested
in sending their children. Interest in switching schools grew dramatically when
parents were offered the option of transferring their children to a private school.*

Interest in School Choice Among Parents with Children in Failing Schools

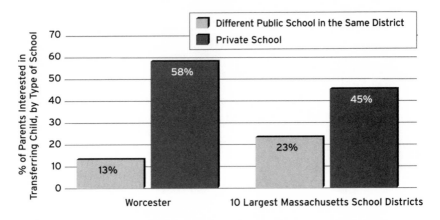

Note: Survey of a stratified random sample of 1,000 public school parents conducted in
the summer of 2003. Worcester sub-sample was 250 parents.
SOURCE: Author.

made adequate yearly progress said they were interested in another school.
Consistent with these responses, parents appeared to be satisfied with their
public schools. Eighty-seven percent of parents with children in schools that
made adequate progress gave their school an A or a B, as did 80 percent of
parents with children in underperforming schools.

However, interest in choice spiked when the options included private
schools. Fully 58 percent of parents with children in underperforming schools
said that they would rather send their child to a private school than their current public school (see figure 22.2), compared with 39 percent of parents with
children in schools that made adequate progress. When asked, "If costs were
not an obstacle, which type of school would you most like your child to
attend?" 49 percent of parents with children in underperforming schools
picked a private school, 44 percent a public school in their district, 4 percent
a public school outside of the district, and just 2 percent a charter school.

The clause "if costs were not an obstacle" apparently freed up some parents' imaginations to consider elite (read: expensive) private schools. When asked to name a preferred private school, roughly half named independent private schools (the most popular being Worcester Academy and Milton Academy), with tuitions that eclipse the values of even the most generous school vouchers offered in public and private programs across the country. The rest identified a Catholic or Protestant day school, most of which were located within or near the city of Worcester.

Misalignments of information, interests, and schooling options have effectively limited NCLB's influence in Worcester. Those parents who qualify for public school choice and supplemental services are the least likely to know it; fewer than one in ten parents with children in schools that failed to make adequate progress could correctly identify their school's status. Meanwhile, Worcester parents are most interested in pursuing schooling alternatives that NCLB does not furnish.

The Road Ahead

In Worcester distrust of NCLB runs rampant. While many principals extol the benefits of using student achievement data as a diagnostic tool, officials downtown remain deeply suspicious of the longer-term consequences that will accompany repeated failures to make adequate yearly progress. Notes Caradonio, "We're screwed. This whole thing has been set up to make sure it looks bad so we can bring in the miracle drugs, the vouchers, and all this is very clear." School Committee member Kathleen Toomey expressed much the same sentiment to the town newspaper. "[NCLB] is one way to promote flight out of city schools," she said. "Proponents of charter schools will be able to say, 'Look, see, those public schools are not working.'" Local officials have assumed a defensive posture, poised at every opportunity to minimize the impact of a law that they think is designed to set them up for failure.

Some short-term solutions may encourage higher participation rates. It is sheer folly, for instance, to expect school districts to vigorously implement an accountability scheme that disrupts their school assignment procedures, drains money from their coffers, and threatens their administrative autonomy. Until an independent organization is established that disseminates information about which schools are underperforming, which students qualify for choice and supplemental services, and which providers are available, there is little reason to expect that NCLB will induce an exodus of students from underperforming schools.

However, even if an independent agency were established, a massive real-location of students and resources would be unlikely. The district will continue to pursue its strategies of blame avoidance. If the survey results are any indication, few qualifying families appear likely to switch to a different public school. And as the number of schools failing to make adequate progress grows, the number of options remaining for families will only dwindle.

WILLIAM G. HOWELL is associate professor of government at Harvard University.

CHAPTER TWENTY-THREE

Selling Supplemental Services

Siobhan Gorman

During the summer of 2002, Martha Fritchley was leafing through the Yellow Pages in search of tutoring firms. As an assistant superintendent of the Hall County school system in Georgia, Fritchley needed to enlist firms to tutor children in four underperforming schools in order to comply with the federal No Child Left Behind Act. She was particularly interested in home-based tutoring, and she happened on the local franchise of a company called Club Z.

Fritchley called the franchise's owner, Scott Morchower. While Morchower was unaware of the new federal law's tutoring provision, he was of course receptive to the idea. He offered his services to several more districts as well, becoming the sole provider in the 2002–2003 academic year of tutoring services for Forsyth County's seventy-five struggling students. Some of those students jumped as many as three grade levels.

"The results we came out with were awesome," says Morchower. So awesome, in fact, that he worked himself out of a contract: all the schools in Forsyth County left the failing schools list, meaning that their students were no longer eligible for tutoring services. During the 2002–2003 school year, students in the supplemental services program made up 20 percent of his business; Morchower figured they would account for 40 percent in 2003–2004. Instead, they again made up 20 percent. With such an unpredictable flow of clients, how should Morchower factor children from the federal program into his business plan? "I wish I knew," he says. "That's the $10 million question."

By some estimates it's actually the $2 billion question. That's how much additional revenue some tutoring providers say could be up for grabs in this new federally funded marketplace. But so far, less than 10 percent of eligible students are electing to participate, according to providers' estimates. Morchower said one of his toughest challenges is convincing parents that the service is free to them. Parents will often hang up on him because they think he's a telemarketer, he says. And sometimes parents simply don't want to acknowledge that their child needs help. "Even when I come out to the house, they ask, 'What's wrong with my kid?'" Morchower says.

These tutoring services, known in the law as "supplemental services," arguably represent the federal government's largest free-market experiment in education. In the rush to capture market share, more than 1,000 tutoring providers have signed up for the program. But market uncertainty, combined with differences in how school districts are administering the law, has produced some extremely rocky terrain for these firms. While most providers maintain an optimistic if-you-build-it-they-will-come mindset, the unevenness of parental participation and program implementation is causing significant anxiety.

The New Marketplace

Under the No Child Left Behind Act of 2001, supplemental educational services are funded by school districts with a portion of their allocation from the U.S. Department of Education. Georgia was early to implement its program; most states were just getting on board during the 2003–2004 academic year.

States first approve a group of tutoring providers. Then districts draw up their own contract with a subset of those providers; districts themselves can also serve as providers. Once the districts notify parents of their options, parents can enroll with a provider of their choosing.

Within this new marketplace, school districts hold enormous power as a result of their dual role—as both program administrator and potential provider. Districts also have little incentive to inform parents of the money available to them for tutoring, since districts get to keep any unused funds. Some providers allege that districts are not actually setting aside the money as required by law. "We've seen districts where the federal per-pupil allocation says it's $1,800 and the district will say it's $1,100," said one provider. "What happens to that other $700?"

The district's dual role also gives rise to a conflict of interest. The concern is that districts enjoy an unfair advantage over other providers because of their direct access to parents. Jeffrey Cohen, president of Catapult Learning (the tutoring firm formerly known as Sylvan Education Solutions), says that he has seen letters sent out by the district that automatically sign children up for the district's program unless the parent affirmatively decides to go with a different provider. "There's not a level playing field," he says.

To overcome these obstacles, most large providers are going around the districts by beefing up their own marketing efforts. Some providers, like Catapult Learning, are running ads and touting their programs with leaflets or promoters who go door-to-door, to shopping malls, and, when allowed, to the school.

Before No Child Left Behind, about $2 billion was spent each year in the retail tutoring market, according to Educate Inc., a national tutoring company formerly known as Sylvan Learning Systems and Catapult Learning's parent company. Half of the tutoring providers were small local companies and individuals, while the other half were regional or national firms. In addition to the retail tutoring market, a few companies, such as Catapult Learning, made an effort to promote public-private partnerships in tutoring, but the marketplace was not well defined.

It has been difficult to get a handle on the scope of the market for publicly funded tutoring created by the No Child Left Behind Act because the program is new and has so many moving parts. According to the U.S. Department of Education, private firms represented 72 percent of providers as of spring 2004. Of all providers, 6 percent were faith-based institutions and 10 percent were online tutoring firms. About a quarter of the providers were part of the public school system. Within a given state, public schools represent anywhere from zero to 80 percent of the providers. Likewise, among the states, online providers compose anywhere from zero to 47 percent of the available options.

This nascent marketplace has all the components of a high school melodrama; there is the popular crowd, the bullies, the overachievers, the earnest do-gooders, and the geeks. (The leading roles are played, in order, by large corporate tutoring providers; school districts; smaller national providers; local, largely nonprofit organizations; and online tutors.) At present, large corporate providers and school districts seem to be ruling the marketplace. And their shares are likely to increase as the program matures because of their ability to meet market demands. But without a chaperone in this new free-market niche in public education, it's been a schoolyard free-for-all.

The Popular Crowd

Jeffrey Cohen was following the supplemental services program long before it became law. As president of Catapult Learning, Cohen saw enormous potential for expansion under a federally funded tutoring program because it mirrored what he had already been doing for fifteen years—partnering with low-income schools to bolster their academic programs.

With their glossy brochures and brand recognition, large corporate providers are the popular kids. While there are 60 corporate tutoring providers that can be considered national firms, only a handful of them are real players. This small, elite group has the potential to garner a large market share because many of its members are approved in twenty to thirty states. They have also been tutoring K–12 clients for many years. So these companies are well positioned to scale up their business without enormous start-up costs, enabling them to take advantage of a growing, if unpredictable, market.

Catapult Learning's business model in this new marketplace is largely the same as before, with one exception: while Cohen deals solely with schools in his regular business, under supplemental services, he must get approved by the state, contract with a district, and then sell his product directly to parents.

Cohen says the supplemental services program offers him two opportunities: (1) to reach many more children, whose schools would not otherwise pay for Catapult's services; and (2) to build relationships with school districts, which could lead to further business outside the federal program.

At the beginning of the 2003–2004 school year, Catapult Learning was approved in thirty-one states. During the year, the firm served 25,000 students through the supplemental services program, up from 6,000 students the previous year. Catapult charges anywhere between $40 and $80 an hour. In the coming years, Cohen says his supplemental services enrollment will be in the "tens of thousands"; down the line, it could double his pre-supplemental services enrollment of 70,000 students. So far, though, Catapult remains in investment mode. "The first year, the program certainly wasn't profitable," Cohen says. His strategy is to ensure that Catapult is operating in as many locations as possible so that it is poised to take advantage of new business as parental demand picks up.

In contrast to Catapult's efforts to market directly to parents, Princeton Review, which is now approved in twenty-seven states, has taken a school-based tack, negotiating with districts in the hopes of becoming a district's or a school's sole provider. The goal is to avoid the headaches of working with school districts that are dragging their feet in implementing their programs. "I don't look at this as a retail business, like putting up billboards on the highways," says Rob Cohen, executive vice president of the company's K–12 division. "I'm looking for districts to call us up."

During the 2003–2004 school year, Princeton Review served 6,000 supplemental services students. Within the next few years, Cohen says his company could be serving as many as 10,000. "I believe we're running supplemental services, on a marginal basis, profitably today," he says.

A third strategy among big tutoring companies—a strategy popular among retail tutoring companies that operate from a storefront, like Huntington Learning Centers—is to continue just as they have been doing. These companies get state approval, contract with districts, and then open their doors. Transportation to these tutoring centers, which are often located in suburban strip malls, is up to the parents. For companies like Huntington, says Russ Miller, vice president for new business development, this presents the biggest challenge: getting students to come. Huntington is evaluating two new options for reaching supplemental services students. One is to establish centers in urban areas. The other is to partner with schools—in a strategy similar to Princeton Review's—to make the school a kind of learning center.

Competitors expected one player in this category, Edison Schools, to jump into the market immediately. Instead, Edison did not begin marketing itself as a tutoring provider until the late spring of 2003, after a year-long research effort. So far, the national school-management firm has gotten approved in only fifteen states. Nonetheless, largely due to the contract Edison signed with the New York City school system, its enrollment has grown quickly: the firm served 12,500 students in the 2003–2004 school year, said Joel Rose, who heads up Edison's supplemental services division, known as Newton Learning. Edison is among the companies with the most to gain from a successful supplemental services program because its core business depends on building relationships with school districts.

The Bullies

John Liechty knows a market when he sees one. At the beginning of the 2003–2004 school year, 186,000 of the nearly 750,000 students in the Los Angeles Unified School District were eligible for supplemental services (see table 23.1). As the associate superintendent for extended-day programs, Liechty wanted to keep the tutoring money in the district. He also saw the program as a chance to tap new ideas from private companies. So he applied to the state to be a supplemental services provider and then designed a Saturday school program that would contract out the curriculum and teaching to private providers.

While each district's reach is limited in scope, school districts, with their ability to be a provider and to control the district-wide funding, have an enormous amount of control over the tutoring options available. That level

Table 23.1. Approved Supplemental Services Providers in Chicago and Los Angeles for the 2004–2005 School Year

Chicago Public Schools	Los Angeles Unified School District
# Eligible for Tutoring Services: 270,000 of Chicago's 440,000 students	**# Eligible for Tutoring Services:** 230,000 of L.A.'s 750,000 students
At Stake: Under NCLB, the district must use at least 20 percent of its $263 million in Title I-A funding for supplemental services and choice programs.	**At Stake:** Under NCLB, the district must use at least 20 percent of its $361 million in Title I-A funding for supplemental services and choice programs.
In 2003–2004: 57,000 of 133,000 eligible students received tutoring	**In 2003–2004:** 18,550 of 186,000 eligible students received tutoring
% Tutored by Chicago Public Schools in 2003–2004: 74 percent	**% Tutored by LAUSD in 2003–2004:** 66 percent

Approved Providers:	Approved Providers:
Chicago School District	Beyond the Bell Learning Centers (LAUSD)
Achieve3000	A+ Educational
Babbage Net School, Inc.	ABC-Learn, Inc.
Brainfuse Online Instruction	Advanced Academics Inc.
Cambridge Educational Services	Boys and Girls Clubs of America
CS&C-Julex Learning	Brainfuse One-to-One Tutoring
EdSolutions, Inc.	Bresee Foundation
Failure Free Reading	Century/Learning Initiatives for Today
Gateway Learning Center	Club Z! In-Home Tutoring
HOSTS Learning	Education Station, A Sylvan Partnership
Huntington Learning Centers, Inc.	Educational & Tutoring Services
I CAN Learn Education System	Failure Free Reading
Kaplan K12 Learning Services	Huntington Learning Centers, Inc.
Kumon North America, Inc.	Kumon Math & Reading Centers
Lindamood-Bell Learning Processes	Math*Ability, Inc.
One-to-One Learning Center	Newton Learning
Princeton Review, Inc.	People Making Progress – Chess/Test Tutors
Progressive Learning	Professional Tutors of America, Inc.
Reading in Motion	Project IMPACT
SCORE! Educational Centers, Inc.	Say Yes! To Life
Socratic Learning, Inc.	SCORE! Educational Centers, Inc.
Sylvan Learning Systems, Inc.	SmartKids Tutoring & Learning Centers
Ventures Education Systems Corp.	SMARTHINKING, Inc.
Teachers Academy for Math & Science	Tutors of the Inland Empire
Wicker Park Learning Center	

SOURCES: Chicago Public Schools; Illinois State Board of Education; Los Angeles Unified School District; *Chicago Sun-Times; Chicago Tribune.*

of control offers up the opportunity for districts to bully other providers, and they are wielding that power in both obvious and subtle ways. Some districts, like Los Angeles, use their status to contract with private providers. Others, like Toledo Public Schools, have opted to develop their own programs.

In Los Angeles, about two-thirds of the 18,550 students who signed up for tutoring in the 2003–2004 school year joined the district's "Beyond the Bell" program (the other third signed up directly with the provider of their choice). Liechty is responsible for running the district's tutoring program and for administering the supplemental services program, which includes twenty-four different providers who have signed contracts with the district.

Each of the district's six tutoring centers is run by a different company, like Kaplan or CompassLearning. "Each one of those centers becomes almost a lab," Liechty says. "I'm looking for everybody and anybody to partner with." Liechty says the benefit of this arrangement is that the district can exercise more quality control and can bargain down the price. Liechty hopes to increase enrollment in the next several years to between 20,000 and 25,000 students. He also needs to figure out how to meet the children's needs without dipping into general district funds. So far, he is operating at a deficit, which he estimated at somewhere between $40,000 and $400,000.

Liechty says that while he tries to run the district's program fairly, he acknowledges that the district has an inside track with parents. "We don't hide that," he says. "There's no question the district is going to have an advantage." In addition, the money going to private providers comes out of a pot of federal money that districts have historically counted as their own, and they are understandably reluctant to lose those funds.

The Overachievers

Mark Lucas was skeptical about the opportunities presented by the new federal tutoring program. As the CEO and founder of Club Z's national operation, he wasn't sure the federal money would ever reach the pockets of for-profit providers. But when some Club Z franchises were awarded contracts, Lucas's royalties increased tenfold. That got his attention.

Meet the overachievers. Club Z is one of a number of smaller, national corporate players that have an opportunity to tap into an important niche: parents who want the reliability of a national company but the feel of a local tutor.

Launched in 1995, Club Z's claim to fame is that it offers in-home tutoring. Across the country, Club Z's regular program serves 50,000 students a year. After Lucas saw the surge in royalty checks, he decided the whole company should get into supplemental services, and he applied for state approval. In the 2003–2004 school year, Club Z was approved in twenty-five states and served 7,000 children through the supplemental services program. That's more than competitive with his more-established counterparts. Lucas antici-pates that within two years, he'll be serving around 10,000 students through supplemental services.

"One of the reasons we're so popular is we go to the home," Lucas says. How can he do it? Club Z trains a bevy of local tutors and then calls on them as needed and pays them only for the hours they work. Overhead costs are minimal, and Lucas says that Club Z is able to attract better tutors because it pays them half of the $35 hourly rate. He says that compares favorably with his larger competitors, which pay their tutors around $9 an hour. And Club Z isn't much more expensive than, say, Princeton Review, which charges around $25 an hour. So Club Z offers parents fewer hours of tutoring, but one-on-one and at home.

The Earnest Do-Gooders

The federal tutoring program has been a boon for Pastor Darius Pridgen at True Bethel Baptist Church in Buffalo, New York. A former school board member, Pridgen started a math tutoring program at his church four years ago to help students pass New York's graduation requirement. But with a $4,000 budget and an all-volunteer tutoring force, the program was "mediocre," Prid-gen says. But after a state assemblyman suggested he take advantage of the federal tutoring money, Pridgen says, "the picture has changed dramatically." After it joined forces with the housing project next door—home to many children who attend a failing school nearby—True Bethel's program doubled in size from 50 to 100 children.

A number of community-based groups, including YMCAs, Boys and Girls Clubs, and churches, have added or expanded tutoring operations because of the federal tutoring money. Similarly, a number of 21st Century Community Learning Centers, established by the federal government in the 1990s to pro-vide after-school care, are entering the supplemental services market.

Nonprofits such as these may represent the largest proportion of providers nationwide because they're the clean-up crew. When the national companies decide a given area isn't going to boost their bottom line, local organizations are the only option parents have outside the public schools.

At True Bethel, Pridgen has switched from volunteer to hired tutors, and a certified teacher is on-site during the after-school program—all enabled by the new $100,000 budget, $80,000 of which comes from supplemental serv-ices. A member of the congregation, a math teacher, offered to work with a few colleagues to write the curriculum. While the program was previously available only to members of the congregation, this one is open to everyone, and the church provides limited transportation with its own bus.

The Geeks

In the spring of 2002, Massachusetts's state department of education called Burck Smith. His start-up company, SMARTHINKING, offered live, online, one-on-one tutoring 24 hours a day to college students. Department officials asked if SMARTHINKING would be able to offer a similar service for struggling 10th graders who needed to pass the state test. Smith, who had founded SMARTHINKING in 1999, thought he'd give it a shot. "We'd always thought we'd move into high-school tutoring," he said. "The overlap between high school and college tutoring is really dramatic."

The geeks are doggedly trying to make virtual tutoring as good as the real thing. Representing perhaps less than 1 percent of the more than 1,000 unique providers nationally and 10 percent of the 1,718 approved providers in each state, online tutoring firms are still an unknown quantity. But they could fill an important niche in serving students who don't want to or can't get to a site-based provider. Other major providers, such as Catapult Learning, are exploring ways to establish online tutoring services.

SMARTHINKING is now approved in 15 states, and it served 200 children during the 2003–2004 academic year, though Smith had hoped to reach 800. He attributes the low turnout to increased competition from other providers in the program's second year. Smith is facing the same low-participation problems as his competitors, but he has a unique problem with attendance. Smith learned from his program in Massachusetts that students are more likely to attend when they have to show up at a supervised center to log in. So he's pursuing that option where possible.

Nevertheless, Smith believes that his online business model is perfect for the supplemental services program. While other companies need a critical mass of students to ensure profitability, Smith doesn't. Furthermore, he has no fixed costs associated with delivering his program—beyond what he has already spent to develop the software. SMARTHINKING has quality advantages, too, says Smith. With a decentralized business model, he can get higher-quality employees; more than 80 percent of his tutors have master's or doctoral degrees. He also provides Spanish-speaking tutors when necessary. And it's no trouble to bring his services to scale if there's a surge in interest. In a few years, Smith hopes to be serving 10,000 supplemental services students.

Survival of the Largest

As this marketplace matures, both experts and a number of providers say two big winners will emerge: corporate providers and school districts. Those organizations possess the greatest resources, the greatest capacity to reach parents and children, and the scale to absorb the unpredictability inherent in this marketplace.

Ultimately, those two groups may join forces. A number of large corporate providers said that the supplemental services program may end up looking a lot like the one in Los Angeles, in which the district contracts with a few big companies to deliver the tutoring. "I think the largest provider nationwide will be schools," says Rob Cohen of Princeton Review. "They have all the teachers. They have all the buildings." And they have the greatest ability to deliver the children.

Cohen thinks this is a good thing. While he acknowledges that providing the services directly to children is more profitable, he may be able to get a greater share of a new market that sells materials to public schools than he can in the current marketplace. "Providing services to the No. 1 provider [districts] is going to be a fine place to be in the market," he says. And it may well be the best way to ensure that the districts have incentives both to participate and to monitor private providers.

In this Darwin-meets-public-education school reform, performance will (hopefully) matter a lot, too. That detail is not lost on most large providers. "The playing field has grown tremendously. Those who will rise to the top will be those who are getting results," said Huntington's Miller. "They're going to gauge the results by their test scores' going up. That's going to be the bottom line: Did the scores improve, and if they did, which provider did the student work with?"

That's the ideal, anyway.

SIOBHAN GORMAN is a reporter for the *National Journal*.